Economic Issues in SAARC Context

Economic Issues in SAARC Context

Anil Bhuimali
Chandan K. Mukhopadhyay

ABHIJEET PUBLICATIONS
DELHI 110094

ABHIJEET PUBLICATIONS
2/46 Tukhmeerpur Extension
Delhi 110094
Phones: 011-22960492, 65698474
e-mail: abhijeetpublication@gmail.com
abhijeet_singh1@indiatimes.com

ECONOMIC ISSUES IN SAARC CONTEXT

First Published 2008

ISBN 978-81-89886-69-1

PRINTED IN INDIA

Published by J.K. Singh for Abhijeet Publications, Delhi 110094, Lasertypeset by Gaurav Graphics, Delhi and Printed at Himanshu Printers, Delhi.

Introductory Preface

Most of the advanced countries of the world have significantly lowered trade restrictions especially since the Second World War. There are two approaches with regard to reducing or lifting trade restrictions. The first approach is the reciprocal reduction in trade barriers on a nondiscriminatory basis. The second approach is forming groups of nations typically on a regional basis. On such economic group in South Asia is the SAARC—a union of eight South Asian nations. The present book is the outcome of UGC Special Assistance Programme (SAP) of the Department of Economics, University of North Bengal started since 2004. Faculties and research scholars of this Department have contributed 14 papers most of which are based on economic problems of the SAARC and South Asian countries. However, some papers are related to national economic problems and one paper is related to mathematical exposition of the LeChatelier Principle for determining short-run and long-run price elasticity relationships in factor and commodity markets. The contributors are Chandan Kumar Mukhopadhyay, Amit Kundu, Sanchari Roy Mukherjee, Panchali Sengupta, Kanak Kanti Bagchi, Nirupam Gope, Anil Bhuimali, Sidhartha Sankar Laha, Shyam Charan Barma, Tulika Kar, Kamanand Dev, Tamash Ranjan Majumdar, KanchanDutta, and Biswajit Maitra.

II

The basic objective of any time series model is to generate forecasting about the likelihood of future events based on past and current information. Chandan Kumar Mukhapadhyay and Amit Kundu in their paper have estimated ARIMA forecast for gross domestic product (GDP) in the economy of India for the period 1984-2005. The model has been used for generating one period ahead forecast for the GDP series. The forecasts are efficient. Such forecasts may help policy makers take measures in order to influence the relevant economic variables.

Women in every society have to perform a lot of works apart from economically productive ones. Rural women also play an important part in farm operations and in enhancing the quality of life. But the contributions they make remain hidden due to some social barriers and gender bias. Sanchari Roy Mukherjee and Panchali Segupta's paper examines the economics of rural work and gender divisions of labour between men and women in the rural setting based on time allocation survey of poor rural households engaged in agriculture and allied activities. The involvement of women in various forms of economic and non-economic activities is also explored exploring the probable reasons for gender differential in rural work participation.

Migration is a complex phenomenon that raises a lot of questions. Most people move for economic reasons. Many migrate for better paying jobs in new areas especially to escape poverty or low living standards. Some migrate for cultural pressures or adverse political conditions. Kanak Kanti Bagchi and Nirupam Gope in their paper delineate the push and pool factors of migration and other facets of socio-economic life of in-migrant rickshaw pullers and construction workers in Siliguri Municipal Corporation area.

India especially since 1985 has initiated a serious rethinking of its trade policy since the start of this decade

(1980s). Indo-US relationship has taken a new turn. Regular interaction and enhanced mutual understanding have given a new direction of this relationship. In their paper Anil Bhuimali and Sidhartha Sankar Laha highlight the pattern of Indo-US trade in the post-reform period with the help of IIT index on the basis of time series data for 1991-2005. They have constructed the IIT index for resource based labour-intensive, scale-intensive, differentiated 2-digit commodities.

India, since 1950-51, has been pursuing economic policies aimed at maximizing the well-being of its citizens. India's foreign trade also has undergone significant changes in terms of volume, composition and direction and it has contributed in some measure to the country's development effort by making available to its indispensable raw materials and capital goods key to infrastructural and technological improvement. Anil Bhuimali and Sidhartha Sankar Laha in their paper examine in detail, how trade has contributed to the growth of the Indian economy in terms of export performance, employment generation, foreign exchange earning and soon in the context of liberalized trade regime. Time series-analysis has been done to evaluate India's IIT, intensity of IIT across sections in multilateral trade and to measure India's overall IIT.

The basic object of any forecast exercise is to aid decision making. The decision making management, production planning, central banking practices, traffic management and even military operations. C. K. Mukhopadhyay and Shyam Charan Barma in their paper have made ARIMA forecasts for exchange rate quoted in Indo-Nepal trade. Box-Jenkins methodology is adopted for building ARIMA model. Quarterly data for the study cover the period ranging from the first quarter of 1973 to the second quarter of 2006. The forecast as the analysis suggests is efficient.

The trade reform in India has integrated the Indian economy with the world economy more intensively and as a result there have been remarkable changes in the volume and direction of its trade cover. Anil Bhuimali and Tulika Kar's paper highlights main features of new trade policy, trade policy changes under globalization perspective, liberalization of exchange rate regime and EXIM policy, export performance, composition of exports and what is more impact of import liberalization on export performance.

Estimating an econometric relationship first and then using this relationship in formulating economic policy prescription is the current practice of most of economic works. The implicit assumption of this type of exercise is that the econometric relationship will remain stable under different scenarios. But this assumption as Lucas argues, is falls. Chandan Kumar Mukhapadhyay and Shyam Charan Barma's paper examines the stability of the causal relationship between consumer price level and money supply over the period 1987-2005. Structural changes in such relationship have been identified through Recursive Residual Tests. Causal relationship between consumar price level and money supply has been found to vary in two different sub-periods.

The tourist potential of any location depends, as Edward Bergman (1996) observes, on the region's accessibility to the core countries, its quality and number of accommodations, and its cultural physical attractions. Anil Bhuimali and Kamanand Dev in their paper seek to assess the impact of tourism development on mountain environment of Nepal. Tourism in Himalayas, as the paper examines; provides income and employment opportunities in remote and relatively inaccessible areas. The paper concludes that too much tourism may lead to over-harvesting of Himalayan resources and environmental degradation.

Box-Jenkins introduced ARIMA model for forecasting a variable. Chandan Kumar Mukhopadhyay and Amit Kundu's paper makes an attempt for estimating for an ARIMA model for GDP in the economy of Sri Lanka.

The forecasts adequately volatility of GDP series and are found to be efficient.

The idea that long-run demand and supply are typically more elastic than shot-run demand and supply is common in economic literature. LeChatelier principle proves this intuitive proposition rigorously. Tamash Ranjan Majumdar's paper provides a mathematical exposition of this principle for the determination of the relationship between short-run and long-run price elasticities for the factor-demand and commodity-supply functions derived from profit maximization hypothesis. The analysis shows that the long run price elasticity with fewer restrictions on variables than in the short-run is at least as large as the short-run price elasticity.

A debate has developed to explain the relationship between budget deficit and interest. Neo-classical theory tells that budget deficit leads to an increase in interest rate which in torn results in crowding out of private investment while the followers of Keynesian idea stress upon rise in interest rate following a budget deficit which in turn stimulates savings and helps capital formation. Chandan Kumar Mukhopadhyay and Kanchan Dutta in their paper reject the Recardian Equivalence Theorem and find that there exists a long-run as well as short-run dynamics in the relationship where unidirectional Granger Causality runs from budget deficit to interest rate over the period 1979-2001 in the economy of Sri Lanka.

Fiscal Policy has a prominent and far- reaching role in economic development. Efficiency of fiscal policy depends on how government regulates fiscal instruments through budgetary management. Chandan Kumar Mukhapadhyay and Biswajit Maitra in their paper examine if there exists any long-run causal relationship between expenditure and revenue in the economy of Maldives over the period 1980-2006. Expenditure and revenue series are found efficient. The impulse response functions indicate that revenue shocks are more important in constituting long-run base of both revenue and expenditure profiles.

Variance Decomposition Study conforms that shocks transmitted through revenue channel the major part of variations in both revenue and expenditure above their corresponding long-run levels.

Vector Autoregressive model (VAR) developed by Christopher Sim is designed for forecasting the interrelated variables by analyzing the dynamic impact of the random disturbances of the system. Chandan Kumar Mukhopadhyay and Biswajit Maitra's paper makes an attempt to find dynamic adjustment of Rupee-Dollar exchange rate variation following internal and external monetary shocks. Appling VAR model and Impulse Response Functions with co-integrated filtered time series it aims at identifying the nature of the shocks and their impulses. It is found that short-run variations in exchange rate are mainly a monetary phenomenon. In the short run variation in exchange rate, domestic monetary shocks dominate the foreign monetary shocks. Data show that exchange rate maintains stable long-run equilibrium relationship between domestic and foreign money supply.

The editors express their gratitudes and thanks for the cooperation and willingness to work for a purpose shown by all the contributors.

ANIL BHUIMALI
C.K. MUKHOPADHYAY

Contributors

1. Chandan Kumar Mukhopadhyay, Department of Economics, North Bengal University.
2. Biswajit Maitra, Registered Ph.D. Scholar, Department of Economics, North Bengal University.
3. Sidhartha Sankar Laha, DACEEFO, North Bengal University.
4. Shyam Charan Barma, Registered Ph.D. Scholar, Department of Economics, North Bengal University.
5. Tamash Ranjan Majumdar, Department of Economics, North Bengal University.
6. Anil Bhuimali, Department of Economics, North Bengal University.
7. Amit Kundu, Registered Ph.D. Scholar, Department of Economics, North Bengal University.
8. Tulika Kar, Tarai Kalipada Mahila Mahavidyalaya.
9. Kanak Kanti Bagchi, Department of Economics, North Bengal University.
10. Kamanand Dev, SAARC Fellow, Department of Economics, North Bengal University.
11. Kanchan Datta, St. Joseph College, Darjeeling.
12. Sanchari Roy Mukherjee, Department of Economics, North Bengal University.
13. Panchali Sengupta, Registered Ph.D. Scholar, Department of Economics, North Bengal University.

Contents

1

'Efficient' and 'Minimum Mean Squared Error' ARIMA Forecast for GDP in the Economy of India by the Box-Jenkins (BJ) Methodology

CHANDAN KUMAR MUKHOPADHYAY* & AMIT KUNDU**

Abstract

ARIMA [(1, 6), 1, 0] Model has been estimated as the univariate process for GDP series in India for the period 1984-2005. The model has been used for generating one period ahead forecasts for the GDP series. The forecasts are "efficient".

Key Words: ACF, ARIMA, ARMA, PACF.

Introduction: Forecasts - Meaning

The main purpose for constructing a time series model is to generate forecasting. A forecast is a quantitative estimate about the likelihood of future events which is developed on the basis of past and current information.

* Professor, Department of Economics, North Bengal University.

** Registered Doctoral Scholar, North Bengal University.

This information is embodied in the form of a model. By extrapolating models beyond the period over which they were estimated, one can make forecasts about future events.

Forecasts frequently are used as guides for private and public policy making process. A forecast of a high rate of inflation that is based on the assumption of a large budget deficit may lead policy makers to alter their budget plans, or a forecast of an increased world demand for crude oil may lead shipbuilders to invest in new tankers.

Moreover, forecast provides guidelines for model building. A forecast, which is found to be way off target when actual data become available, provides information which may lead to the revision of the model which generated the forecast.

Relevance of Forecast

In formulating policy decision it is essential to be able to forecast the value of economic magnitude. Such forecasts will enable the policy-markets to judge whether it is necessary to take any measures in order to influence the relevant economic variables.

For examples, the government may want to decide its employment policy. It is necessary to know what the current information of employment is as well as what the level of employment will be in five years time, if no measures whatsoever is taken by the government.

With econometric techniques we may. make forecast about the level of employment. If this level is too low, the government will take appropriate measures to avoid its occurrence. If the forecast value of employment is higher than the expected labour force, the government must take different measures in order to avoid inflation.

Thus forecasts are frequently used as guides for public and private policy as well as decision making process. Consequently, forecasting has become increasingly important both for the regulation of developed economics as well as for the planning of the economic development of less developed countries.

Importance of Forecast for GDP

National income has emerged as the most important variable in any macro economic study because of the fact that all other macroeconomic variables are related to national income implicitly or national explicitly. For example, in Keynesian economics, consumption; savings, employment, demand for money and tax proceeds etc are explicit functions of national income. Again, interest rates and investment etc are implicitly related to national income. So the importance of national income in macro-economic studies was stressed upon even by the classical writers and, therefore, they were engrossed with the determination of national income. They identified the attainment of full employment income level as the panacea for all economic problems.

Keynes, on the other hand, was not that enthusiastic about 'full employment' income. He, instead, stressed upon the determination of "under-employment" equilibrium level of income. Again Friedman devoted himself in the determination of nominal income level.

In Keynesian and Friedmanian systems forecast for national income (GDP) occupies a very important role since the future values of all the macro-economic variables are tied to forecast value of GDP. However, in these systems GDP forecast appears as an exogenous variable and it is determined outside the system. If the equilibrium values of the concerned variables cannot be determined when the GDP forecast is not available, the system remains indeterminate.

Rational Expectationists or the New Classical economists have developed 'Observationally Equivalent' economic models where expected national income appears as the endogenous variable. Consequently, many of macroeconomic variable at period t emerge as a function of expected income at period t +1. The forecast for GDP is also determined within the system.

Rational expectations model are usually 'Over Identified'. As a result, the forecast values for GDP at time t+1 are not 'unique'. Consequently, the values of all other endogenous variables are not 'unique'. In such situation forecasts for GDP play an important role for the system. Once the most plausible forecast for GDP is chosen, then the values of all other macro-economic variables are solved for the chosen forecast values of GDP.

Special Relevance Of GDP Forecast In The Keynsian System

In the Keynsian 'Over-Identified' system 'conditional' forecast for GDP plays an important role. This is explained through the following example.

Let us consider the following model consisting of two equations:

$$C_t = \alpha + \beta Y_t + u_t \qquad 1.1$$

$$Y_t = C_t + I_t + G_t \qquad 1.2$$

where $u_t \sim \text{iid } N(0,\sigma^2_u)$

The appropriate method of estimation of the model is "Two-Stage Least Square"(2SLS) Method. In the first stage ILS (Indirect least Square) Method is applied on equation (1.2) for getting the conditional expectation (forecast) of Y_t (GDP).

The relevant Reduced Form Equations (RFEs) are:

$$C_t = \alpha/(1-\beta) + \beta/(1-\beta)\ I_t + \beta/(1-\beta)\ G_t + 1/(1-\beta)\ u_t$$

$$\text{or, } C_t = \pi_{11} + \pi_{12}\ I_t + \pi_{13}\ G_t + v_t \qquad 1.3$$

where $v_t = \beta/(1-\beta)\ u_t$

Again,

$$Y_t = \alpha/(1-\beta) + 1/(1-\beta)\ I_t + 1/(1-\beta)\ G_t + 1/(1-\beta)\ u_t$$

$$\text{or, } Y_t = \pi_{21} + \pi_{22}\ I_t + \pi_{23}\ G_t + w_t \qquad 1.4$$

where $w_t = 1/(1-\beta)\ u_t$

Now applying OLS on (1.4) we have,

$\hat{Y}_t = \hat{\Pi}21 + \hat{\Pi}\,22I_t + \hat{\Pi}\,23G_t$ 1.5

$\hat{Y}_t = E[Y_t / \Omega_t]$ 1.6

where $\Omega_t = \{ I_t, G_t \}$

Consequently, Y_t represents the 'Conditional Forecasts' for Y_t (GDP) such that

$e_t = Y_t - \hat{Y}_t$

where e_t represents the vector of forecasts errors.

Now applying $Y_t = \hat{Y}_t + e_t$ in the structural equation (1.1) we have,

$C_t = \alpha + \beta\,\hat{Y}_t + Z_t$ 1.7

where $Z_t = (u_t + \beta e_t)$ is a compound error term.

Now applying OLS on eqn. (1.7) we have

$\underline{\beta} = \Sigma\, S_{mcy} \,/\, \Sigma S_{myy}$ 1.8

where β, the 2SLS estimator β , is consistent such that

$$\operatorname*{plim}_{n \to \infty} = \beta$$

Thus, it is evident that the key to the solution of the Keynesian system is the forecast (Conditional Expectation) of GDP. Most of the Keynesian system is marked by the presence of the national income identity like eqn (1.2). Consequently, the forecast (Conditional Expectation) of GDP plays the vital role in deriving determinable equilibrium values of other endogenous variables in the system.

Econometric Forecast

An econometric equation is estimated in order to show the relationship among variables concerned. Economic theory and/or economic rationality specifies the relationship which is expressed as an equation. This equation is estimated to examine the exact relationship among the variables concerned.

For example, economic theory holds that a company's sale proceeds (S_t) depends on its own advertising expenditure (A_t) and its competitors advertising expenditure (C_t) i.e,

$S_t = f(A_t, C_t)$,

In order to know the exact relationship between St and the independent variables (A_t, C_t),the following equation is estimated.

$$S_t = \beta_0 + \beta_1 A_t + \beta_2 C_t + u_t \quad 1.9$$

where u_t ~ iid $N(\sigma^2_u)$

The estimated equation is

$$\hat{S}_t = \hat{\beta}_0 + \hat{\beta}_1 A_t + \hat{\beta}_2 C_t \quad 1.10$$

Now equation (1.9) can be used to generate forecast for S_{t+1} provided the values of A_{t+1} and C_{t+1} are known with certainty Thas forecast of S_t is a conditional forecast.

Such econometric forecasts are beset with several limitations.

First, there may be error in the specification of the equation. Consequently, the estimation may suffer from "Mis-specification Bias".

Second, most of the econometric equations specify instantaneous relationship. Consequently, forecasting for the dependent variable becomes "conditional" by nature and depends on the forecast values of independent variable. In that case we need separate econometric equation for each independent variable. This gives forth a "round about" problem in forecasting.

Third, the residuals of the estimated equation are not used for forecasting even though these residuals constitute a very important source of information for forecasting. Consequently, the forecast becomes "biased" and "inefficient". This constitutes the main limitation for econometric forecasting.

Transfer Function Forecasting

Econometric equations are converted to Transfer Function Equations for the purpose of forecasting. Transfer Functions Equations are constituted by adding AR (Auto Regressive) structure of residuals to the econometric equation.

For example, let us assume that the residuals of the equation (1.9) follow AR (1) structure such that

$u_t = \rho\, u_{t-1} + \varepsilon_t$ 1.11

where $u_t \sim$ iid $N(0,\sigma^2_\varepsilon)$

or, $u_t - \rho\, u_{t-1} = \varepsilon_t$

or, $u_t\,(1-\rho L) = \varepsilon_t$

or, $u_t = \varepsilon_t\,/(1-\rho L)$ 1.12

Now putting eqn (1.12) in to eqn (1.10) we have

$S_t = \beta_0 + \beta_1 A_t + \beta_2 C_t + \varepsilon_t\,/(1-\varepsilon L)$ 1.13

where $\varepsilon_t \sim$ iid $N(0,\sigma^2_\varepsilon)$

or, $S_t - \beta_0 - \beta_1 A_t - \beta_2 C_t = \varepsilon_t\,/(1-\rho L)$

or, $(1-\rho L)(S_t - \beta_0 - \beta_1 A_t - \beta_2 C_t) = \varepsilon_t$

or, $(1-\rho L)\,S_t - (1-\rho L)\,\beta_0 - \beta_1 A_t(1-\rho L) - \beta_2 C_t\,(1-\rho L) = \varepsilon_t$

or, $S_t - \rho_1\, S_{t-1} - \beta^*_0 - \beta_1 A_t - \beta_1 \rho A_{t-1} - \beta_2 C_t + \beta_2\, \rho C_{t-1} = \varepsilon_t$

or, $S_t = \beta_0 + \rho S_{t-1} + \beta_1 A_t - \beta_1 \rho A_{t-1} + \beta_2 C_t - \beta_2\, \rho C_{t-1} + \varepsilon_t$

or, $S_t = \beta^*_0 + \rho S_{t-1} + \beta_1 A_t - \beta'_1 \rho A_{t-1} + \beta_2 C_t - \beta_2{}' \rho C_{t-1} + \varepsilon_t$ 1.14

The equation (1.14) represents the Transfer Function Equation. Here the residuals are $\varepsilon_t \sim$ iid $N(0,\sigma^2_\varepsilon)$. The residuals of the equation seem to be AR (0). Consequently, the forecasting power of the equation improves. However, Transfer Function Forecasting may be inefficient because of the presence of "Mis-specification Bias".

ARIMA Forecasting

Limitations of the Econometric and Transfer Function Forecastings are being avoided through ARIMA forecasting. In ARIMA forecasting 'Univariate Structure' of any sequence $\{X_t\}$ is identified and estimated. That structure is used for forecasting.

The past and present realizations of the sequence $\{X_t\}$ are used for constructing univariate ARIMA (p, d, q) which is assumed to be the stochastic process generating the sequence. If the economic structure remains unchanged next period /periods, then the stochastic process will also remain unchanged. Consequently, the identified univariate structure for the $\{X_t\}$ sequence will also remain unchanged. In that case, the realization of $\{X_t\}$at period t+1 can be determined and this realization is considered to be forecast for X_t at period t+1.

In ARIMA forecasting the residuals usually follow ARIMA (0, 0, 0). There exists no specification bias in the construction of the univariate structure. Moreover, no a priori economic rationality is required for the construction of the univariate structure. The entire process of information provided by the realization of the $\{X_t\}$ sequence are being exploited for making forecast. Consequently, the forecast, though 'a theoretic', is 'efficient'.

Methodological Issues

Introduction: Stationary Series

In case of stationary time series statistical properties such as mean, variance, autocorrelation, etc. are all constant over time. Most statistical forecasting methods are based on the assumption that the time series can be rendered approximately stationary through the use of mathematical transformations. A stationarized series is relatively easy to predict. The predictions for the stationarized series can then be 'untransformed,' by reversing whatever mathematical transformations were previously used, to obtain predictions for the original series. Thus, finding the sequence of transformations needed to stationarize a time series often provides important clues in the search of an appropriate forecasting model.

Another reason for trying to stationarize a time series is to be able to obtain meaningful sample statistics such as means, variances, and correlations with other variables.

Such statistics are useful as descriptors of future behavior only if the series is stationary. As an example, if the series is consistently increasing over time, the sample mean and variance will grow with the size of the sample, and they will always underestimate the mean and variance in future periods. So if the mean and variance of a series are not well-defined, then neither are its correlations with other variables.

Stationarity Through De-Trending and Differencing

Most business and economic time series are far from stationary when expressed in their original units of measurement. Even after deflation or seasonal adjustment these will typically still exhibit trends, cycles, random-walking, and other non-stationary behavior. If the series has a stable long-run trend and tends to revert to the trend line following a disturbance, it may be possible to stationarize it by de-trending. Such a series is said to be trend -stationary. However, sometimes even de-trending is not sufficient to make the series stationary. In such case it may be necessary to transform it into a series of period-to-period and/or season-to-season differences. If the mean, variance, and autocorrelations of the original series are not constant in time, even after detrending, perhaps the statistics of the changes in the series between periods or between seasons will be constant. Such a series is said to be difference-stationary.

Testing for Stationarity: Unit Root Test

It is necessary to know whether the underlying stochastic process is invariant with time. If the process is non-stationary, it is difficult to represent the time series over past and future intervals of time by an algebraic model. If stochastic process is stationary, then the process can be modeled through an equation with fixed coefficients and that model can be estimated from the past data. Stationarity is examined through Unit Root Tests like

Dickey-Fuller (DF) Test, ADF Test, Phillips-Perron Test and Correlogram analysis.

In the DF test it is assumed that the error terms are uncorrelated. But in case where the error term is correlated, the Augmented Dickey Fuller test is used. This test is conducted by adding the lagged values of the dependent variable in the equation. Phillips and Perron use nonparametric statistical methods to take care of the serial co-rrelation in the error terms owing to structural shift in the stochastic process.

Let us consider a sequence $\{y_t\}$ such that

$Y_t = Y_{t-1} + \varepsilon_t$ 2.1

where Y_t and Y_{t-1} are the present and the immediate past values of a variable respectively; and et is a stationary error term.

Equation (2.1) can be expressed in the following form:

$Y_t = (1+\theta)\ Y_{t-1} + \varepsilon_t$ 2.2

Or, $Y_t = qY_{t-1} + \varepsilon_t$

where q is an arbitrary parameter. When q=1, Equation (2.2) equals Equation (2.1). After rearranging Equation (2.2), the following equation is obtained:

$\Delta\ Y_t = Y_t - Y_{t-1} = \theta\ Y_{t-1} + \varepsilon_t$ 2.3

If q equals 1 and e_t is stationary, then $Y_t \sim I\ (1)$. Dickey and Fuller considered the following three different equations to test for the presence of unit roots:

$\Delta Y_t = \theta\ Y_{t-1} + \varepsilon_t$ 2.4

$\Delta\ Y_t = a_0 + \theta\ Y_{t-1} + \varepsilon_t$ 2.5

$\Delta Y_t = a_0 + \theta\ Y_{t-1} + a_{2t}t + \varepsilon_t$ 2.6

The differences depend on the presence of a0, constant (drift) and $a_{2t}t$, deterministic term (time trend). The above equations represent a process depending only one lag value. The test can be extended for higher order autoregressive process. The extended DF test for higher order equations is known as the ADF test. In a 'p' order autoregressive process, Equations (2.4) – (2.6) can be presented as

$$\Delta Y_t = \theta Y_{t-1} + \sum_{j=1}^{p} \gamma_j \Delta Y_{t-j} + \varepsilon_t \quad 2.7$$

$$\Delta Y_t = a0 + \theta Y_{t-1} + \sum_{j=1}^{p} \gamma_j \Delta Y_{t-j} + \varepsilon_t \quad 2.8$$

$$\Delta Y_t = a0 + \theta Y_{t-1} + a_{2t} + \sum_{j=1}^{p} \gamma_j \Delta Y_{t-j} + \varepsilon_t \quad 2.9$$

where a_0 and t are the constant and time trend, respectively.

An important assumption of the DF test is that the error term et is independent and identically distributed. The ADF test adjusts the DF test by adding the lagged difference terms of the regressand. However, Phillips and Perron (1988) use nonparametric statistical methods to examine stationarity without adding lagged difference terms.

Theoretical Basis of ARIMA Model

The publication by Box and Jenkins (1976) of Time Series Analysis: Forecasting and Control ushered in new generation of forecasting tools. Popularly known as the Box-Jenkins methodology, but technically known as the ARIMA methodology, the emphasis of these methods is not on constructing single-equation or simultaneous–equation models but on analyzing the probabilistic or stochastic properties of economic time series on their own under the philosophy of letting the data speak for themselves.

Unlike the regression models, in which Y_t is explained by k regressors, X_1 , X_2, X_3, …,X_k, the BJ-type time series models allow Y_t to be explained by past , or lagged values of Y_t itself and stochastic error terms. For this reason, ARIMA models are sometimes called 'atheoretic' models because these are not derived from any economic theory-while economic theories are often the basis of simultaneous-equation models.

Let $\{Y_t\}$ be a time series sequence for t = 1,....T. If we model Y_t as

$$Y_t - \delta = a_1 (Y_{t-1} - \delta) + u_t \qquad 2.10$$

where δ is the mean of Y and where $u_t \sim$ ii $dN(0, \sigma^2\varepsilon)$, then we say that Y_t follows a first order autoregressive process or AR(1). Here the value of Y at time t depends on its value in the previous time period and a random term. In other words, this model says that the forecast value of Y at time t is simply some proportion (a_1) of its value at time (t-1) plus a random shock or disturbance at time t. Again the values are expressed around their mean values.

But if we consider this model,

$$Y_t - \delta = \alpha_1 (Y_{t-1} - \delta) + \alpha_2 (Y_{t-2} - \delta) + u_t \qquad 2.11$$

then we say that Y_t follows a second order autoregressive process or AR(2) process.

In general we can have

$$Y_t - \delta = \alpha_1(Y_{t-1} - \delta) + \alpha_2(Y_{t-2} - \delta) + \ldots\ldots + \alpha_p(Y_{t-p} - \delta) + u_t \qquad 2.12$$

in which case Y_t is a *p*th- order autoregressive or AR(p) process.

The AR process just discussed is not the only mechanism that may have generated {Y}.

Suppose we model Y_t as follows:

$$Y_t = \mu + \beta_1 u_{t-1} + v_t \qquad 2.13$$

where μ is a constant and u_t is the white noise stochastic error term. Here Y at time t is equal to a constant plus a moving average of the current and past error terms. Thus, in the present case, we say that Y_t follows a first-order moving average, or an MA (1) process. But if Y_t follows the expression

$$Y_t = \mu + \beta_1 u_{t-1} + \beta_2 u_{t-2} + v_{1t} \qquad 2.14$$

then it is an MA(2) process. More generally,

$$Y_t = \mu + \beta_1 u_{t-1} + \beta_2 u_{t-2} + \ldots\ldots + \beta_q u_{t-q} + v_{2t} \qquad 2.15$$

is an MA(q) process. In short, a moving average process is simply a linear combination of white noise error terms.

Of course, it is quite likely that Y possesses characteristics of both AR and MA and is, therefore, ARMA. Thus, Y_t follows an ARMA(1,1) process if it can be written as

$$Y_t = \theta + \alpha_1 Y_{t-1} + \beta_1 u_{t-1} + w_t \qquad 2.16$$

where θ presents the constant term.

In general, in an ARMA(p,q) process, there will be p autoregressive and q moving average terms.

Economic time series are usually nonstationary, since these are integrated. These need differencing for attaining stationarity. If a time series is integrated of order 1, its first differences are I (0), and it is stationary. Similarly, if a time series is I (2), its second difference is I (0). In general, if a time series is I(d), after differencing it d times we obtain an I(0)· series.

Therefore, if we have to difference a time series d times to make it stationary and then apply the ARMA (p, q) model to it, we say that the original time series is ARIMA (p, d, q). It is then an Autoregressive Integrated Moving Average time series, where p denotes the number of autoregressive terms, d represents the number of times the series has to be differenced before it becomes stationary, and q is the number of moving average terms.

ARIMA Structure: The Box-Jenkins (BJ) Methodology

The ARIMA structure of a stationary variable may be obtained through the following procedure consisting of four separate steps.

Step 1. Identification: This relates to finding out the appropriate values of p, d and q. The correlogram and partial correlogram may be an aid in this task.

Step 2. Estimation: Having identified the appropriate p and q values, the next stage is to estimate the parameters of the autoregressive and moving average terms included in the model.

Step 3. Diagnostic Checking: Having chosen a particular ARIMA model, and having estimated its parameters, one needs to examine whether the chosen model fits the data reasonably well, for it is possible that another ARIMA model might do the job as well. This is why Box-Jenkins ARIMA modeling is more an art than a science.

Step 4. Forecasting: One of the reasons behind the popularity of the ARIMA modeling is its success in forecasting. In many cases, the forecasts obtained by this method are more reliable than those obtained from the traditional econometric modeling, particularly for short term forecast.

Model Estimation: Further Elaboration

Let the ARIMA (p, d, q) model be

$$\varphi(\beta)\ \Delta^d\ y_t\ =\ \varphi(\beta)\ \omega_t\ =\ \theta_2(\beta)\varepsilon_t \qquad 2.17$$

with $\varphi(\beta) = 1- \varphi 1\ \beta - \varphi_2\beta^2-\ldots\ldots\ldots- \varphi_p\ \beta_p$

and $\theta\ (\beta) = 1- \theta_1\ \beta - \theta_2\beta^2-\ldots\ldots\ldots- \theta_q\ \beta^q$

Eqn (2.17) can be expressed in terms of error term series ε_t such that

$$\varepsilon_t = \theta^{-1}\ (\beta)\ \varphi(\beta)\ \omega_t \qquad 2.18$$

where

$\omega_t = \Delta^d\ y_t$

The objective in estimation is to find a set of autoregressive parameters $(\varphi_1, \varphi_2,\ldots\ \varphi_p)$ and a set of moving average parameters $(\theta_1,\ldots\ldots\ \theta_q)$ which minimize the sum of squared errors

$$S\ (\varphi_1,\ \ldots\ldots\ldots\ldots,\ \varphi_p\ ,\ \theta_1\ ,\ldots,\ \theta_q) = \Sigma_t\varepsilon^2_t \qquad 2.19$$

Now let us assume that the error terms ε_1, ... ε_t are all normally distributed and independent with mean 0 and variance σ^2_ε. Then the conditional log-likelihood function associated with parameter values $(\varphi_1,\ \ldots\ldots\ldots\ldots,\ \varphi_p\ ,\ \theta_1\ ,\ldots,\ \theta_q\ ,\ \sigma_\varepsilon)$ is given by

$$L = -T\ \log\ \sigma_\varepsilon\ -\ S(\varphi_1,\ \ldots,\ \varphi_p,\ \theta_1\ ,\ldots,\ \theta_q)/\ 2\sigma^2_\varepsilon \qquad 2.20$$

Here L is the conditional logarithmic likelihood

function. Consequently,

$$\varepsilon_1 = \omega_1 - \varphi_1 \omega_0 - \varphi_2\omega_{-1} - \ldots\ldots\ldots - \varphi_p \omega_{-p+1} + \theta_1\varepsilon_0 + \ldots\ldots\ldots + \theta_q \varepsilon_{-q+1} \quad 2.21$$

Equation (2.20) shows that the maximum-likelihood estimate of the model's parameters is given by the minimization of the sum of squared residuals. Thus, under the assumption of normally distributed errors, the maximum-likelihood estimate is the same as least-square-estimate.

Minimum Mean-Square- Error Forecasts

Optimum forecasts are 'forecasts with minimum mean-square forecast error'. Thus the forecast $y_T(l)$ will be so chosen that $E[e^2 (l)] = E\{[y_{T+e} - \hat{y}_T (l)]^2\}$ is minimized. This forecast is the conditional expectation of y_{T+l} such that

$$\hat{y}_{T+l} = E [y_{T+l} / y_T, y_{T-1}, \ldots, y_1] \quad 2.22$$

Eqn (2.22) gives the minimum mean-square-error forecast.

Eqn (2.17) can be written as

$$\varphi(\beta) (1-\beta)^d y_t = \theta(\beta)\varepsilon_t \quad 2.23$$

since $\Delta = 1-\beta$. Therefore,

$$y_t = \varphi\text{-}1 \ (\beta) (1-\beta)^{-d} \theta(\beta)\varepsilon_t = \Psi(\beta)\varepsilon_t = \sum_{j\text{-}0} \Psi_j\varepsilon_{t-j} \quad 2.24$$

Eqn (2.24) expresses the ARIMA model as a purely moving average process of infinite order. Then

$$y_{T+l} = \Psi_0\varepsilon_{T+l} + \Psi_1\varepsilon_{T+l-1} + \ldots\ldots\ldots\ldots + \Psi_l\varepsilon_T + \Psi_{l+1}\varepsilon_{T-1} + \ldots..$$
$$=\Psi'_0\varepsilon_{T+l}+\Psi_1\varepsilon_{T+l-1}+ \ldots\ldots\ldots\ldots +\Psi_{l-1}\varepsilon_{T+1}+\sum_{j\text{-}0}\Psi_{l+j}\varepsilon_{T-j} \quad 2.25$$

In equation (2.25) the infinite sum has been divided into two parts. The second part begins with the term $\Psi_j\varepsilon_T$ and thus describing information up to and including time period T.

However, the forecast $\hat{y}T(l)$ can be based only on information available up to time T. Now forecast can be written as a weighted sum of those error terms, ε_T, ε_{T-1} ,... . Then the desired forecast is

$$\hat{y}_T(l) = \sum_{j-0} \Psi^*_{l+j}\varepsilon_{T-j} \qquad 2.26$$

where the weights are chosen optimally to minimize the mean square forecast error. Then using Eqn (2.25) and (2.26) we get

$$e_T(l) = y_{T+l} - \hat{y}T(l)$$

$$=\Psi_0\varepsilon_{t+l} + \Psi_1\varepsilon_{t+l-1} + \ldots\ldots\ldots\ldots + \Psi_{l-1}\varepsilon_{T+1} + \sum_{j-0}(\Psi_{l+j} - \Psi^*_{l+j})\varepsilon_{T-j} \qquad 2.27$$

Since by assumption $E(\varepsilon_i, \varepsilon_j) = 0$ for $i \neq j$, the mean-square forecast is

$$E[e^2_t(l)] = (\Psi^2_0 + \Psi^2_1 + \ldots\ldots\ldots + \Psi^2_{l-1})\sigma^2\varepsilon + \sum_{j-0}(\Psi_{l+j} - \Psi^*_{l+j})^2\sigma^2\varepsilon \qquad 2.28$$

Then this expression is minimized by setting the "optimum" weights Ψ^*_{l+j} equal to true weights Ψ_{l+j}, for j= 0,1, ... In that case optimal forecast $\hat{y}T(l)$ just becomes the conditional expectation of y_{T+l}. Consequently,

$$\hat{y}_T(l) = \sum\Psi_{l+j}\varepsilon_{T-j} = E[y_{T+l} / y_{t'} \ldots y^1] \qquad 2.29$$

Eqn (2.29) provides the basic principal for estimations of forecast from ARIMA models.

Computation of A Forecast

Let the ARIMA (p,d,q) model be

$$\omega_t = \varphi\omega_{t-1} + \ldots\ldots + \varphi_p\omega_{t-p} + \varepsilon_t - \theta_1\varepsilon_{t-1} - \ldots - \theta_q\varepsilon_{t-q} + \delta \qquad 2.30$$

where $y_t = \Sigma^d\omega_t$

The one period forecast of ω_t is $\hat{\omega}_t(1)$. Now from eqn (2.30) we get

$$\omega_{T+1} = \varphi_1\omega_T + \ldots\ldots + \varphi_p\omega_{T-p+1} + \varepsilon_{t+1} - \theta_1\varepsilon_T - \ldots\theta_q\varepsilon_{T-q} + \delta \qquad 2.31$$

Now taking conditional expected value of ω_{T+1} in equation (2.31) we get

$$\hat{\omega}_T(1) = E[\omega_{T+1} / \omega_T, \ldots]$$

$$=\varphi_1\omega_T + \ldots\ldots + \varphi_p\omega_{T-p+1} - \theta_1\varepsilon_T - \ldots - \theta_q\varepsilon_{T-q+1} + \delta \qquad 2.32$$

where $\hat{\varepsilon}_T$, $\hat{\varepsilon}_{T-1}$ etc are the observed residuals and the expected value of ε_{T+1} is 0.

Now using the one-period forecast $\hat{\omega}_T(1)$, one can obtain two-period forecast, $\hat{\omega}_T(2)$ such that

$\hat{\omega}_T(2)=E[\omega_{T+2}/\omega_T,..]$

$=\varphi_1\omega_T(1)+\varphi_2\omega_T+\ldots\ldots +\varphi_p\omega_{T-p+2}-\theta_1\hat{\varepsilon}_T-\ldots. -\theta q\hat{\varepsilon}_{T-q+2}+\delta$ 2.33

The two-period forecast is then used to produce the three period forecast, and so on until the l-period forecast $\hat{\omega}_T(l)$ is reached:

$\hat{\omega}_T(l)=\varphi_1\hat{\omega}_{T(l-1)}+\ldots+\varphi_l\omega_T+\ldots+\varphi_p\omega_{T-p+l}-\theta_1\hat{\varepsilon}_T-\ldots-\theta_q\hat{\varepsilon}_{T-q+l}+\delta$ 2.34

If l > p and l >q, this forecast will be

$\hat{\omega}_T(l)=\varphi_1\hat{\omega}_{T(l-1)}+\ldots\ldots\ldots\ldots+\varphi_{p(l-p)}$ 2.35

Once the differenced series ω_T has been forecasted, a forecast can be obtained for the original series y_t simply by summing $\hat{\omega}_t$ 'd' times.

Data

The study involves the use of annual data set for GDP in India. The data cover the period running from 1984 to 2005. The data have been collected from various issues of IFS (International Financial Statistics) where the base period is 2000. Log series of the data have been used.

Building ARIMA Model for GDP Data and Forecasting

To fit an ARIMA model we have used the data for GDP for the period 1984 to 2005. The model identification needs examination of stationarity of the series concerned.

Stationarity Test

The stationarity test of the variable GDP has been performed by using ADF test, PP test and Correlogram analysis. These are being presented below.

Augmented Dickey-FullerTests for Unit Roots

The results of the Augmented Dickey-Fuller Tests for Unit Roots on GDP are being presented through the Tables-1, 2 and 3. A summary of the results is being presented through the Table-3.

Table 1: The Results of the Augmented Dickey-Fuller Tests on GDP at Level

Null Hypothesis: LOGGDP has a unit root

Exogenous: Constant, Linear Trend

Lag Length: 8 (Automatic based on SIC, MAXLAG=8)

		t-Statistic	*Prob.**
Augmented Dickey-Fuller test statistic		-0.978484	0.9108
Test critical values:	1% level	-4.886426	
	5% level	-3.828975	
	10% level	-3.362984	

*MacKinnon (1996) one-sided p-values.

Augmented Dickey-Fuller Test Equation

Dependent Variable: D(LOGGDP)

Method: Least Squares

Sample(adjusted): 1993 2005

Included observations: 13 after adjusting endpoints

Variable	*Coefficient*	*Std. Error*	*t-Statistic*	*Prob.*
LOGGDP(-1)	-0.447017	0.456846	-0.978484	0.4310
D(LOGGDP(-1))	0.102559	0.378054	0.271280	0.8116
C	1.540627	1.346234	1.144397	0.3709
@TREND(1984)	0.023814	0.028471	0.836426	0.4909
R-squared	0.995671	Mean dependent var		0.054446
Adjusted R-squared	0.974025	S.D. dependent var		0.017028
S.E. of regression	0.002744	Akaike info criterion		-9.137995
Sum squared resid	1.51E-05	Schwarz criterion		-8.659961
Log likelihood	70.39697	F-statistic		45.99889
Durbin-Watson stat	3.060577	Prob(F-statistic)		0.021459

Table 2: The Results of the Augmented Dickey-Fuller Tests on GDP at 1st Difference

Null Hypothesis: D(LOGGDP) has a unit root

Exogenous: Constant, Linear Trend

Lag Length: 8 (Automatic based on SIC, MAXLAG=8)

	t-Statistic	*Prob.**

Augmented Dickey-Fuller test statistic		-6.815005	0.0009
Test critical values:	1% level	-4.992279	
	5% level	-3.875302	
	10% level	-3.388330	

*MacKinnon (1996) one-sided p-values.

Augmented Dickey-Fuller Test Equation

Dependent Variable: D(LOGGDP,2)

Method: Least Squares

Included observations: 12 after adjusting endpoints

Variable	*Coefficient*	*Std. Error*	*t-Statistic*	*Prob.*
D(LOGGDP(-1))	-6.406744	0.940094	-6.815005	0.0928
D(LOGGDP(-1),2)	3.812225	0.585475	6.511341	0.0970
C	0.533930	0.080910	6.599098	0.0957
@TREND(1984)	-0.009891	0.001605	-6.163403	0.1024
R-squared	0.999205	Mean dependent var		-0.003258
Adjusted R-squared	0.991254	S.D. dependent var		0.011190
S.E. of regression	0.001046	Akaike info criterion		-11.53831
Sum squared resid	1.10E-06	Schwarz criterion		-11.09381
Log likelihood	80.22983	F-statistic		125.6738
Durbin-Watson stat	2.342817	Prob(F-statistic)		0.069318

Table 3
Augmented Dickey Fuller Test (Unit Root Test)

Null Hypothesis: The variables (GDP) has unit root.

Exogenous: Constant, Linear Trend

Lag Length: (Automatic based on SIC, MAXLAG=8)

Variable	*ADF.Test Statistic*	*Prob.* value*	*Lag length*	*Mackinnon Critical Value* 1%	5%	10%
Log(GDP) at level	-0.978484	0.9108	8	-4.886426	-3.828975	-3.362984
Log(GDP) at 1st difference	-6.815005	0.0009	8	-4.992279	-3.875302	-3.388330

The Findings

The Table 3 gives forth the following observations:

Unit Root hypothesis is accepted for the variable log GDP at the level by Augmented Dickey Fuller test. But Unit Root test is rejected for the variable GDP (in log) at the 1st difference. It means that GDP becomes stationary at 1st difference.

Phillips – Perron Unit Root Test

The results of Phillips- Perron tests for Unit Root test on variables (GDP) are being presented in the Tables 4 and 5.

Table 4: The Results of the Phillips – Perron Tests on GDP at Level

Null Hypothesis: LOGGDP has a unit root

Exogenous: Constant, Linear Trend

Bandwidth: 2 (Newey-West using Bartlett kernel)

		Adj. t-Stat	*Prob.**
Phillips-Perron test statistic		-0.505082	0.9745
Test critical values:	1% level	-4.467895	
	5% level	-3.644963	
	10% level	-3.261452	

*MacKinnon (1996) one-sided p-values.

Residual variance (no correction) 0.000159

HAC corrected variance (Bartlett kernel) 0.000275

Phillips-Perron Test Equation

Dependent Variable: D(LOGGDP)

Method: Least Squares

Included observations: 21 after adjusting endpoints

Variable	*Coefficient*	*Std. Error*	*t-Statistic*	*Prob.*
LOGGDP(-1)	-0.005076	0.085162	-0.059608	0.9531
C	0.084919	0.281902	0.301234	0.7667
@TREND(1984)	-0.000730	0.005068	-0.144129	0.8870
R-squared	0.196972	Mean dependent var		0.056776

Adjusted R-squared	0.107746	S.D. dependent var	0.014422
S.E. of regression	0.013623	Akaike info criterion	-5.622555
Sum squared resid	0.003341	Schwarz criterion	-5.473337
Log likelihood	62.03683	F-statistic	2.207573
Durbin-Watson stat	1.047974	Prob(F-statistic)	0.138860

Table 5: The Results of the Phillips – Perron Tests on GDP at 1st Difference

Null Hypothesis: D(LOGGDP) has a unit root

Exogenous: Constant, Linear Trend

Bandwidth: 0 (Newey-West using Bartlett kernel)

		Adj. t-Stat	Prob.*
Phillips-Perron test statistic		-2.602056	0.2828
Test critical values:	1% level	-4.498307	
	5% level	-3.658446	
	10% level	-3.268973	

*MacKinnon (1996) one-sided p-values.

Residual variance (no correction)	
	0.000125
HAC corrected variance (Bartlett kernel)	0.000125

Phillips-Perron Test Equation

Dependent Variable: D(LOGGDP,2)

Method: Least Squares

Sample(adjusted): 1986 2005

Included observations: 20 after adjusting endpoints

Variable	*Coefficient*	*Std. Error*	*t-Statistic*	*Prob.*
D(LOGGDP(-1))	-0.553336	0.212653	-2.602056	0.0186
C	0.039650	0.016124	2.459022	0.0250
@TREND(1984)	-0.000709	0.000532	-1.333670	0.1999
R-squared	0.196972	Mean dependent var		0.056776
R-squared	0.285372	Mean dependent var		3.37E-05
Adjusted R-squared	0.201298	S.D. dependent var		0.013565
S.E. of regression	0.012123	Akaike info criterion		-5.849902
Sum squared resid	0.002499	Schwarz criterion		-5.700542
Log likelihood	61.49902	F-statistic		3.394292
Durbin-Watson stat	2.086030	Prob(F-statistic)		0.057502

Table 6: Phillips-Perron Unit Root Test

Variable	*Phillips-Perron Test Statistic*	*Prob.* value*	*Bandwith*	*Mackinnon Critical Value* 1%	5%	10%
Log(GDP) at level	-0.505082	0.9745	2	-4.467895	-3.644963	-3.261452
Log(GDP) at 1st difference	-2.602056	0.2828	0	-4.498307	-3.658446	-3.268973

The Findings

Presence of Unit Root is accepted for the variable GDP (in log) at the level by the Phillips-Perron test. But presence of Unit Root is not totally rejected for the variable GDP (in log) at the 1st difference.

Correlogram Analysis For Stationarity

The stationarity of the GDP at level has been further examined through the study of their Auto Correlation Functions (ACFs) and Partial Autocorrelation Functions (PACFs). Figure 3 represents the ACFs and PACFs of the variable concerned.

It is observed from the Figure 1 that

(i) the ACF exhibits a dying-out pattern for the spikes,

(ii) there exists only one single spike at lag one.

These observations indicate that the GDP series at level is non-stationary and needs differencing. The ACF and PACF of the first differenced series of GDP are being given by the Figure 2.

The Figure 2 shows that

(i) the ACF is free from the dying-out pattern of spikes, and

(ii) the PACF does not contain any significant spike at lag one.

These observations testify for the stationarity of the first differenced GDP series. Consequently the GDP series is I (1) and d=1.

Figure 1: Correlogram of GDP at Level Data

Sample: 1984 2005
Included observations: 22

Autocorrelation	Partial Correlation		AC	PAC	Q-Stat	Prob
		1	0.872	0.872	19.097	0.000
		2	0.742	-0.071	33.649	0.000
		3	0.612	-0.081	44.050	0.000
		4	0.482	-0.078	50.862	0.000
		5	0.355	-0.073	54.784	0.000
		6	0.230	-0.087	56.537	0.000
		7	0.109	-0.086	56.957	0.000
		8	-0.006	-0.085	56.958	0.000
		9	-0.113	-0.080	57.478	0.000
		10	-0.205	-0.056	59.323	0.000
		11	-0.282	-0.059	63.140	0.000
		12	-0.342	-0.047	69.322	0.000

Figure 2: Correlogram of GDP at 1st Difference

Sample: 1984 2005
Included observations: 21

Autocorrelation	Partial Correlation		AC	PAC	Q-Stat	Prob
		1	0.579	0.579	8.0900	0.004
		2	0.432	0.146	12.843	0.002
		3	0.310	0.019	15.430	0.001
		4	0.040	-0.280	15.476	0.004
		5	0.158	0.296	16.225	0.006
		6	-0.174	-0.530	17.204	0.009
		7	-0.403	-0.276	22.806	0.002
		8	-0.350	0.070	27.347	0.001
		9	-0.382	0.259	33.235	0.000
		10	-0.214	-0.164	35.241	0.000
		11	-0.197	-0.045	37.123	0.000
		12	-0.214	0.142	39.585	0.000

Identification of The Model:

AR(p) Structure Identification:

It is further observed from the Figure-2 that

(i) the PACF contains significant spikes at lag 1 and also at lag 6.

(ii) the ACF also contains significant spikes at lag 1 and at lag 2.

These indicate that the first differenced GDP (?Yt) series defines an AR(1,6) structure.

Consequently, the estimable AR (1,6) model is

$$\Delta Y_t = \alpha + \alpha_1 \Delta Y_{t-1} + \alpha_2 \Delta Y_{t-6} + u_t \qquad 1$$

Results of Estimation

The estimated equation is as follows:

$$\Delta Y_t = 0.046734 + 0.682028\ \Delta Y_{t-1} - 0.480074\ \Delta Y_{t-6} \qquad 2$$

S.E.	(0.017934)	(0.203226)	(0.264384)
t-Stats	(2.605809)	(3.356003)	(-1.815818)
Prob.	(0.0230)	(0.0057)	(0.0945)

R^2 =0.507881, Adj R^2 = 0.425861, DW=2.501418, F=6.192165

Findings:

The equation 2 shows that

(i) $\hat{\beta}_1$ is found be significant at 1% level,

(ii) $\hat{\beta}_2$ is found be significant at 5% level

(iii) $\hat{\alpha}$ is significant at 1% level,

(iv) the equation is free from autocorrelation since DW=2.501418.

Figure –3

Correlogram of Residual of Equation-2

Sample: 1984 2005
Included observations: 15

Autocorrelation	Partial Correlation		AC	PAC	Q-Stat	Prob
		1	-0.268	-0.268	1.3103	0.252
		2	-0.103	-0.189	1.5191	0.468
		3	0.128	0.050	1.8663	0.601
		4	-0.303	-0.300	3.9955	0.407
		5	0.253	0.133	5.6323	0.344
		6	0.113	0.152	5.9942	0.424
		7	-0.299	-0.177	8.8374	0.265
		8	0.084	-0.112	9.0957	0.334
		9	-0.104	-0.101	9.5569	0.388
		10	0.037	0.034	9.6278	0.474
		11	0.015	-0.199	9.6421	0.563
		12	-0.091	-0.073	10.351	0.585

MA (q) Structure Identification:

The ACF and PACF of the residuals of the equation (2) are being plotted in Figure-3. The Figure-3 indicates that

(i) the ACF contains no significant spike,

(ii) the PACF also contains no significant spike.

These observations testify for MA (0) structure for ΔY_t.

ARIMA [(1, 6), 1, 0] Forecasts For Y_t

ARIMA [(1, 6), 1, 0] model as given by the equation 1 has been used for generating one period ahead forecast for Y_t . The time plots of GDP (Y_t) and the corresponding forecast (Y_f) are being presented through the Figure-4.4. Y_f is found to be almost coinciding with Yt over the period concerned.

Figure –4

The Time Plots of the GDP Level Data and the Corresponding ARIMA [(1, 6), 1, 0] Forecasts.

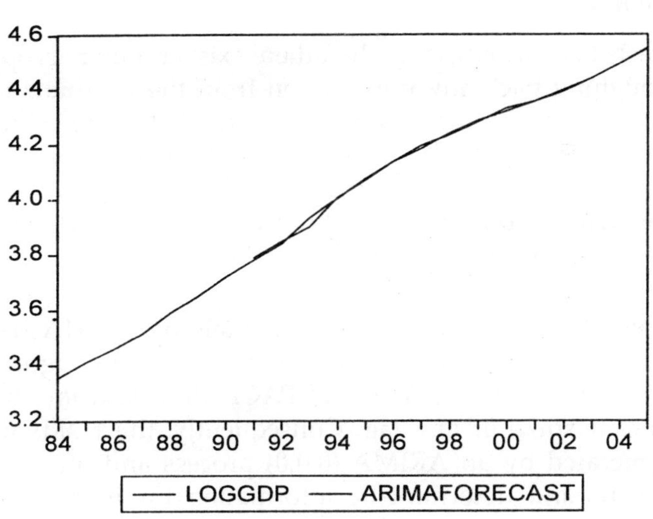

Findings from the Figure- 4

The Figure-4 shows that

(i) the ARIMA [(1, 6), 1, 0] forecasts almost coincide with the GDP level data.

(ii) GDP data set is marked by the absence of unusual volatility over the range 1984-2005.

Figure -.5

The Time Plot of Forecast Errors

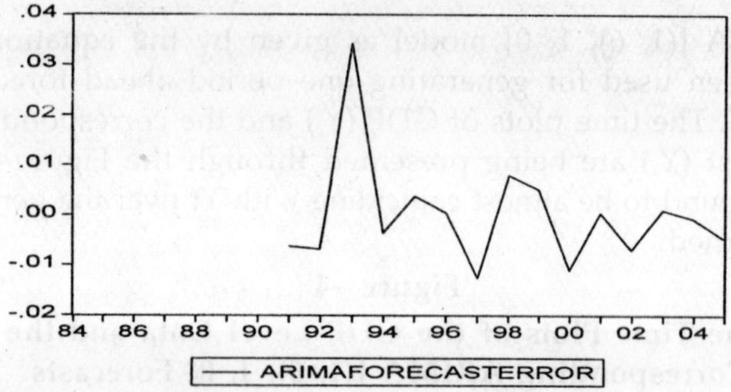

Efficiency of Forecasts:

Forecasts become efficient when there exists no more scope of ploughing back any information from the residuals to improve upon the forecast. If the residuals (e_t) are white noise such that e_t ~ iid N (0, $\sigma^2\varepsilon$), then these errors would have no AR (Auto regressive) structure at all. Consequently, no more information can be obtained from the errors and the errors would not represent any significant loss of information.

The ACF and PACF of the residuals of ARIMA [(1, 6), 1, 0] equation 3 are given by the Figure-3. The Figure-3 shows that both the ACF and PACF are free from any significant spike at any lag. Consequently, the residuals are generated by an ARIMA (0,0,0) process and offer no systematic and deterministic information for improving upon the forecast.

The forecasts become unbiased and and efficient if the forecast residuals are free from auto-correlation and heteroscedasticity. ARIMA (0,0,0) structure for the residuals indicates that residuals are free from autocorrelation. It, therefore, becomes imperative to examine if the residuals are heteroscedastic.

Heteroscedasticity of the Residuals:

The presence of high volatility followed by low volatility is indicative of heterocsedastic variance of the residuals. Since there is no cluster in the forecast error and Residual Mean Square is equal to 0.000116023, there is no heteroscedasticity in the residual and there is no need to estimate ARCH or GARCH Model.

Efficiency of ARIMA Forecasts-Further Examination:

In Time Domain analysis, a given time series of variable Xt is assumed to be generated by a stochastic process. Consequently, for any $\{X_t\}$ series there must be a sequence presenting stochastic process and the sequence is nothing by the realization of the process over time.

In any time series analysis, a researcher seeks to unearth the stochastic process generating the given sequence $\{X_t\}$. If that identified stochastic process is the "true" stochastic process behind the sequence $\{X_t\}$, then the stochastic process can be used to generate the future realization of the variable. These future realizations are the forecasts for the variable concerned. As a matter of fact, the original use of time series analysis was primarily as an aid to forecasting.

The stochastic process for any sequence $\{X_t\}$ is usually captured by an ARIMA (p,d,q) process and this ARIMA (p,d,q) process is used to make forecasts for the variable X_t. If these forecasts truly match the future realization of $\{X_t\}$, then forecasts are considered to be "efficient".

However, the forecasts are known to day while it takes considerable time to know the future realizations of the sequence $\{X_t\}$. As a result, these exists no scope for verifying on the spot whether forecasts are really acceptable. Yet there exist specific criteria for a priori verification of efficiency of forecasts.

Efficiency Criteria for Forecasts:

In time series analysis, forecasts are taken to be efficient if

(i) forecast RMSE is the minimum
(ii) forecast residuals are white noise such that these follow ARIMA(0,0,0) process
(iii) forecast residuals are not heteroscedastic
(iv) the correlogram structure of the forecasts is in unision with that of the forecast variable at level.

Verification of Correlogram Structure:

Consequently, we are left with the forth consideration involving examination of the unision of correlogram structures of forecasts and GDP data set at level. This is being considered below.

Fig-6 as reproduced here presents the correlogram of the GDP level datain the economy of India. The correlogram of the GDP forecasts is given by Fig-7.

One correlogram is found to be in conformity with the other since both the correlograms exhibit

(i) non-stationarity with dying out pattern of spikes at the ACF with a singular significant spike at the PACF at lag 1.
(ii) negative insignificant spikes at lag 2 and at onward lags.
(iii) sum of significant spikes in ACF in Fig-6 is 0.572 while that in ACF in Fig-7 is 0.556.

Figure –6
Correlogram of GDP at Level Data(India).

Sample: 1984 2005
Included observations: 22

Autocorrelation	Partial Correlation		AC	PAC	Q-Stat	Prob
		1	0.872	0.872	19.097	0.000
		2	0.742	-0.071	33.649	0.000
		3	0.612	-0.081	44.050	0.000
		4	0.482	-0.078	50.862	0.000
		5	0.355	-0.073	54.784	0.000
		6	0.230	-0.087	56.537	0.000
		7	0.109	-0.086	56.957	0.000
		8	-0.006	-0.085	56.958	0.000
		9	-0.113	-0.080	57.478	0.000
		10	-0.205	-0.056	59.323	0.000
		11	-0.282	-0.059	63.140	0.000
		12	-0.342	-0.047	69.322	0.000

Figure-7
Correlogram of ARIMA[(1,6),1,0] Forecasts

Sample: 1984 2005
Included observations: 15

Autocorrelation	Partial Correlation		AC	PAC	Q-Stat	Prob
		1	0.786	0.786	11.267	0.001
		2	0.580	-0.101	17.869	0.000
		3	0.379	-0.117	20.916	0.000
		4	0.213	-0.049	21.972	0.000
		5	0.066	-0.090	22.083	0.001
		6	-0.069	-0.108	22.217	0.001
		7	-0.179	-0.079	23.233	0.002
		8	-0.271	-0.100	25.905	0.001
		9	-0.344	-0.103	30.939	0.000
		10	-0.385	-0.064	38.504	0.000
		11	-0.403	-0.077	48.838	0.000
		12	-0.386	-0.038	61.478	0.000

Conclusion

ARIMA model offers a good technique for predicting the magnitude of the variable. Its strength lies in the fact that the method is suitable for any time series with any pattern of change and it does not require the forecaster to choose a priori the value of any parameter. Its limitations include its requirement of a long time series. Often it is called a "Black Box" model. Like any other method, this technique also does not guarantee perfect forecasts. Nevertheless, it can successfully be used for forecasting long time series data.

In this study GDP was found to be generated by ARIMA [(1, 6), 1, 0] model and this model was used for forecasting GDP. The ARIMA [(1, 6), 1, 0] forecasts were found to be efficient since there is no heteroscedasticity of forecast residuals.

Accordingly ARIMA [(1, 6), 1, 0] forecasts have been found to be "efficient". ARIMA [(1, 6), 1, 0] model, therefore, appears to be the appropriate model for forecasting GDP in the economy of India.

REFERENCES

Abhayaratne, A.S.P., (1996). "Foreign Trade and Economic Growth Evidence from Sri Lanka", 1960-1992. *Applied Economics Letters* 3, 567-570.

Akaike, H., (1969). "Fitting Autoregressive Models for Prediction". *Annals of the Institute of Statistical Mathematics* 21, 243-247.

Anderson, B.D.O., Moore J.B.(1979). *Optimal Filtering*. Prentice-Hall, Englewood Cliffs.

Aoki, M. (1987). *State Space Modeling of Time Series.* Springer- Verlag, Berlin.

Archibald BC (1900). "Parameter Space of The Holt-Winters' Model." *International Journal of Forecasting*, 6, 199-209.

Arnade, C., Vasavada, U., (1995). "Causality Between Productivity and Exports in Agriculture: Evidence from Asia and Latin America." *Journal of Agricultural Economics* 46, 174-186.

Assimakopoulos, V., Nikolopoulos, K. (2000). "The Theta Model: a Decomposition Approach to Forecasting." *International Journal of Forecasting*, 16, 199-209.

Bahmani-Oskooee, M., Mohtad, H., Shabsigh, G., 1991. "Export, Growth and Causality in LDCs: a Re-examination". *Journal of Development Economics* 36, 405-415.

Blalock, G., Gertler, P.J., (2004). "Learning from Exporting Revisited in A Less Developed Setting". *Journal of Development Economics* 75, 397-416.

Boero, G. and Marrocu, E,: (2002), "The Performance of Non-linear Exchange Rate Models: A Forecasting Comparison", *Journal of Forecasting* 21, 512-3-542.

Bowerman, B.L., O'Connel, R.T., Koehler, A.B. (2005). *Forecasting Time Series and Regression: An Applied Approach.* Thomson Brooks/ Cole, Belmont CA.

Box, George, and Gwily M. Jenkins. *Time Series Analysis, Forecasting, and Control*. San Francisco: Holden Day, (1976).

Box, G.E.P. and Jenkins, G.M.: (1970), *Time Series Analysis, Forecasting and Control,* Holden- Day, San Francisco.

Brailsford, T. J. and Faff, R.W. (1996): "An Evaluation of Volatility Forecasting Techniques", *Journal of Banking and Finance,* 20, 419-438.

Brannas, K. and De Gooijer, J.G.: (1994), "Autoregressive-Asymmetric Moving Average Model for Business Cycle Data", *Journal of Forecasting* 13, 529-544.

Brockwell, P.J., Davis, R.A. (1991). *Time series: Theory and Methods.* Springer-Verlag, New York, 2nd edition.

Chatfield, C., Yar, M. (1991). "Prediction Intervals for Multiplicative3 Holt-Winters." *International Journal of Forecasting,* 7, 31-37.

Choi, I., (1993). "Asymptotic Normality of The Least-Squares Estimates for Higher-Order Autoregressive Integrated Process with Some Applications". *Econometric Theory* 9, 263-282.

Clements, M.P. and Hendry, D.F.: (1999), *Forecasting Non-stationary Economic Time Series,* MIT Press, Cambridge, MA.

Clements, M.P., Franses, P.H. and Swanson, N.R.: (2004), "Forecasting Economic and Financial Time-Series with Non-linear Models", *International Journal of Forecasting* 20, 169-183

Deutsch, M., Granger, C.W.J. and Terasvirta, T. (1994), "The Combination of Forecasts Using Changing Weights", *International Journal of Forecasting* 10, 47-57.

Diebold, F., and R. Mariano (1995): "Comparing Predictive Accuracy". *Journal of Business and Economic Statistics,* 13, 253-263.

Enders, Walter. "ARIMA and Cointegration Tests of Purchasing Power Parity." *Review of Economics and Statistics* 70 (Agu. 1988), 504-08.

Gardner Jr ES, McKenzie E (1985). "Forecasting Trends in Time Series." *Management Science,* 31(100, 1237-1246.

Garner Jr ES (1985). "Exponential Smoothing: The State of The Art." *Journal of Forecasting,* 4, 1-28.

Goodrich RL (2000). "The Forecast Methodology." *International Journal of Forecasting,* 16(4), 533-535.

Granger, C.W.J., (1963). "Economic Processes Involving Feedback". *Information and Control* 6, 28-48.

Granger, C.W. J. and Pesaran, M.H.: (2000), "Economic and Statistical Measures of Forecast Accuracy", *Journal of Forecasting* 19, 537-560.

Granger, C.W. J. and Terasvirta, T.: (1991), "Experiments in Modeling Non-linear Relationships Between Time Series", in M. Casdagli and S. Eubank(eds), *Nonlinear Modeling and Forecasting,* Addison-Wesley, Redwood City, pp. 189-197.

Hamilton, J.D.: (1994), *Time Series Analysis,* Princeton University Press, Princeton, NJ.

Hannan EJ, Rissanen J (1982). "Recursive Estimation of Mixed Autoregressive-Moving Average Order." *Biometrika,* 69(1), 81-94.

Harvey, A.C. (1989): *Forecasting, Structural Time Series and Kalman Filter.* Cambridge University Press.

Harvey, D., S. Leybourene, and S. Newbold (1997): "Testing the Equality of Prediction Mean Squared Errors". *International Journal of Forecasting,* 13, 281-291.

Hendry, D.F. (1997)."The Econometrics of Macroeconomic Forecasting." *The Economic Journal,* 107(444), 1330-1357.

Hendry, D.F. and Clements, M.P.: (2003), "Economic Forecasting: Some Lessons From Recent Research", *Economic Modeling* 20, 301-329.

Hyndman, R.J., Billah, B. (2003). "Unmasking the Theta Method." *International Journal of Forecasting,* 19(2), 287-290.

Hyndman, R.J., Koehler, A.B., Snyder, R.D. (2008). *Forecasting with Exponential Smoothing: The State Space Approach,* Springer.

Hyndman, R.J., Koehler, A.B., Snyder, R.D., Grose, S. (2002). "A State Space Framework for Automatic Forecasting Using Exponential Smoothing Methods." *International Journal of Forecasting,* 18(3), 439-454.

Islam, M.N., (1998). "Export Expansion and Economic Growth: Testing for Cointegration and Causality". *Applied Economics* 30,415-425.

Lall, S. (1996). *Learning from the Asian Tigers.* Macmillan, London.

Lall. S., (2004). "Reinventing Industrial Strategy: The Role of Government Policy in Building Industrial Competitiveness." Working Paper (-2004, Trade and Industrial Policy Strategies, Johannesburg.

Liu LM (1989). "Identification of Seasonal ARIMA Models Using a Filtering Method." *Communications in Statistics,* Part A : Theory & Methods, 18, 2279-2288.

Maddala, D.S.: (1977), *Econometrics,* McGraw-Hill, New York.

Makridakis, S. Wheelwright, S.C., Hyndman, R.J. (1998). *Forecasting: Methods and Applications.* John Wiley & Sons, New York, 3rd edition.

Melard G, Pasteels JM (2000). "Automatic ARIMA Modeling Including Intervention, Using Time Series Expert Software." *International Journal of Forecasting,* 16, 497-508.

McLeod, A., and W.Li,(1983) "Diagnostic Checking ARMA Time Series Models Using Squared Residual Correlations." *Journal of Time Series Analysis* 4, 269-73.

Mincer, J. and Zarnowitz, V.: (1969), "The Evaluation of Economic Forecasts," in J. Mincer (ed.), *Economic Forecasts and Expectations,* National Bureau of Economic Research, New York.

Ord, J.K., Lowe, S. (1996). "Automatic Forecasting." *American Statistician,* 50(1), 88-94.

Petrucelli, J., and S. Woolford. (1984), "A Threshold AR(1) Model." *Journal of Applied Probability* 21 ,270-86.

Pindyck, R.S.D.L. Rubinfeld (2001) Econometric Models and Economic Forecasts (4th Edn), Irwin-McGraw-Hill, *Applied Economics* 26, 1145-1157.

Sharma, S.C., Dhakal, D., (1994). "Causal Analysis Between Exports and Economic Growth in Developing Countries". *Applied Economics* 26, 1145-1157.

Siegel, S. and Castellan, N.J. (1988): *Nonparametric Statistics.* McGraw-Hill: London.

Watson, M. W. and Engle, R.F.: (1985), "Testing for Regression Coefficient Stability with a Stationary AR(1) Alternative", *Review of Economics and Statistics* 67, 341-346.

West, Mike, and Jeff Harrison. (1989), *Bayesian Forecasting and Dynamic Models*. New York: Springer-Verlag,

West, K.D.: (2006), "Forecast Evaluation", in G. Elliott, C. W. J. Granger and A. Timmermann (eds.), *Handbook of Economic Forecasting*, Elsevier, Amsterdam.

2

Gender Differentials in Rural Work: An Assessment in a Regional Context

SANCHARI ROY MUKHERJEE* & PANCHALI SENGUPTA**

Abstract

The paper examines the economics of rural work and gender divisions of labour between men and women within the rural household, based on a recent time allocation survey of poor rural households engaged in agriculture and allied activities. The involvement of women in various forms of economic and non-economic activities is also explored, using stylised questionnaire methods for capturing the nature of women's work and latent gender structures whicht create disparities between men's and women's work in agricultural households.

Key Words: Time Allocation Study, SNA, Ex-SNA, Non-SNA ,Gender Disparity

* Reader in Economics, North Bengal University.

** Research Scholar, Dept. of Economics, North Bengal University.

Introduction

Foundational Issues

Economic disparities between countries and regions become visible when differences in the market value of labour are assessed in monetary terms. Disparities in gender terms are often invisible. Wage disparity is deeply entrenched in developing economies, where women are paid less after working identical or even longer hours than men. Women are estimated to support 53 percent of the total burden of work in developing countries. Nearly half of this however is unpaid household or community work. The duties of Third World women can be placed into three categories: reproductive and nurturing, family and household management, and productive and/ or income-generating roles (Momsen, 1991). Studies have shown that in developing countries women, especially poor women, work an average of 12 to 18 hours a day compared to an average of 8 to 12 hours a day for men. Among the tasks women perform are subsistence farming, food production and processing, traditional weaving and sewing, soap-making, petty trading, craft-making, baking, shop-keeping, procuring energy fuel and water, household work, payment of children's school fees, animal care, caring for the elderly, and raising children. Historically, women have performed mostly laborious gender-assigned duties with skills and tools passed down from generation to generation.

In developing societies, men climb faster on the developmental scale since they are more gender capable of utilizing the new earning opportunities that accompany development. Women on the other hand are burdened in this respect by the social and economic handicaps that shackle their independent development. Inequalities in social welfare, education and employment opportunities, and low participation in decision making appear more stark in the case of women than in the male segment of developing society. Gender development problems are rooted both in *i)* biological differences between the sex's and *ii)* inbuilt discrimination within the social and economic systems.

There are high degrees of inter-state and inter-district variations in gender roles in agriculture, environment and rural production. Women have extensive workloads with dual responsibility for farm and household production. In rural India, women have an active role and extensive involvement in livestock production, forest resource use and fishery processing. Women's work is getting harder and more time consuming due to ecological degradation and changing agricultural technologies and practices. Women contribute considerably to household income through farm and non-farm activities as well as through work as landless agricultural labourers.

Gender disparity is replicated also by the rural-urban divide. With rural production still contributing 72.18 percent of the value generated by the Indian economy in 1991 (Narasimhan, 1999:27), gender disparities have stronger implications for rural women than for their urban contemporaries. Working hours for rural women considerably exceed those for men. Empowerment of women lags specifically because of gender discrimination within intra-household relationships. The context needs to be addressed by examining gender division of labour and gender decision making roles both within and without the household. Despite widespread administrative acceptance of the UNDP index measures, they do not represent a woman's self perception of her predicament. The gender aspects made visible through the GDI are calibrated towards earnings rather than towards women's work. The social aspect of gender remains entirely hidden behind such indices. Since the UN World Conference on Women held at Beijing in 1995, feminist perspectives have been well articulated in terms of strategic gender needs (SGN) versus personal gender needs (PGN), and 'positive discrimination'. By itself, the increased earning ability of a woman offers a personal escape from property. No escape is offered however from the self-perpetuating character of gender discrimination within society. While GDI measures focus on PGN aspects, indices such as the Gender Empowerment Measure have evolved around the SGN aspect, namely the placement of women within the social decision making process.

Women's Economic Status in the Society

Anthropologists have approached the measurement of women's participation from a different viewpoint: that of the overall sexual division of labour (Brown, 1970). Many feminists have argued that all sexual inequalities are based on the sexual division of labour and that its abolition would result in overall equality between the sexes (Dixon, 1978). While performing a number of important tasks in the rural sector, women continue to be handicapped in many ways. Women all over the world suffer from a common disadvantage in that they seldom hold ownership rights over land in their own name (Mandelbaun 1959, Gore 1968, Ghai 1984 Charyulu and Reddy, 1987 Mencher 1986). In rural society, access to other resources i.e. credit, fertilizers, training etc are often determined by access to and control over land. Family traditions, inheritance systems and women's acceptance of subordination stand in the way). Even land reform programmes in most regions overlook the interests of women producer with the result that their economic insecurity has increased. These findings were supported by several empirical researches (Tadesse 1982, Sen 1983, Ahmed 1984).

In India, as the women folk are left with no alternative to earn their livelihood they are pushed into less skilled, low paying, more time consuming and drudgery prone activities (Kaur 1987, Verma 1992). Discussing the diminishing female work participation rate since 1901 in India, Sailabala Debi (1987) attributes this to the decline of traditional household and cottage based industries that employed women to a great extent. The segmentation of female labour market has led to the confinement of women to few occupations enabling the employers to pay them low wages (Banerjee, 1985 Mukhopadhya 1975). An inter-state analysis of women's participation in labour force revealed a high participation rate in the states of northeast where tribals following a matriarchal society constitute an important percentage of the overall population. The rate is unduly low in large and populous states like UP, Punjab, West Bengal, Bihar, Rajasthan, etc. (Sen, 1988). In Bastar District of Rajasthan, a large number of women were found to be involved in mining, factory, building construction and even in domestic service. They were picked up by contractor's trucks early in the morning but paid lower wages for similar work performed by men (Ranade 1975, Joshi 1989).

An opinion has therefore arisen among women economists to recast gender development on an Indian canvas. Bina Agarwal (1994) has exhaustively studied women's command over property in India, identifying the issue as a critical gap in the economic analysis of gender. Indira Hirway and Mahadevia (1996) have drawn attention towards the role of women's work patterns and the importance of women's living condition and personal security, while assessing prevailing levels of gender inequality in India. Unlike the typical measure of women's work that have been used in the recent UNDP indices, women's work in rural India is generally unpaid. Much of this work is done within the household, and can be truly measured not in income-terms, but in terms of time expended. An important elaboration of the women's work concept through Time Allocation Studies (TAS) suitable to rural women's work in India has been proposed by Devaki Jain (1996). It may be noted that the contribution made by women during unpaid household and community work represents sizeable household savings rather than income. Even then, the lack of direct money-income often minimizes the social importance of women's work.

Methodology and Relevance of Time Allocation Study

Time Use Study and Profile of Study Region

Time-use data can reveal the details of an individual's "daily life with a combination of specificity and comprehensiveness" not achieved in any other type of survey data (United Nations, 1997a). Statistics produced from such an exhaustive coverage of how individuals spend their time can paint an integrated picture of how various activities- paid and unpaid work, volunteer work, domestic work, leisure and personal activities-are interrelated in the lives of the general population and its various subsectors. With time-use data it is possible to determine what, how, why and how long activities are carried out. When properly collected and analysed, time-use data can allow for relating time-allocation patterns to the demographic and socio-economic status of the individual. The attempt of United Nations Statistical Division in extending the production boundary of the Systems of National Accounts (SNA), 1993 has led to the inclusion of the activities of unpaid work into the national accounting system as satellite accounts. This extended production boundary of SNA 1993 provides a better understanding of women's contribution to the economy.

In Indian Time Use, the activities were classified in three categories, namely System of National Accounts (SNA) activities (primary, secondary and tertiary activities – classified in market-oriented economic activity, and non-market economic activities within SNA production boundary), extended SNA activities (household maintenance, care for children, sick and elderly, community and organizational volunteer work), and non SNA activities (learning, personal care, leisure time...) to correctly capture and organize women's activity (economic and non economic).

In the present study primary data were collected for both males and females regarding the various types of work done by them. In the rural economy, mobility of female labour is restricted up to a certain extent, as is indicated in various studies. In the present study, the aim is to highlight the contribution of women in the rural household economy. The method used here is basically qualitative and includes time use studies where a questionnaire was designed to collect detailed information on the time spent by the individual members of the household in different activities that are both paid and unpaid. A stratified four stage sampling design , with districts as the first units, blocks as the second stage units, villages as the third stage units and households as the fourth (ultimate) stage units had been adopted for the survey. Questionnaire was designed to collect information on daily time use by male and female members of the households and thus fifty male respondents and fifty spouses were interrogated at the time of survey in each of the district to avoid bias in the data. Thus the total number of respondents for the study stood at 200 with equal gender division.

A process of stratified purposive random sampling has been used for each village in the district, where both men and women are available and are jointly engaged in the production process. In addition, the presence of both parties is imperative for the investigation. The sample population was from a mixed population belonging to lower, middle and higher income groups and from a mixed social background of SC, ST and Muslims. The data collected in the process is used meaningfully to reveal the time expended on various activities by the respondents and also the average time spent on different housework and agricultural activities by men and women.

The northern part of West Bengal is popularly known as North Bengal and comprises of six districts of Darjeeling, Jalpaiguri, Cooch Behar, Uttar Dinajpur, Dakshin Dinajpur and Malda, moving from north to south. Except the district of Darjeeling, the rest of the districts are in the plains and are primarily rural districts. The two districts where the present study is located, namely,

Jalpaiguri and Cooch Behar, are primarily agrarian in character, where the major rural workforce depends on agriculture or some form of artisanal activity for their livelihood. Jalpaiguri however, has vast tracts of forest lands and a significant belt of tea gardens in the Dooars region. Cooch Behar, an erstwhile princely state, has a dominant agricultural population.

Although the two districts are similar with a large section of the population being engaged in agriculture and related activities, the dominant cropping patterns of the two are dissimilar and consequently the time differentials at work is expected, although the nature of work may not differ totally. Thus, the two districts chosen from the six northern districts of West Bengal was a conscious choice for the purpose of the study. The villages in the districts were selected on the basis of both secondary and primary information. Demographic details, geographical features and economic background were collected from secondary sources. On the other hand, details of women's employment and participation in various activities of livelihood were obtained from women respondents by making personal contacts. The socio-demographic characteristics of the study villages are presented in tables below. The villages in the Jalpaiguri districts are Chaparerpar, Chadirjher and Salkumarhat. These villages are agrarian in nature and the rural folk are mostly dependent on agriculture. The villages are dominated by Hindus. The major crops raised are rice and jute. In the absence of irrigation facilities, agriculture is dependent on water fro the wells, ponds and rainfall. Literacy rates are above 60 percent in two of the selected villages while it is greater than 70 percent in Chaparerpar. Chandirjher and Salkuma.hat are interior villages that suffer from inadequate transportation facilities, but the facilities are comparatively better for Chaparerpar as it is located alongside the highway.

Table 1: Social and Demographic Characteristics of the Study Villages of Jalpaiguri District, Census 2001

Characteristics	*Chaparerpar*	*Chandirjher*	*Salkumarhat*
No of households	715	834	1118
Population	3498	4059	5439
Males	1819	2097	2800
Females	1679	1962	2639
Sex ratio(per 1000 males)	923	936	942
Family Size	4.9	4.9	4.9
Literacy rate(%)	71.4	65.4	64
Male literacy rate (%)	70.2	65.9	64.5
Female literacy rate(%)	52.2	45.5	42.5
Work participation rate(%)	31.4	34.9	49.5
Male cultivator (%)	23	34.1	42.9
Female Cultivator (%)	5	31.9	42.6
Male Agricultural labour (%)	20.4	20	22.1
Female Agricultural labour (%)	47.5	52.4	37.4

Source: Registrar General of Census, 2001.

Table 2: Social and Demographic Characteristics of Study Villages of Cooch-Behar District, Census 2001

Characteristics	*Hemkumari*	*Jangalbas*
No of household	3029	386
Population	15174	1812
Males	7817	941
Females	7357	871
Sex ratio(per 1000 males)	941	926
Family Size	5.0	4.7
Literacy ratio(%)	62.7	61.6
Males literacy rate (%)	60.3	57.1
Females literacy rate(%)	38.4	42.7
Work participation rate(%)	29.5	29
Female Cultivator (%)	17.5	28.6
Male Cultivator (%)	47.6	37.5
Female Agricultural labour (%)	66.5	30.4
Male Agricultural labour (%)	43.1	28.8

Source: Registrar General of Census, 2001.

Village survey has been done on the basis of following categorized activities:

A) SNA activities: The activities include SNA1 Land preparation, SNA2 Crop husbandry, SNA3 Post-harvest activities, SNA4 Crop protection, SNA5 Kitchen gardening, SNA6 Market sales & purchases, SNA7 Livestock tending, SNA8 Livestock grazing, SNA9 Making dung cakes, SNA10Poultry rearing, SNA11Water & fuel collection, SNA12 Processing & storage, SNA13 Dwelling construction, SNA14 Well/Irrigation construction, SNA15 Common infrastructure, SNA16 Making handicrafts SNA17 Market purchase & sales.

B) Extended SNA activities: In extended SNA activities, the activities are XNA1 cooking & cleaning, XNA2 Childcare, XNA3 Care of elderly, XNA4 Community work, XNA5 Education & tutoring, XNA6 Training programmes.

C) Non-SNA activities: Non-SNA activities include those activities that are performed for self care, maintenance of health and hygiene etc. These include NNA1Leisure, NNA2 Personal care, NNA3 Social conversation, NNA4 Rest & relaxation.

Results and Findings

While studying the various activities performed by the rural folk, differences in the focus of activities could be identified. Women workforces in Jalpaiguri district are involved in artisanal activities other than the usual agricultural and household activities, whereas, women in Cooch Behar district are heavily engaged in their household chores and primary agricultural activities. The rural men in Jalpaiguri district are also engaged in constructional activities like building construction, well/irrigation construction etc., but in Cooch Behar district majority of the men are engaged in agriculture and allied activities and they seldom keep their land fallow. Thus, crop diversification could be found in Cooch Behar district while demanding more time involvement from the men.

A comparative analysis of relative time contribution on different activities by men and women can be now undertaken with the help of the following figures. It is clear from the Figure-1, that, females in Jalpaiguri district spend much more time in activities related to care of children; cooking and cleaning as compared to males while males spend time on those activities which are remunerative SNA activities. After spending a larger portion of their time in caring of children and household maintenance, the women in Jalpaiguri district happen to spend a still larger portion of their total time on non remunerative SNA work. From the survey, it is also noticed that both the men and women spend significant number of hours for rest and relaxation in Cooch Behar, when compared to Jalpaiguri. The reason behind this is the less hesitant reporting on the part of the respondents in Cooch Behar, while respondents from Jalpaiguri underrated their leisure hours while trying to project the arduous nature of agricultural work. Participation of male labour force in Extended SNA activities is found to be smaller compared to their female counterpart.

Figure 1

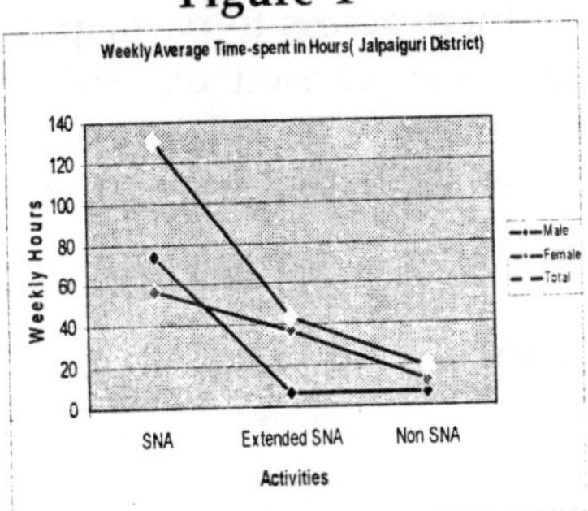

Figure 2

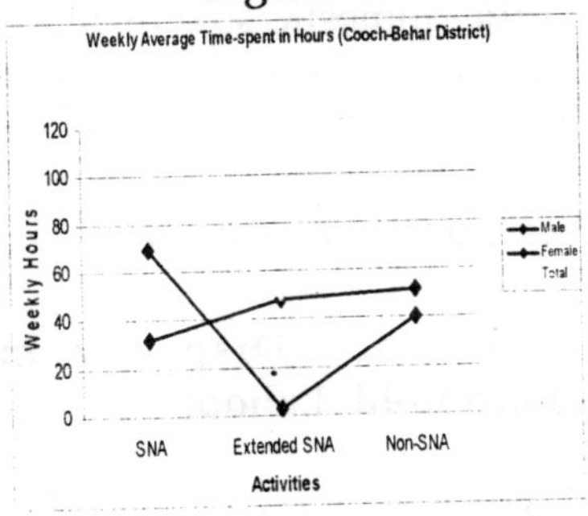

We can make a comparative estimation of the relative contribution of men and women in terms of hours spent in SNA, XNA and NNA activities from the above two figures. It is observed from the figures that percentage of weekly hours expended by women on XNA activities is much higher than the percentage of weekly hours expended by men on XNA activities. Thus, it is clear that women shoulder the heaviest burden in domestic core i.e. cooking, cleaning, care of children and community work whereas their male counterparts are mostly engaged in those activities which require physical strength like land preparing, crop protection etc. Again, work which needs sustained effort and endurance have been assigned to women like fetching water, poultry rearing, and post harvest activities like threshing, winnowing. All the matters involving money are dominated, rather monopolized by the men. Although, the gender involvement in various activities is mostly socially defined, women have a pivotal role in livestock management and household management.

The pattern of work carried out solely by women such as post harvest activities (threshing, winnowing) water-fuel collection, child care, livestock tending restrict women in the domestic sphere and limit there access to participate outside the home. Whereas activities carried out solely by men like market sales and purchases, crop husbandry and construction are those activities, which gave them the power of decision-making.

C) Gender Disparity measure and Division of Household Labour

Disparity Indexing on Work

On the basis of the time spent on different activities by men and women in rural household economy the paper attempts to index gender disparity (GDI) to show the contribution of women in agriculture. It is undoubtedly impossible to measure the love and affection of a mother to her children but one can give them recognition of those works which are performed by them within household chores to help their family and through activities that are income saving as well as income generating like tending animals, poultry rearing etc. These activities are non remunerative, where these tasks are performed during their leisure time. In rural areas, women have to do non remunerative SNA activities, Ex-SNA activities and also the Non SNA activities throughout their waking hours which results in excessive work burden on their shoulders. Often, they become the only source of earning and act as principle bread winner for their family. More often than not, their work remains optional or supplementary but one cannot obliterate their participation in the household and their sacrifices for the well being of the family and society at large.

The methodology for the gender disparity measure used here is taken from Human Development Report, 1995. The absolute differences in average time spent by males and females in different categories of activities in SNA, Extended SNA and Non-SNA have been taken and combined to arrive at a composite index of gender disparity for two districts. If ai represents the absolute difference of the amount of weekly average time spent by men and women in different SNA, Ex-SNA and Non-SNA activities, then for any component of the activity, the individual indices can be find out by the general given formula as:

$$\frac{\text{Actual } a_i \text{ value} - \text{Minimum } a_i \text{ value}}{\text{Maximum } a_i \text{ value} - \text{Minimum } a_i \text{ value}} = \text{GDI}$$

Table: 3 Measure of Gender Disparity in Jalpaiguri District (Activity wise)

Activities		Weekly Average Time Spent Male	Female	Absolute Difference	Gender Disparity Index
SNA1	Land preparation	41.02	31.22	9.8	1.00
SNA2	Crop husbandry	1.36	0	1.36	0.13
SNA3	Post-harvest activities	0	1.56	1.56	0.15
SNA4	Crop protection	1.59	0.04	1.55	0.15
SNA5	Kitchen gardening	0.2	1.19	0.99	0.09
SNA6	Market sales & purchases	0.73	0	0.73	0.07
SNA7	Livestock tending	0	6.08	6.08	0.62
SNA8	Livestock grazing	1.39	0.49	0.9	0.09
SNA9	Making dung cakes	0	3.36	3.36	0.34
SNA10	Poultry rearing	0	0.95	0.95	0.09
SNA11	Water & fuel collection	0	0.76	0.76	0.07
SNA12	Processing & storage	0.89	0.14	0.75	0.07
SNA13	Dwelling construction	9.28	1.12	8.16	0.83
SNA14	Well/Irrigation construction	1.02	0	1.02	0.10
SNA15	Common infrastructure	10.08	8.26	1.82	0.18
SNA16	Making handicrafts	0	2.03	2.03	0.20
SNA17	Market purchase & sales	0	0.04	0.04	0.00
XNA1	Cooking & cleaning	0	21.7	21.7	1.00
XNA2	Childcare	0	6.22	6.22	0.27
XNA3	Care of elderly	0	1.12	1.12	0.02
XNA4	Community work	1.54	2.06	0.52	0.00
XNA5	Education & tutoring	0.21	1.33	1.12	0.02
XNA6	Training programmes	0	0.56	0.56	0.00
NNA1	Leisure	4.15	4.2	0.05	0.00
NNA2	Personal care	0	3.34	3.34	0.91
NNA3	Social conversation	0.07	3.71	3.64	1.00
NNA4	Rest & relaxation	5.84	5.72	0.12	0.02
Combined SNA		73.37	57.11	16.26	0.40
Combined Ex-SNA		6.4	37.19	30.29	1.00
Combined Non-SNA		6.41	12.77	6.36	0.00

Source: TU Survey data.

The results of the gender disparity measure in different activities of the two districts are shown in table 3 and table 4. If we look at the combined activities of the two districts, a higher gender disparity index with a value of 1.00 is observed for the Extended SNA activities in each district implying that females undertake the sole responsibility of household management which includes numerous activities like cooking, cleaning etc. Men are reluctant to take initiative in sharing responsibility in household chores but conscious and cautious about their decision making role in household expenditure. In Non-SNA work, there is less disparity i.e. men and women both enjoy free and spare time. For SNA activities, GDI are 0.40 and 0.76 in Jalpaiguri and Cooch Behar respectively, indicating favourable male position in terms of paid SNA activities. It has been noticed earlier that in each district that the men-folk are primarily engaged in those activities that are paid and they spend most of their time on the SNA activities which are remunerative. If one considers the GDI for individual activities then it will be very clear that GDI favours males only on activities like land preparation, dwelling construction, common infrastructure, while GDI is weighted in favour of females for SNA activities like livestock tending, making dung cakes, making handicrafts which are non remunerative. Women are given those activities which need sustained efforts and energy. This phenomenon substantiates the traditional concept of gender division of labour that is pre-conditioned by social values, primitive socio-cultural norms and prejudices etc., relegating women to a subordinate position within the family while preventing women from entering the public domain.

Table 4: Measure of Gender Disparity in Cooch Behar District (Activity wise)

Activities		*Weekly Average Time Spent*		*Absolute Difference*	*Gender Disparity Index*
		Male	*Female*		
SNA1	Land preparation	29.84	10.54	19.3	1.00
SNA2	Crop husbandry	7.69	1.44	6.25	0.32
SNA3	Post-harvest activities	6.43	2.43	4.00	0.20
SNA4	Crop protection	3.1	0.84	2.26	0.11
SNA5	Kitchen gardening	0.71	2.42	1.71	0.09
SNA6	Market sales & purchases	2	0	2	0.10
SNA7	Livestock tending	2.9	2.8	0.1	0.00
SNA8	Livestock grazing	2.76	2.38	0.38	0.02
SNA9	Making dung cakes	0.23	2.57	2.34	0.12
SNA10	Poultry rearing	0.94	1.83	0.89	0.04
SNA11	Water & fuel collection	1.48	2.66	1.18	0.06
SNA12	Processing & storage	1.87	0.4	1.47	0.07
SNA13	Dwelling construction	2.56	1.68	0.88	0.04
SNA14	Well/Irrigation construction	1.52	0	1.52	0.07
SNA15	Common infrastructure	5.34	1.82	3.52	0.18
SNA16	Making handicrafts	0	0	0	0.00
SNA17	Market purchase & sales	0	0	0	0.00
XNA1	Cooking & cleaning	0.28	30.34	30.06	1.00
XNA2	Childcare	0.63	12.92	12.29	0.40
XNA3	Care of elderly	0.21	1.82	1.61	0.05
XNA4	Community work	0.37	0.51	0.14	0.00
XNA5	Education & tutoring	0.88	2.16	1.28	0.03
XNA6	Training programmes	0.19	0.36	0.17	0.00
NNA1	Leisure	2.66	3.32	0.66	0.00
NNA2	Personal care	0.75	1.9	1,15	0.07
NNA3	Social conversation	1.77	4.01	2.24	0.24
NNA4	Rest & relaxation	35.14	42.4	7.26	1.00
Combined SNA		69.37	31.79	37.58	0.76
Combined Ex-SNA		2.56	48.12	45.56	1.00
Combined Non-SNA		40.32	51.63	11.31	0.00

Source: TU Survey data.

Conclusion

Gender discrimination is all pervasive, cutting across social, political and economic life. In any organizational set-up, if women are discriminated on the grounds of gender issues and are denied the positions of power or are denied the opportunities to participate in the decision making process, effectiveness of the organization would definitely get affected. Transformation within our social structures to make invisible contribution of women visible is imperative to improve on the subordinate position of women in society. The work participation rate (WPR) in India (Census 2001) is higher for males than females, both in rural and urban areas. However, even though female participation in economic activities are low, but her total hours of work, including work within household are not less than the total time of work by the male. Thus, if data and analysis were disaggregated in terms of gender work participation in both private and public sphere, then redefining 'work' would reflect the contributions of women more meaningfully. Indispensable but unpaid home-based activities pursued by women are not reflected in the statistics on labour force. It is because little quantitative information relating to non-monetized household activities performed by women are available. If the entire ranges of both economic and non-economic activities of women are properly accounted for, their work participation rates as well as their contribution to agricultural development will definitely exceed those of men. By ignoring the contribution and development of women, no nation can ever reach the stage of development in any sector at which it ought to be and could be and thus the role of women in agriculture and household spheres has to be rendered visible.

REFERENCES

Agarwal, B. 1994. *A Field of One's Own*, CUP, Cambridge.

Ahmed, Z. 1984. "Rural Women and their Work: Dependence and Alternatives for change". *International Labour Review*. Vol. 123, No. 1, Jan-Feb, pp. 71-84.

Banerjee. N. 1985. "Women's Work and Discrimination", In: Jain, D and Banerjee, N. (ed) *Tyranny of the Household*. New Delhi. Vikas Publishing House.

Banerjee, Nirmala (2005): 'Economics of Gender Roles', Paper presented at the CWS-Sachetana Seminar on Women and Development: West Bengal Scenario, 1-2 February, Centre for Women's Studies, University of North Bengal.

Brown, C. and Penchman, J. 1970. *Gender in Workplace*, Washington, Brookings.

Central Statistical Organisation, 2000. "Report of the Time Use Survey", Ministry of Statistics and Programme Implementation, Government of India, New Delhi.

Charyulu, U.V.N. and Reddy, G.N. 1987 "Rural Women: Decision Making, Public Participation and other Basic Needs". *The Indian Journal of Social Work*, Vol. XLVII, No-4 Jan, pp. 407-415.

Debi, S. (1991) "Contribution of Women to Agricultural Production in Orissa", In: Mahajan, V.S. (ed) *Women's Contribution to India's Economic and Social Development*. N.D: Deep & Deep Publications, pp. 59.

Debi, L.A. 1987. *Rural Women: Management in Farm and Home*. New Delhi, Northern Book Centre.

Dixon , R.B. 1978. "Rural Development and Women's Economic Roles in Asia", In: Das, M.S., Gupta, V.K., *Social Status of Women in Developing Countries*. N.D: M.D. Publications Pvt Ltd. 1995

Ghai, D. 1984. Resource, Power and Women. Proceedings of the African and Asian Inter-Regional Workshop on Strategies for Improving the Employment Conditions of Rural Women, ILO, Geneva.

Gore. M.S. 1968. *Urbanization and Family Change*, Bombay: Popular Prakashan.

Hirway, I. and Mahadevia, D. 1996 ' Critique of Gender Development Index : Towards an Alternative', *Economic and Political Weekly*, 31(43): WS 87-96.

Jain, D. 1996: 'Valuing Work: Time as a Measure', *Economic and Political Weekly*, Vol. XXXI, No- 43, Oct.-26.

Joshi. U. 1989: Improving the Status of Rural Women, *Social Welfare*. Vol. XXXVI, No.-2-3, June-July.

Kaur, S. 1987. *Women in rural Development*. New Delhi: Mittal Publication.

Mendelbaum and David, G. 1959. *Society in India*, California: California University Press.

Mencher, J. 1982. 'Women 's work and Poverty: Their Contributions to Household Maintenance in Southern Indian States'. Paper presented at the conference on Women and Income Control in the Third World. New York: Columbia University, pp 7-9.

Mencher, Joan P. & Deborah D'Amico (1986): 'Kerala Women as Labourers and Supervisors: Implications for Women and Development', in Leela Dube, Eleanor Leacock, Shirley Ardener (eds.): *Invisibility and Power: Essays in Women and Society and Development*, Oxford University Press, New York

Momsen, J.H. (1991). *Women and Development in the Third World*. New York: Routledge

Mukhopadhyay, S. 1975. Women in Indian Labour force: A case of Market Segmentation of women in Indian Labour force, *Demography India*, Vol. 4, No. 2, pp. 345-364.

Narasimhan, S. 1999. *Empowering Women*, Sage, New Delhi

Ranade. S.N. 1975: *Women Construction Workers*, New Delhi: Allied Publishers, pp. 1.

Sen.G.1983. "Women Agricultural Labourers: Regional vatiations in Incidence an Employment". Working paper No. 168, Mimeographed p. 168, Trivandrum; Centre for Development Studies.

Sen, G. 1988."Paddy Production, Processing and Women Workers in India—The South versus the North-east". Paper presented at the Conference on Women in Rice farming, 26-30 September, Phillipines: IRRI, LOS Bonus.

Shimray, U. A. (2004): 'Women's Work in Naga Society: Household Work, Workforce Participation and Division of Labour', *Economic & Political Weekly*, 39(17):1698-1711

Tadesse. Z. 1982. `The Impact of Land Reforms on Women: A case of Ethiopia' in Beneria, L. (ed) *Women and Development the Sexual Division of Labour in Rural Societies*, New York.

UN (2005): Guide to Producing Statistics on Time Use: Measuring Paid & Unpaid Work, Department of Economic & Social Affairs, United Nations Statistics Division, New York

UNDP (1995): Human Development Report 1995: Gender & Human Development, United Nations Development Programme (UNDP), Oxford University Press, New York

UNDP (2005): 'Technical Notes', Human Development Report 2005: International Cooperation at a Crossroads: Aid, Trade and Security in an Unequal World, United Nations Development Programme (UNDP), Oxford University Press, New York

Verma, S.K. 1992. *Women in Agriculture: A Socio-Economic Analysis*. New Delhi: Concept Publishing Company. pp. 117-118.

3

People on the Shift: Character and Significance of Migration in Urban Informal Sector

KANAK KANTI BAGCHI* & NIRUPAM GOPE**

A large volume of inter and intra district in-migration of workers can be found in Siliguri Municipal Corporation Area (SMCA) induced by push factors such as reduced income opportunities at villages, inadequate harvests, low wages etc. and pull factors like easy absorption in the unorganised sector, better access to public services such as electricity, clinics, schools, as well as better recreation facilities in the city. There is no denying the fact that apathy towards villages also is swelling the ranks of job hunters. The present paper delineates the push and pull factors of migration and other facets of socio-economic life of in-migrant rickshaw pullers and construction workers in SMCA.

Key Words: Migration, Living Condition.

* Professor, Department of Economics, North Bengal.

** Senior Lecturer, Dinhata College, Dinhata, Cooch Behar.

I. Introduction

There is extensive debate on the factors that cause populations to shift, from those which emphasize individual rationality and household behavior to those which cite the structural logic of capitalist development (De Haan and Rogaly, 2002). The sources of early migration flows were primarily agro-ecological, related to population expansion to new settlements or to conquests (e.g. Eaton, 1984). Mass departure from one area to another in search of a better livelihood is a key feature of human history. Forces driving migration are many and complex. Streams differ in duration, basis, purpose and migrant characteristics. Migration often involves longer working hours, poor living and working conditions, social isolation and poor access to basic amenities. Recent evidence based on NSS data in case of internal migration figures for 1992–1993 and 1999–2000, and indirectly supported by the census, suggests an increase in migration rates—from 24.7 per cent to 26.6 per cent over that period (Government of India, 1993, 2000). This evidence suggests that the proportion of migrants of both sexes, in both rural and urban areas, increased during the last decade of the 20th century.

Migration in India is predominantly confined to short distance, with around 60 per cent of migrants changing their residence within the district of enumeration and over 20 per cent within the state of enumeration while the rest move across the state boundaries (Government of India, 1991). A significant proportion of women migrate over short distances, mainly following marriage. For inter-state migration, a similar trend is observed. Developed states show high inter-state immigration while poor states, barring Madhya Pradesh, show low rates of total and male immigration. Rates of interstate lifetime emigration are complementary to the above trends (Srivastava, 1998). Based on place of last residence and on place of birth, migrants are generally classified into four migration streams. Rural areas are still the main destination for migrants, but urban destinations are more important for male migrants (49 per cent of male migrants moved to urban destinations in 1991, compared to 29.5 per cent female migrants) (Government of India, 1991). Between 1992–1993 and 1999–2000, NSS data indicate an increase in urban migration, but this is mainly due to urban-urban flows (Srivastava and Bhattacharya, 2002). More recent studies have reconfirmed that migration is a significant livelihood strategy for poor households in several regions of India (Mosse et al, 2002; Haberfeld et al, 1999; Rogaly et al, 2001).

In India, as in most other developing economies, macro economic policy prejudices against the informal sector continued for a long time. Again it is commonly believed that strict labour laws, firmness in the labour markets and growing global competition have pushed the use of capital-intensive technology which has accelerated the growth of employment in the informal sector, compelling the informal sector to absorb most of the additional job aspirants. There is a large volume of inter and intra district migration in the Siliguri Municipal Corporation Area (SMCA) induced by reduced income opportunities at villages, inadequate harvests, low wages in villages, easy absorption in the unorganised sector and better access to public services such as electricity, clinics, schools, as well as better prospects for recreation in the city. With the multitudes of rural families migrating to cities due to lack of opportunities in rural areas and in search of a better job in the city, the formal sector finds it difficult to offer jobs to the migrants. It is ultimately the informal economic sector that absorbs these migrants and provides them opportunities to find jobs, create entrepreneurship and raise incomes above the rural levels. Economic forces are very important in influencing migration to SMCA and the person, who migrates, gains most from it.

There is no denying of the fact that apathy towards village life is also one of the factors contributing to the increasing number of job seekers in the cities. The traditional profession in the villages no longer charm to most of the members of the younger generation. Because of the social stigma, people are hesitant to take up menial jobs in the village but prefer to work on such jobs in the cities where they are strangers. Land is only asset on which village people fall back upon. But of late, there has been a tremendous pressure on land because of manifold rise in population. Following the mechanization and modernization of agricultural operations, more and more people are being rendered redundant. It is increasingly becoming clear that deployment of manual labour on agricultural operations almost reached a saturation point and thereby aggravating the problem of disguised unemployment. The main important factor contributing to the emergence of this class of wage earners is poverty. What is worse, a sizeable number of these wage earners have got large families to support. The small holdings are becoming economically unviable because of frequent migration. Unemployed or underemployed people flock to the cities in search of employment and the easiest job in commensurate with their ability and skill is that of rickshaw pulling (a three-wheel cart driven by human being) and then largely the job of unskilled construction worker. Another equally important factor is charm and attraction which city life holds. The glamour and charm of the city appeals to the naïve mind of rustic and they crave to be in a city at whatever cost.

The objective of the present study is to explore the character and significance of in-migration of workers in urban informal sector with special reference to rickshaw pullers and construction workers in Siliguri Municipal Corporation Area (SMCA) in the district of Darjeeling of the state of West Bengal. The study is based on a field survey where primary data have been collected from selected numbers of rickshaw pullers and construction workers. For collecting primary data on Rickshaw Pullers (RPs) we purposively selected 12 rickshaw stands at busy road crossings from different locations of the city. Again for collecting primary data from Construction Workers (CWs), we purposively selected 12 civil construction sites from different parts of the city. Selected RPs and CWs of all age groups were interviewed using a structured questionnaire and the workers were compensated for the time spent with us. The total size of the sample is 410 workers comprising of 205 RPs and 205 CWs. Primary data has been collected through personal interaction with the respondents. In total 2 sets of questionnaires have been used one each for the RPs and CWs.

The paper is organized as follows. Section II deals with migration and gender profiles of the two selected categories of workers. Section III delineates the reasons for migration. In Section IV comparison between RPs and CWs has been made in respect of income and consumption on the basis of migration status. Summary of findings and conclusions have been placed in the final section.

II. Types of Migration and Gender Profile

Field survey data reveal that people from diverse areas of the state do not take part equally in rickshaw pulling as well as in construction work. Nature of migration according to home district is not homogenous between RPs and CWs [p<3.0604.10-19]. Majority of in-migrant RPs belong to the districts of Jalpaiguri and Uttar Dinajpur from which more than half (nearly 56 per cent) of the sample RPs have come (Table-1). In case of CWs, two largest contributing districts are Jalpaiguri and Coochbehar from which more than two third (nearly 87 per cent) of the sample CWs had come. Interstate migrants were found only among RPs with 3.82 per cent. Intra-district migration is higher among RPs (15.29 per cent) than CWs (10.94per cent). Thus on a close scrutiny we find that for RPs, a larger proportion of pullers have come from south of Jalpaiguri (about 32 per cent) and for CWs, a larger portion of workers have come from east of Jalpaiguri (about 28 per cent). Jalpaiguri alone contributes more than 52 per cent of both RPs and construction workers taken together.

Table 1
Distribution of Migrant RPs and CWs According to Home Districts

District	*Rickshaw Pullers*	*Construction Workers*
Inter State	6[3.82]	0
Intra District	24[15.29]	22[10.94]
Coochbehar	30[19.10]	35[17.41]
Jalpaiguri	48[30.59]	140[69.66]
Malda	4[2.54]	4[1.99]
Mursidabad	5[3.18]	0
Uttar Dinajpur	40[25.48]	0
Total	157[76.59]	201[98.05]
Native	48[23.41]	4[1.95]
Grand Total	205[100]	205[100]

Note: Column percentage in brackets.

Source: Field Survey.

Migration status is not homogenous between RPs and CWs [p<1.05.10-20]. Of the total RPs and CWs, migrants among the CWs are higher (98.05 per cent) than the RPs (76.59 per cent) (Table-2). Temporary migrants among the RPs (56.68 per cent) are higher than that of CWs with only 19.40per cent and conversely, circular migrants among the CWs (68.56 per cent) are higher than the RPs with 34.39per cent. Again higher percentage of permanent migrants is seen among CWs (11.94 per cent) than RPs (8.93per cent). The reason behind the higher percentage of temporary migrants among the RPs is that earnings from pulling rickshaws in Siliguri are much higher than in other adjacent towns.

Table 2: Distribution of RPs and CWs According to Migration Status

	Non-Migrants	*Migrants*			*Total Migrants*
		Temporary	*Permanent*	*Circular*	
Rickshaw Pullers	48 [23.41]	89 [56.68]	14 [8.93]	54 [34.39]	157 [76.59]

Construction Workers	4 [1.95]	39 [19.40]	24 [11.94]	138 [68.56]	201 [98.05]

Note: Row percentage in brackets.
Source: Field Survey.

Average rickshaw rent for hired rickshaws varies with the nature of migrating pullers (Table-3). Average rent paid by the pullers is the highest among the temporary migrants (Rs.27.26) as opposed to permanent (Rs. 25.66) and circular (Rs. 24.04) migrants. On the contrary, native RPs paid the lowest rental for their hired rickshaws @ Rs. 22.50 per day. Thus the rent on hired rickshaws depends on the degree of permanence of the rickshaw pullers in Siliguri town.

Table 3: Distribution of RPs According to Average Rickshaw Rent per Day and Nature of Migration

	Temporary	*Permanent*	*Circular*	*Native*
Average Rent Paid Per Day [Rs]	27.26	25.66	24.04	22.50

Source: Field Survey.

Gender profile of CWs by nature of migration is illustrated in Table-4. Gender profile is not homogenous between RPs and CWs [p<0.00011]. Among the temporary and circular migrants, majority belongs to the category of male CWs (76.93 per cent and 81.15 per cent). Among the permanent migrants, major proportion constitutes the female workers with 58.34per cent. Majority of both male and female CWs are circular migrants by nature.

Table 4

Gender Profile and Nature of Migration [CWs]

	Temporary	*Permanent*	*Circular*	*Native*	*Total*
Male	30[76.93]	10[41.66]	112[81.15]	4[100]	156[76.09]
Female	9[23.07]	14[58.34]	26[18.85]	0	49[23.91]
Total	39[100]	24[100]	138[100]	4[100]	205[100]

Note: Column percentage in brackets
Source: Field Survey

Table 5: Migration Status of RPs and CWs by Duration of Work

Category & duration	*Construction Work at SMCA*				*Rickshaw Pulling at SMCA*			
	1-4	*5-15*	*15+*	*Total*	*1-4*	*5 -15*	*15+*	*TOTAL*
Native	2[50]	2[50]	0	4[100]	20[42]	22[46]	6[12]	48
	[3.18]	[1.62]		[1.96]	[29.42]	[19.47]	[25.00]	[23.41]
				Migrant				
Temporary/Seasonal	21[54]	16[41]	2[5]	39[100]	22[25]	55[62]	12[13]	89[100]
	[34.42]	[13.12]	[11.11]	[19.40]	[45.84]	[60.45]	[66.67]	[56.68]
Permanent	6[25][9.84]	14[58]	4[17]	24[100]	8[57]	6[43]	0	14[100]
	[9.84]	[11.48]	[22.21]	[11.94]	[16.66]	[6.59]	0	[8.93]
Circular	34[24]	92[67]	12[9]	138[100]	18[33]	30[56]	6[11]	54[100]
	[55.73]	[75.40]	[66.68]	[68.56]	[37.50]	[32.96]	[33.33]	[34.39]
Total	61[30]	122[61]	18[9]	201[100]	48[31]	91[58]	18[11]	57[100]
	[96.84]	[98.38]	[100.00]	[98.06]	[70.58]	[80.55]	[75.00]	57[100]
Grand Total	63[31]	124[60]	18[9]	205[100]	68[33]	113[55]	24[12]	205[100]
	[100]	[100]	[100]	[100]	[100]	[100]	[100]	[100]

Notes :(i) Column percentage in brackets, (ii)1-4 years=new joiners;5-15 years=core joiners;15+years=deep joiners

Source: Field Survey.

If we compare the migration status by duration of work at SMCA among RPs and CWs (Table-5), then we can see that higher percentage of native worker is found among RPs. Thus native people are more inclined in favour of pulling rickshaws rather than working at construction sites. Again, among all the migrant CWs, major proportion is circulatory by nature (1-4 years -55.73 per cent; 5-15 years -75.40 per cent; 15+ years -66.68 per cent) and among all the joiners of migrant RPs, major portion constitutes temporary migrants (1-4 years-45.84 per cent; 5-15 years -60.45 per cent; 15+ years -66.67 per cent). Thus major portion of migrant CWs are coming from adjacent regions of Siliguri town and major portion of the migrant RPs are coming regions far away from Siliguri town.

As far as new joiner workers are concerned, higher percentage of native workers has been found in rickshaw pulling [29.42 per cent] than in construction work [3.18 per cent]. Thus young native peoples are more inclined to rickshaw pulling rather than to construction work. Our survey revealed that, among the temporary migrant CWs, new joiner CWs [54 per cent] hold higher percentage than core [41 per cent] and deep joiner [5 per cent] CWs. In case of rickshaw pulling, core joiner RPs hold higher percentage than new and deep joiner RPs among temporary migrant RPs. Higher percentage of new joiner RPs has been found among the permanently migrant RPs and on the other hand, the core joiner CWs hold higher percentage among permanently migrant CWs. In case of circular migrant workers, core joiner workers constitute major proportion both in rickshaw pulling and in construction work.

III. Reasons of Migration

Movement is an integral part of human existence. Factors motivating migration are complex and intertwined. Motives for migration are frequently multiple. People move for a combination of several reasons, and they are not always aware of all the factors motivating their moves. Though many people are coming with the intention of permanent job, often circumstances force them to grab the opportunities by any manner. The majority of the workers came to the city only after being unable to maintain themselves in the villages.

Causes of migration are not homogenous between RPs and CWs [p<. 002]. A preponderant majority of both RPs (81.55 per cent) and CWs (69.65 per cent) leave their villages because of inadeauate earnings (Chart-1). Again the great majority of them leave their ancestral homes only when forced to do, either by lack of employment or by unsatisfactory social conditions. Migration owing to unsatisfactory working condition is more prevalent in rickshaw pulling [15.28 per cent] than in construction work [6.96 per cent]. Migration owing to unemployment problem in villages has been found more rampant among CWs [45.77 per cent] than among the RPs [30.57 per cent].

Push Factors

Migration, any type, whether documented or undocumented, forced or voluntary can be explained in terms of push-pull factors. Push factors attribute to the negative characteristics operating at the center of origin whereas pull factors identify the positive characteristics at the center of destination. There are essentially two types of migrants. One is owing to persecution for various reasons, and the other is economic reason. Persecution is essentially either for political or religious reasons. In such cases, the persons are given asylum to adopt other places. An economic migrant does not receive these privileges. Push factor that worked predominantly among both the RPs and CWs is "economic depression or poverty" which accounts 49.04per cent for RPs and 40.29 per cent for CWs. Here all the push factors which they have outlined during interview are economic in nature [Chart-2]. Push factor for migration is not homogenous between RPs and CWs [p<. 00083].

Pull Factors

Motivation for migration can be explained by involuntary similes- centrifugal and centripetal forces. The centrifugal desire does not have strong effect if the receptive desire is weak. The centrifugal impulse attribute to the push factors operating at the centre of origin, whereas the receptive impulse relates to pull factors that identify the positive characteristics at the center of destination. It appears that economic opportunities in terms of job availability in primary and informal sectors, economic stability, and easy absorption in SMCA worked as centripetal force for migrants. Such receptive forces are strengthened by centrifugal forces and have possibly caused migrants to come at SMCA. These can be easily established from the following opinion of the respondents of Chart-3. Preponderant majority of both RPs [53.50 per cent) and CWs (51.24 per cent) migrated to SMCA due to higher job opportunity in relation to other areas of north Bengal. Easy absorption and strong economic stability of Siliguri were the other pull factors stated by our surveyed respondents.

Chart 1

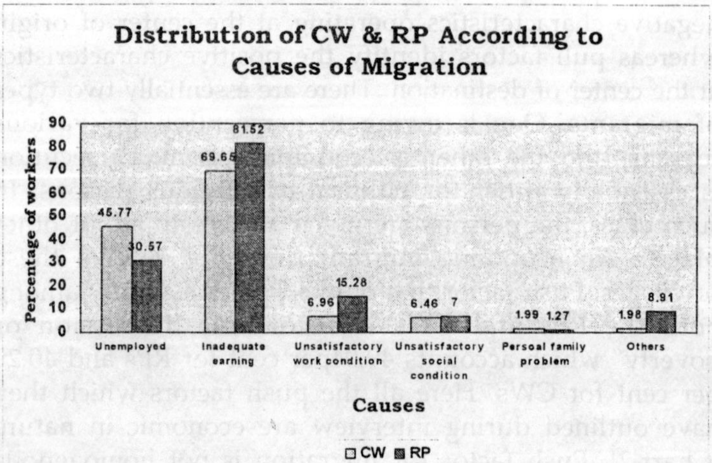

Chart 2

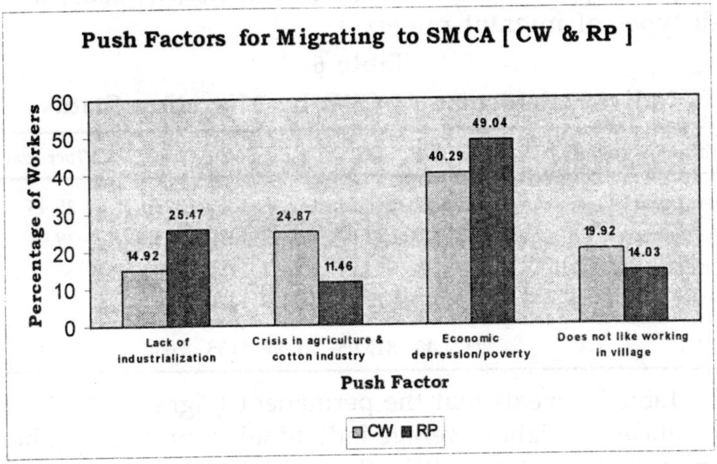

Chart 3

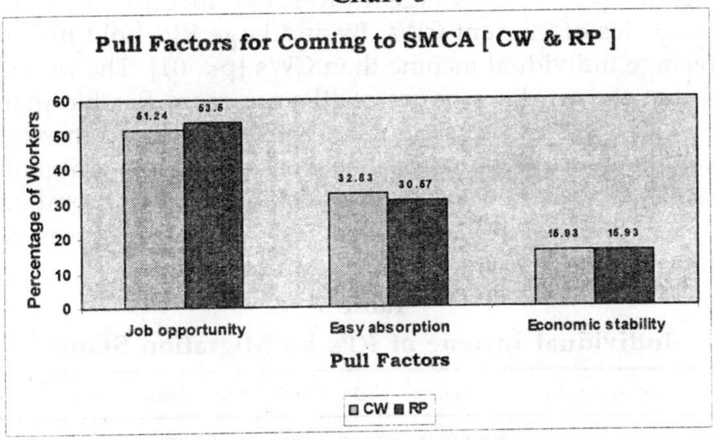

IV. Comparison by Migration Status

Individual Income

As far as individual income is concerned, there is no significant difference in average individual incomes among migrant CWs [Table-6]. Somehow native CWs manage to grip higher individual average income [Rs. 2860] than all types of migrant pullers.

Table 6

Individual Income of CWs by Migration Status

Nature of migration	*Mean*	*S.D.*	*S.E.*	*Min*	*Max*	*CV[per cent]*
Temporary	2156.47	548.31	132.98	1365	3250	25.43
Permanent	2005.00	582.57	168.17	1210	2850	29.06
Circular	2473.91	884.81	106.52	1155	7600	35.77
Native	2860.00	622.25	440.00	2420	3300	21.76
Total	2371.40	815.05	81.50	1155	7600	34.37

Table-7 reveals that the permanent migrant RPs have significantly higher average individual income than other categories of migrant RPs. It can be found from Table-7 that all categories of migrant pullers have significantly higher [p<. 01] average individual income than all categories of migrant CWs. By and large RPs hold higher average individual income than CWs [p<. 01]. The reason is that the working hours of RPs are more flexible than the CWs. RPs can work in the night shift also and thereby, can augment their income. But working in the night shift for the CWs is rare in the Siliguri Municipal Corporation area and therefore, CWs have little scope of increasing their income by working for additional hours.

Table 7

Individual Income of RPs by Migration Status

Nature of migration	*Mean*	*S.D.*	*S.E.*	*Min*	*Max*	*CV[per cent]*
Temporary	2993.81**	624.50	96.36	2080	4500	20.86
Permanent	3921.43**	788.38	297.98	3000	5300	20.10
Circular	3379.63**	582.35	112.07	2250	4200	17.23
Native	3530.42	654.70	133.64	2700	5400	18.54
Total	3291.70**	685.16	68.52	2080	5400	20.81

Note: **highly significant [p<. 01]

Household Income

Barring the natives, there is no significant difference in total average household income earned by the migrant CWs [Table-8]. But native CWs [Rs.8110.01] earn significantly higher average household income than migrant CWs.

Table 8

Household Income of CWs by Migration Status

Nature of migration	*Mean*	*S.D.*	*S.E.*	*Min*	*Max*	*CV[per cent]*
Temporary	3281.76	1024.29	248.43	1650	5150	31.21
Permanent	3633.42	1681.54	485.42	1690	7280	46.28
Circular	3891.16	1856.02	223.44	1350	13400	47.70
Native	8110.01	1682.91	1190.00	6920	9300	20.75
Total	3841.01	1818.60	181.86	1350	13400	47.35

In case of RPs, there is no significant difference of average household income except for temporary migrants [Table-9]. Temporary migrant RPs earn significantly less average household income [Rs.3425.64] than native and other categories of migrant RPs. Significantly higher average household income is found among the permanent [Rs.5135.71] [p<.05] and circular [Rs.4917.78] [p<.01] migrant RPs than permanent [Rs.3633.42] CWs.

Table 9

Household Income of RPs by Migration Status

Nature of migration	*Mean*	*S.D.*	*S.E.*	*Min*	*Max*	*CV[per cent]*
Temporary	3425.64	768.76	118.62	2250	5050	22.44
Permanent	5135.71*	1304.07	492.89	3000	7100	25.39
Circular	4917.78**	1506.31	289.89	2250	8700	30.63
Native	5502.50	2348.02	479.29	3000	10100	42.67
Total	4446.67**	1741.03	174.10	2250	10100	39.15

Note: *significant [p<. 05]

**Highly significant [p<. 01]

and circular [Rs.3891.16] migrant CWs. The average household income of RPs [Rs.4446.67] is significantly higher than CWs [Rs.3841.01] [p<.01].

Table 10

Individual Consumption of CWs by Migration Status

Nature of Migration	*Mean*	*S.D.*	*S.E.*	*CV[per cent]*	*Min*	*Max*
Temporary	2167.0	675.42	163.81	31.17	1200	3800
Permanent	1805.83	533.27	153.94	29.53	880	2500
Circular	2175.51	618.58	74.47	28.43	1000	6000
Native	2050.00	353.55	250.00	17.25	1800	2300
Total	2127.20	619.63	61.96	29.13	880	6000

Individual Consumption

Table 10 shows that there is no significant difference in individual average consumption expenditure among all migrant CWs. In case of RPs also, no significant differences has been found in the case of individual average consumption expenditure [Table-11]. With the exception of native RPs, all categories of migrant RPs are subject to significantly higher individual average consumption than that of CWs.

Table 11

Individual Consumption of RPs by Migration Status

Nature of Migration	*Mean*	*S.D.*	*S.E.*	*Min*	*Max*	*CV[per cent]*
Temporary	2646.95**	386.94	59.71	14.62	2080	3550
Permanent	2841.43**	434.76	164.32	15.30	2300	3500
Circular	2662.59**	397.35	76.47	14.92	2000	3500
Native	2563.54	490.10	100.04	19.12	1500	3325
Total	2644.77**	418.31	41.85	15.82	1500	3550

Note: **highly significant [p<. 01]

On the whole, the individual average consumption of RPs [Rs.2644.77] is significantly higher than CWs

[Rs.2127.20] [p<. 01]. The reason for higher level of individual consumption by the RPs is explained by the fact that rickshaw pulling being a strenuous job than construction work, the RPs require more food to consume to get more energy than the CWs.

Household Consumption

Barring native CWs there is no significant difference in household consumption among migrant CWs [Table-12].

Table 12

Household Consumption of CWs by Migration Status

Nature of Migration	*Mean*	*S.D.*	*S.E.*	*CV[per cent]*	*Min*	*Max*
Temporary	2803.24	695.31	168.64	24.80	1600	3950
Permanent	2878.33	920.03	265.59	31.96	1690	4900
Circular	3047.25	1300.13	156.52	42.67	1350	10000
Native	5775.00	388.91	275.00	6.73	5500	6050
Total	3040.05	1224.21	122.42	40.27	1350	10000

Temporary migrant RPs have significantly lower consumption expenditure than other migrant RPs [Table-13]. It could be found from the Table-13 that with the exception of native and temporary migrant RPs, permanent and circular migrant RPs have significantly higher household consumption than that of CWs [p<. 05]. Average household consumption of RPs is significantly higher than that of CWs [p<.05].

Table 13

Household Consumption of RPs by Migration Status

Nature of Migration	*Mean*	*S.D.*	*S.E.*	*Min*	*Max*	*CV[per cent]*
Temporary	2825.64	473.57	73.07	16.76	2080	4400
Permanent	3627.14*	756.71	286.01	20.86	2740	5100
Circular	3597.59*	927.56	178.51	25.78	2000	6000
Native	3791.88	1137.57	232.21	30.00	2150	6000
Total	3322.07*	916.25	91.63	27.58	2000	6000

Note: *significant [p<. 05]

V. Summary of Findings and Conclusions

The study shows that family size of RPs and CWs are not homogeneous. Before migrating to SMCA for survival and better livelihood, majority of both RPs and CWs were attached to agriculture as labourers of which CWs holds higher percentage than RPs. Greater proportion of both RPs and CWs has migrated to SMCA owing to inadequate income opportunity in villages. Pattern of migration is not homogenous between RPs and CWs. Interstate migrants were found only among RPs, not among CWs. It is revealed that major portion of migrant CWs are from adjacent places of Siliguri whereas major portion of the migrant RPs are from places far away from Siliguri. Migration pattern in respect of gender is also not homogenous between RPs and CWs. Young native people are more inclined to rickshaw pulling rather than to construction work. Causes of migration are also not similar between RPs and CWs. Push factor for migration is not homogenous between RPs and CWs. All categories of migrant pullers have significantly higher [$p < .01$] average individual income than all categories of migrant CWs. The average household income of RPs (Rs.4446.67) is significantly higher than that of CWs (Rs.3841.01). The individual average consumption of RPs [Rs.2644.77] is significantly higher than that of CWs (Rs.2127.20). Barring native and temporary migrant RPs, permanent and circular migrant RPs have significantly higher household consumption than that of CWs. Average household consumption of RPs is significantly higher than that of CWs.

Thus both push and pull factors have led to immigration of rickshaw pullers and construction workers in SMCA. But push factor are stronger to the rickshaw pullers while pull factor are of similar importance to both the groups of workers. Inadequate earnings or lack of rural employment opportunities as well as poverty are the most important causes behind in-migration of rural workers to the urban informal sector of the SMCA. Thus, the policy implication is that employment and living conditions of workers in rural areas should be improved so that the incidence of rural-urban migration is reduced to a great extent. However, as a result of in-migration of rickshaw pullers and construction workers in SMCA, economy of SMCA as well as household economy of the workers benefits a lot.

Note

Secondary data have been collected from sources like NSSO, different Census reports etc. Data processing has been done both through manual calculation as well as by using computer software. Some descriptive and inferential statistics have been used. Different frequency distributions and relative frequencies have been presented. For those frequency tables, Pearsonian chi-square tests of significance for (a) Goodness of Fit, (b) Homogeneity, and (c) Independence have been done.

For the variables like individual income, household income, individual savings, household savings, individual consumption, household consumption etc, measures of central tendencies like arithmetic mean, dispersions like standard deviation, coefficient of variations, (along with minimum and maximum values) have been calculated to compare the averages and variabilities. Test of significance for equality of means has been done by t-test and F-test. Bivariate and Multivariate regression analysis along with their test of significance have been done. In this case t-test and F-test have been done. Multiple correlation co-efficients have been shown with regression analysis.

REFERENCES

De Haan, A. and Rogaly, B (2002), Introduction: Migrant Workers And Their Role In Rural Change, *Journal of Development Studies*, 37(5): 1-14.

Eaton, R (1984), *The Rise of Islam and Bengal Frontier*, Oxford University Press, Delhi.

Government of India (1991), *Census of India*, 1991.

Government of India. (1993), *National Sample Survey, 1992-1993*, New Delhi.

Government of India (2000), *National Sample Survey, 1999-2000*, New Delhi.

Haberfeld, Y., Menaria, R.K., Sahoo, B.B. and Vyas, R.N. (1999), "Seasonal Migration of Rural Labour in India", *Population Research and Policy Review,* 18(6): 471–87.

Mosse, D., Gupta, S., Mehta, M., Shah, V., Rees, J. and KRIBP Team (2002), "Brokered Livelihoods: Debt, Labour Migration and Development in Tribal Western India", *Journal of Development Studies,* 38(5): 59–88.

Rogaly, B., Biswas, J., Coppard, D., Rafique, A., Rana, K. and Sengupta, A (2001), "Seasonal Migration, Social Change and Migrants Rights, Lessons from West Bengal", *Economic and Political Weekly,* pp. 4547–58.

Srivastava, R.S (1998), "Migration and the Labour Market in India", *Indian Journal of Labour Economics,* 41(4): 583-616.

Srivastava, R.S. and Bhattacharyya, S. (2002), "Globalization, Reforms and Internal Labour Mobility: Analysis of Recent Indian Trends", Paper Presented in September 18-19, 2002 at the Seminar on Labour Mobility and Globalizing World: Conceptual and Empirical Issues, V.V. Giri National Labour Institute, ISLE and IHD, New Delhi.

4

Expansion of Indo-US Trade: A Quantitive Analysis

ANIL BHUIMALI* & SIDHARTHA SANKAR LAHA**

Abstract

This paper highlights the pattern of Indo-US trade relations in the post-reform era with the help of IIT index on the basis time series data for 1991-2005. It has constructed the IIT index for resource-based, labour-intensive, scale-intensive, differentiated 2-digit commodities.

Key Words: Pure Inter-Industry Trade, Resource-Based Commodities, 2-Digit Goods, GL- Indices

Introduction

India's fascination with the planned economy model was beginning to wither away by mid 1980s. Even earlier to that it had been understood that the country's obsession with strictly controlled external trade was becoming increasingly problematic. This had resulted in piecemeal import liberalization measures, essentially directed to export production. In 1985, the Government of India initiated a serious rethinking of its trade policy. After liberalization, USA is world's third largest country by size after Russia and Canada and by population after China and India. It has emerged as one of the most important industrial powers of the world and has substantial influence on world economy. On the other hand, India is the seventh largest and second most populous country in the world. The huge market, continuous enhanced economic growth and large pool of human resources have led the country to emerge as an important country in the developing world. USA and India are the largest democracies of the world. Both have struggled for freedom from the British rule. Peace, justice and equality are the inherent philosophy of both the countries. Of late, Indo-American relationship has taken a new turn. Regular interaction and enhanced mutual understanding have given a new direction to this relationship.

Significance of Indian Economy

Traditional village farming, modern industries and a multitude of support services (The World Fact Book, 2001) characterize Indian economy. The sector wise contributions to GDP include agriculture (25 percent), industry (24 percent) and service (51percent). Since the introduction of the economic reforms in the year 1991, the economy has been growing at the rate of 5-6 percent annually. Indian economic reforms have led to stronger economic growth, higher investment, flows and substantial growth in trade. The changing economic scenario would help India emerge as one of the important destinations of the world market. The continuous economic reforms, stable growth, growing income have made the country as a prosperously growing market in the world.

India's main exports to US are precious stones, metals (worked diamonds & gold jewellery), woven apparel, knit apparel, miscellaneous textile article, fish and sea food

* Professor, Department of Economics, North Bengal University.
** Lecturer, DACEEFO, North Bengal University.

(frozen shrimp), textile floor coverings, iron/steel products, organic chemicals and machinery (taps, valves, transmission shafts, gears, pistons, etc). USA is the single largest market for Indian products followed by the UK, Germany, Japan and Belgium for the year 2004-2005. On the import side, India imports sophisticated machinery (computers and components, gas turbines, telecom, etc), electrical machinery (recording/sound media), medical and surgical equipments/instruments, aircraft, spacecraft (small aircraft), precious stones, metals (diamonds, not mounted or set), jewellery, organic chemicals, plastic, cotton and cotton waste pulp, etc. USA has been the largest import source for India till 1998-99. The share of UK has been slightly higher for the year 2003-2004, followed by US, Belgium, Japan and Germany.

The major features of Indian economy are: *(i)* continuous economic reforms since 1991, *(ii)* stable enhanced economic growth, *(iii)* focus on deregulation and stimulation of foreign investment, *(iv)* large diversified economy, *(v)* strong legal system, *(vi)* free and vibrant press, *(vii)* skilled managerial and technical manpower, *(viii)* important emerging markets in the world, *(ix)* growing middle class population, *(x)* huge market & *(xi)* adequate production base.

The Indian government requires exploiting the strengths of the economy and creating favourable environment for enhancing trade and investment. US, being a major trade partner, may play an important role in this direction.

Significance of USA Economy

USA has emerged as a leading industrial power of the world. The country possesses highly diversified and technologically advanced petroleum, steel, motor vehicles, aerospace, telecommunication, chemicals, electronics, food processing, consumer goods, lumber, mining etc. (The World Fact Book, 2001). It is considered as one of the most powerful countries of the world. Steady growth, low unemployment and rapid advances in technology characterize the economy. It is the largest and most technologically powerful economy in the world with a per capita GDP of $ 36,200. During the year 1994-2004, the country witnessed substantial increase in real output, low inflation rate and an un-employment below 5 percent. The sector wise contributions to GDP include agriculture 2 percent, industry 18 percent and services 80 percent.

The major features of USA economy are: *(i)* continuous technological innovations, *(ii)* strong rate of productivity growth, *(iii)* dynamic organizational changes, *(iv)* conducive public policy, *(v)* faster income growth, *(vi)* low level of inflation, and *(vii)* disappearance of federal budget deficits. These features have made USA a very dynamic and vibrant economy in the world economy.

Methodology for Measurement of IIT

To assess the importance of intra-industry trade on trends in India-US trade, data for India exports to and imports from U.S have been employed for the study over 9 years (1996-97 to 2004-05). Both import and export data are classified and published according to the Harmonized Commodity Description and Coding System (H.S). In the H.S, commodities are classified by what they are made of and not according to their stage of fabrication, their use, or origin. The basic system uses a six-digit number to identify commodities. But our trade data is calculated at a two-digit level H.S, divided into 98 chapters and then aggregated and presented in 21 sections. All trade (exports/ imports) flows are measured on a value basis, in thousands of U.S. dollars. Aggregation of trade data is an issue of importance. The choice of particular level of aggregation of all classification system may lead to a distorted value of calculations. A higher level of aggregation is likely to give a higher level of specialization in intra-industry trade. Thus, it would be preferable to carry out the analysis for quite narrowly defined commodity groups. Since our calculations are done at a two-digit level, our estimates will probably be too high because of the aggregation problem that arises from the fact that the classified groups consist of heterogeneous products. This implies that non-perfect substitutes can be counted as intra-industry trade. The H.S. classification also causes some asymmetry among the chapters since some are more disaggregated than others. For example, computer/machinery (Chapter 84) and electrical equipment (chapter 85) are wide concepts, while wool (chapter-51) and cotton (chapter 52) are more narrowly defined. To overcome the possible incorrectness of H.S at the 2-digit level, we have disaggregated our trade data into country-specific data, which gives cross-sectional comparisons (See Apendix-1). Here we may use the famous Grubel and Lloyd (1975) intra-industry trade index as follows:

$$GL = \frac{(X_i + M_i) - |X_i - M_i|}{(X_i + M_i)} = 1 - \frac{|X_i - M_i|}{(X_i + M_i)} = 1 - B_{ij}$$

Where i = commodity within industry j, that assigned pure Intra-Industry Trade a value of 1 and pure inter-industry trade a value of 0. We have calculated IIT index of Indian-USA trade for years 1996-97 to 2004-2005.

India's Trade with USA

USA is a very significant trading partner of India. If India has decided that increased trade and investment is the basis for economic growth, then the significance of Indo-US trade cannot be over emphasized (Mukherjee, 2000). It requires proper strategy to boost the trade and investment flows. India's export to USA has been increasing substantially. The export has increased from $ 3192.5 million in the year 1991 to $ 13721. 6 million in the year 2005 (See table 1).

Table 1: India's Trade with USA

(US million $)

Year	*Export*	*Import*	*Balance*	*Total Trade*
1991	3192.5	1999.3	1193.2	5191.8
1992	3779.8	1917.1	1862.7	5696.9
1993	4553.7	2778.1	1775.6	7331.8
1994	5309.5	2294.0	3015.5	7603.5
1995	5726.2	3295.8	2430.4	9022.0
1996	6169.5	3328.3	2841.2	9497.8
1997	7322.4	3607.6	3714.8	10930.0
1998	8237.2	3564.4	4672.8	11801.6
1999	9070.8	3687.8	5383.0	12758.6
2000	10686.6	3667.2	7019.4	14353.8
2001	11463.8	3942.5	7521.3	15406.3
2002	12092.5	4131.7	7960.8	16224.2
2003	12742.6	4762.2	7980.4	17504.8
2004	13121.3	5021.3	8100.0	18142.6
2005	13721.6	5692.8	8028.0	19414.4

Source: US Census Bureau, Foreign Trade Division, Washington D.C. 20233.

The export has witnessed 330 percent increase during the period of 15 years. In 2005, the Government of India declared new Foreign Trade Policy (FTP) and new scheme to accelerate growth of exports called "Target Plus". As far as import is concerned, there has been a slow growth in import. The import has increased from $ 1999.3 million in the year 1991 to $ 5692.8 million in the year 2005. The import has increased by 110 percent during last 15 years. As a result of rapid growth in export and comparatively slow growth in import, India is having favourable trade balance with USA. The trade balance has increased from $ 1193.2 million in the year 1991 to $ 8028 million in the year 2005. It has increased 572 percent during the above period. The share of India's export to USA to total India's export has been increasing. It has increased from 18.1 percent in the year 1991 to 23.9 percent in the year 2005. These all are represented in table 2 below.

Table 2: Share of India's Exports to US to Total India's Export

(US million $)

Year	*India's total export*	*India's export to USA*	*Share of India's export to US to total India's export*
1991	17664	3193	18.1
1992	19563	3780	19.3
1993	21553	4554	21.1
1994	25022	5310	21.2
1995	30630	5726	18.7
1996	33105	6170	18.6
1997	35008	7322	20.9
1998	33437	8237	24.6
1999	36316	9071	25.0
2000	42295	10687	25.3
2001	47329	11464	24.2
2002	50213	12093	24.1
2003	51129	12743	24.9
2004	54113	13121	24.3
2005	57207	13721	23.9

Source: W.T.O. International Trade Statistics, 2006.

It is glaring that USA is a very important and strategic market for India because about ¼th of India's total export goes to USA. The analysis of US import shows that India is an insignificant trade partner for USA. India contributes only 0.6 percent of total import of USA in the year 1991. The share has gone up to 0.8 percent in the year 2005 (See table- 3). This shows that India's share in total import of USA is very insignificant. Even China's share in total US import is about 8 percent. Therefore, India requires aggressive marketing and product strategy to enhance the share in the total import of the USA.

Table 3: Share of India's Import to Total Import of USA

(US million $)

Year	*Total import of USA*	*Import from India*	*%age of India's import to total USA import*
1991	508363	3193	0.6
1992	553923	3780	0.7
1993	603438	4554	0.8
1994	689215	5310	0.8
1995	770852	5726	0.7
1996	822025	6170	0.8
1997	899020	7322	0.8
1998	944353	8237	0.9
1999	1059435	9071	0.9
2000	1257636	10687	0.8
2001	1304211	11464	0.8
2002	1396121	12093	0.8
2003	1487210	12743	0.8
2004	1503212	13121	0.9
2005	1781293	13722	0.8

Source: WTO, International Trade Statistics, 2006 (The data relating to India's export to USA has been taken from US Census Bureau of Foreign Trade)

IIT Between India and USA

The concept of Intra-Industry Trade (IIT) is gaining importance in recent years. Trade liberalization increases the contestability of the market performance and progress of IIT should be periodically evaluated for the improvement in the functioning and operation process. A limited number of research works have been undertaken to study the potential, progress of India-USA overall intra-industry trade indices. It is presented in table 4.

Table 4: IIT index between India and USA

Year	*IIT*
1991	0.77
1992	0.67
1993	0.76
1994	0.61
1995	0.73
1996	0.70
1997	0.66
1998	0.60
1999	0.57
2000	0.49
2001	0.52
2002	0.50
2003	0.54
2004	0.55
2005	0.58

Source: Calculated from Table 1.

Figure 1: IIT trend between India and USA

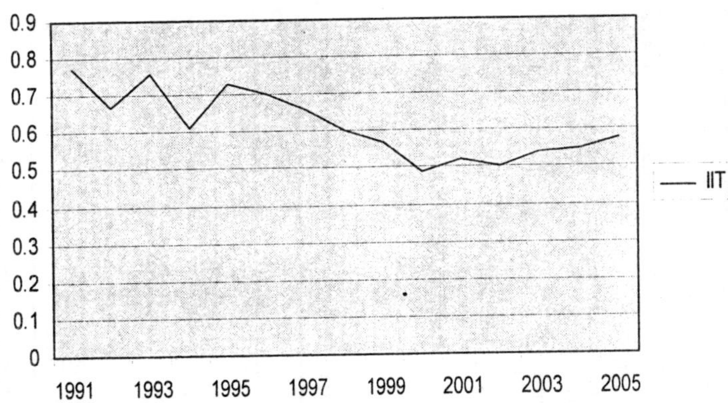

Table 4 indicates that the height GL intra-industry index is 0.77 in the year 1991, In this year some important trade policy reforms have been introduced. These are as follows: *(i)* A large part of administratered licensing of

Table 5: Intra-Industry Trade Index for Resource Based Commodities

Commodity	*1996-97*	*1997-98*	*1998-99*	*1999-00*	*2000-01*	*2001-02*	*2002-03*	*2003-04*	*2004-05*
Resource Based	0.561	0.873	0.696	0.452	0.408	0.635	0.276	0.347	0.617
Live Animals (01-05)	0.027	0.023	0.028	0.022	0.024	0.022	0.023	0.019	0.014
Vegetable Products (06-14)	0.283	0.834	0.228	0. 225	0.280	0.232	0.191	0.249	0.364
Fats and Oils (15)	0.953	0.983	0.518	0.708	0.918	0.953	0.986	0.924	0.912
Prepared Foodstuffs (16-24)	0.884	0.538	0.378	0.727	0.899	0.994	0.812	0.847	0.532
Mineral Products (25-27)	0.364	0.483	0.348	0.534	0.992	0.939	0.521	0.826	0.733
Wood and Wood articles (44 – 46)	0.832	0.916	0.794	0.895	0.684	0.384	0.397	0.396	0.259

Source: Calculated from DGCIS&S data (various year)

Table 6: Intra-Industry Trade Index for Labour -Intensive Commodities

Commodity	*1996-97*	*1997-98*	*1998-99*	*1999-00*	*2000-01*	*2001-02*	*2002-03*	*2003-04*	*2004-05*
Labour-intensive	0.124	0.108	0.104	0.109	0.089	0.137	0.124	0.163	0.175
Hides and Leather (41-43)	0.163	0.099	0.154	0.126	0.083	0.073	0.113	0.077	0.062
Textiles and apparel (50-63)	0.047	0.036	0.342	0.052	0.039	0.136	0.082	0.118	0.070
Foot Wear (64-67)	0.368	0.019	0.010	0.026	0.045	0.320	0.287	0.059	0.020
Gems (71)	0.177	0.179	0.173	0.153	0.119	0.137	0.124	0.172	0.187
Arms (93)	0.361	0.137	1.00	.000	.000	0.432	0.364	0.250	0.588
Miscellaneous Manufactured articles (94-96)	0.417	0.670	0.628	0.462	0.437	0.438	0.422	0.399	0.369
Other (99)	0.381	0.083	0.127	0.133	0.203	0.167	0.357	0.933	0.624

Source: Calculated from DGCIS&S data (various year)

Table 7: Intra-Industry Index for Scale Intensive Commodities

Commodity	*1996-97*	*1997-98*	*1998-99*	*1999-00*	*2000-01*	*2001-02*	*2002-03*	*2003-04*	*2004-05*
Scale Intensive	0.869	0.933	0.863	0.860	0.846	0.889	0.900	0.980	0.989
Chemicals (28-38)	0.742	0.589	0.538	0.482	0.989	0.964	0.913	0.995	0.997
Plastics (39-40)	0.827	0.908	0.937	0.853	0.840	0.978	0.956	0.628	0.728
Pulp and paper (47-49)	0.288	0.139	0.158	0.203	0.306	0.286	0.395	0.334	0.394
Stone/Cement/Ceramics (68-70)	0.431	0.701	0.453	0.414	0.348	0.272	0.164	0.208	0.235
Base metal and Articles (72-83)	0.742	0.507	0.548	0.429	0.408	0.575	0.863	0.501	0.554
Vehicles (86-89)	0.478	0.641	0.719	0.642	0.784	0.995	0.912	0.902	0.960

Source: Calculated from DGCIS&S data (various year).

Table 8: Intra-Industry Trade Index for Differentiated Commodities

Commodity	*1996-97*	*1997-98*	*1998-99*	*1999-00*	*2000-01*	*2001-02*	*2002-03*	*2003-04*	*2004-05*
Differentiated	0.612	0.540	0.573	0.569	0.627	0.504	0.507	0.549	0.511
Mach. & Electrical (84-85)	0.462	0.561	0.437	0.512	0.524	0.503	0.463	0.496	0.460
Optical, Musical inst (90-92)	0.334	0.396	0.416	0.412	0.312	0.404	0.484	0.392	0.401
Antiques and works of art (97-98)	0.881	0.729	0.672	0.749	0.712	0.707	0.569	0.621	0.712

Source: Calculated from DGCIS&S data (various year)

Table 9: Intra-Industry Trade Index for 2-digit Commodities

Commodity	*1996-97*	*1997-98*	*1998-99*	*1999-00*	*2000-01*	*2001-02*	*2002-03*	*2003-04*	*2004-05*
Resource Based	0.561	0.873	0.696	0.452	0.408	0.635	0.276	0.347	0.617
Labour-intensive	0.124	0.108	0.104	0.109	0.089	0.137	0.124	0.163	0.175
Scale Intensive	0.869	0.933	0.863	0.860	0.846	0.889	0.900	0.980	0.989
Differentiated	0.612	0.540	0.573	0.569	0.627	0.504	0.507	0.549	0.511

Source: Calculated from DGCIS&S data (various year)

imports was replaced by import entitlements linked to export earnings. These import entitlements, renamed Exam-scrip, were freely tradable and attracted a premium in the market. *(ii)* The Advance Licensing System (ALS) for exports was simplified so as to improve exporter's access to imported inputs at duty-free rates. *(iii)* The scope of canalization for both exports and imports was narrowed. This calculation clearly shows that India and USA are intra-industry oriented.

To show the comparison with different aggregation of data, first we have calculated index for the total amount of each industry and then each commodity groups within these industries. These are presented in the following tables 5, 6, 7, 8 and 9.

Figure 2: Intra-Industry Trend as Share of India- USA Trade

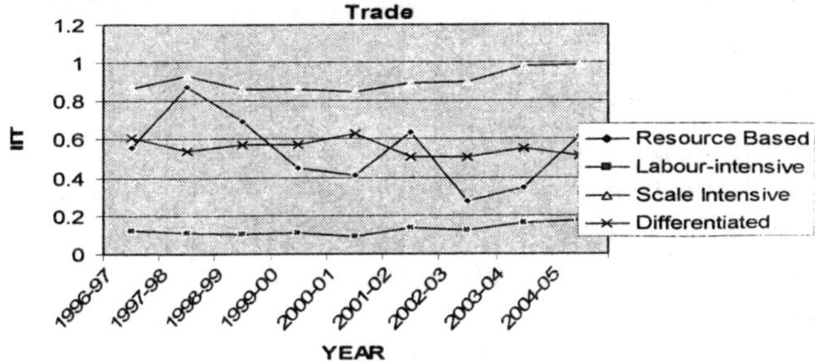

Conclusion

As seen in table 9, the GL index reveals difference between the four commodity groups. The scale-intensive commodities exhibit the highest growth in intra-industry trade. Chemicals have the highest IIT which is 0.997 in the 2004-05 (see table 7). We see an upward trend of this commodity because the EXIM policy (1993) provides a greater thrust exports from agriculture and scale-intensive sectors in which the country had a strong comparative advantage. A new export-promoting capital goods scheme permitting import of capital goods at a concessional 15 percent duty rate was introduced for the service sector. In this year, a significant amount of foreign direct investment in the manufacturing sector led to increased trade in scale-intensive commodities. Over the last three years foreign investment had grown at an average of 100 percent per year. From US$ 20 million in 1993-94, foreign direct investment becomes more than doubled in 1994-1995 (i,e. US $1.31 billion).

Between the other three commodity groups smaller difference in GL indices are revealed, with values well below scale-intensive commodities and the GL average. For the resource based commodity group the values lie between 0.276 in 2002-03 and 0.873 in 1997-98 (see table 5). Fats and Oils are the highly intra-industry oriented goals between India and the USA. Figure 2 reveals the differentiated commodity groups a downward trend in GL indices, whereas an upward trend can be distinguished for both scale-intensive and labour-intensive IIT. However, there have been more fluctuations of the resource-based commodity over the study period. The calculated indices show that Indo-US trade is mostly an intra-industry trade oriented one.

REFERENCES

Abd-el-Rahman, K. (1991): "Firms Competitive and National Comparative Advantages as Joint Determinants of Trade Compositions". *Weltwirtschaftliches Archiv,* 127, pp. 83-97.

Adiseshiah Malcolm, S. (1987): "The Economic Rationale of SAARC" *South Asian Journal,* Vol. 1 No. 1, June-Sep.

Algiri, B. & Ankkuriniemi, Salla & Zampieri, Laura. (2001):"Inter-Industry Specialisation versus Intra-industry Trade : A Regional approach", *Economica Internzionale International Economics,* Vol. LIV, No. 3, August, PP. 299-223.

Annicchiarico, Barbara and Quintieri, Beniamino. (2000): "Aggregated Measures of Intra-Industry Trade: A Critical Comparison". Mimeo, CEIS- University of Rome Tor Vergata.

Aquino, A. (1978): "Intra-Industry Trade and Inter-Industry Specialization as Current Sources of International Trade in Manufactures", *Wehwirtschaftliches Archiv,* 114. pp. 275-296.

Azhar, Abdul K., Elliott, Robert J.R. (2001): "A Note on the Measurement of Trade-Induced Adjustment". Mimeo, University of Manchester

Azhar, Abdul K., Elliott, Robert J.R. and Milner, Chris. (1998): "Static and Dynamic Measurement of IIT and Adjustment: A Geometric Reappraisal", *Weltwirtschaftiliches Archiv,* Vol. 134, pp. 404-422.

Balassa, Bela. (1986): "The Determinants of Intra-industry Specialization in United States Trade", Oxford Economic paper, Vol. 38, No. 2, pp. 220-232.

Briihart, Marius. (1999): Marginal Intra-Industry Trade and Trade-Induced Adjustment: A Survey In: Briilhart, M. and Hine, R.C., *Intra-Industry Trade and Adjustment: The European Experience.* Macmillan, London. (eds)

Briilhart, Marius.(1994): "Marginal Intra-Industry Trade: Measurement and Relevance for the Pattern of Industrial Adjustment". *Weltwirtschaftliches Archiv,* vol. 130, pp. 600-613.

Chakraborty, S. (1988): "Development Experience in South Asia" *Asian Development Review,* Vol. 6. No. 1.

Dagli, Valilal. (1973): *India's Foreign Trade,* Vora and Company Publication Private Limited, New Delhi, India.

Das Gupta, A.K. (1977): "The Problem of International Economic Order", *International Studies,* April-June, Vol. 16.

Dasgupta, B. (2000): International Institutions for Global Trade: The Case for South Asian Free Trade Association. In Dutta, D. (ed.) *Economic Liberalization and Institutional Reform in South Asia: Recent Experiences and Future Prospect,* Atlantic Publishers, New Delhi.

Despande, G.P. (1981):"Long Shadow over South Asia", *Economic and Political Weekly,* No. 21.

Government of India, Director General of Commercial Intelligence and Statistics, Kolkata, (various years)

Dixon, Peter B. and Menon, Jayant. (1995): "Measures of Intra-Industry Trade as Indicators of Factor Market Disruption", *Journal of Economic Record,* vol. 73, pp. 233-237.

Donges, J.B. (1977): "The Third World Demand for a New International Economic Order", *Kyklos,* vol. 30, no. 2.

Financial Times (2004): India Awakes, Special Report on India

Released at the World Economic Forum at Davos, Switzerland, January.

Halder, A. (1976): *India's Export Pattern Analysis on Potential Diversification*, Minerva Association Pvt. Ltd, Calcutta.

Harrison, Anne (1996): "Openers and Growth a Time Series, Cross Country Analysis for Developing Countries", *Journal of Development Economics*, vol. 48, No. 2, pp. 419-447.

Harrison, S. (1965): "Troubled India and Her Neighbours", *Foreign Affair*, January.

Hassan, M.K. (2002): Trade with India and Trade Policies of Bangladesh in Forrest and Alam A.K.M.S. 2002 (ed.) *Towards Greater Sub-regional Economic Cooperation*, Chapter 10, DIDS, Bangladesh.

International Monetary Fund (IMF) (2001): *International Financial Statistics Yearbook*.

Government of India, National Industrial Classification (All Economic Activities), Central Statistical Organisation. Ministry of Statistics and Programme Implementation, New Delhi, 2004.

Tharakan, P.K.M. (1985): Empirical Analysis of the Commodity Composition of Trade in D. Greenaway (eds.) *Current Issues in International Trade: Theory and Policy*, London: Macmillan.

The World Fact Book (2001), Washington, U.S.A.

World Bank (2001): *World Development Indication*, Washington D.C.

World Bank, (2005): *World Development Report*, Oxford University Press.

Wright, Peter, Haynes, Michelle and Upward, Richard. (2001): "Estimating the Wage Costs of Inter-and Intra-Sectoral Adjustment". CEPR Discussion Paper, No. 2710.

Young, A. (1991): "Learning by Doing and the Dynamic Effects of International Trade," *Quarterly Journal of Economics*, vol. 106, no. 2, pp. 369-405.

Young, Allyn A.(1928): "Increasing Returns and Economic Progress", *The Economic Journal*, vol. 38, pp. 527-542.

Appendix -I
Classification key, chapter – section

Section	*Chapter*
Resource-based commodities	*Resource-based commodities*
01-05 Live Animals	01 Live Animals
	02 Meat & Edible Meat Offal
	03 Fish
	04 Dairy Produce
06-14 Vegetable Products	05 Other Animal Products
	06 Live Trees
	07 Edible Vegetables
	08 Edible Fruit & Nuts
	09 Coffee, Tea, Spices
	10 Cereals
	11 Malt & Wheat Gluten
	12 Seeds
	13 Lac, Gums & Resins
15 Fats and Oils	14 Other Vegetables Products
16-24 Prepared Foodstuffs	15 Fats & Oils
	16 Preparations Meat/Fish
	17 Sugars
	18 Cocoa
	19 Prep. Cereals/Flour/Milk
	20 Prep. Vegetables/Fruit/Nuts
	21 Misc. Edible Products
	22 Beverages
	23 Waste from Food Industry
25-27 Mineral Products	24 Tobacco
	25 Salt/Sulphur/Lime/Cement
	26 Ores
	27 Lubricants/Fuels/Oil
44-46 Wood and Wood articles	44 Wood
	45 Cork
	46 Straw
Labour-intensive commodities	*Labour-intensive commodities*
41-43 Hides and Leather	41 Raw Hides & Skins
	42 Articles of Leather
	43 Fur skins
50-63 Textiles and apparel	50 Silk
	51 Wood
	52 Cotton
	53 Paper Yarn
	54 Man-made Filaments
	55 Man-made Staple Fibres

	56 Wadding
	57 Carpets
	58 Special Woven Fabrics
	59 Laminated Textile Fabrics
	60 Knitted Fabrics
	61 Apparel, Knitted
	62 Apparel, not Knitted
	63 Other Textile Articles
64-67 Footwear	64 Footwear
	65 Headgear
	66 Umbrellas, Walking Sticks
	67 Prepared Feathers
71 Gems	71 Jewellery
93 Arms	93 Arms & Ammunition
94-96 Misc. Manufactured articles	94 Furniture
	95 Toys
	96 Misc. Manufactured Articles
99 Others	99 Other
Scale-intensive commodities	*Scale-intensive commodities*
28-38 Chemicals	28 Inorganic Chemicals
	29 Organic Chemicals
	30 Pharmaceutical Products
	31 Fertilizers
	32 Tanning/Dyeing Extracts/Ink
	33 Cosmetics
	34 Soap, Waxes, Pastes
	35 Glues
	36 Explosives
	37 Photographic Goods
	38 Misc. Chemical Products
39-40 Plastics	39 Plastics
	40 Rubber
	47 Wood Pulp
	48 Paper & Paper Board
	49 Books, Newspapers
68-70 Stone/Cement/Ceramics	68 Stone/Plaster/Cement
	69 Ceramic Products
	70 Glass and Glassware
72-83 Base metal and Metal articles	72 Iron and Steel
	73 Articles of Iron or Steel
	74 Copper
	75 Nickel
	76 Aluminium
	78 Lead
	79 Zinc

	80 Tin
	81 Other Base Metals
	82 Tools
	83 Miscellaneous Base Metals
	86 Railway
	87 Cars, Trucks, Autos
	88 Aircraft, Spacecraft
	89 Ships, Boats
Differentiated commodities	*Differentiated commodities*
84-85 Machinery and Electrical Appliances	84 Computer/Machinery 85 Electrical Equipment
90-92 Optical, precision & musical Instruments	90 Optical/Medical Instruments 91 Clocks 92 Musical Instruments
97-98 Antiques and works of art	97 Works of Art 98 Postal Packages & Special Transactions

5

Changing India's Trade Pattern: A Time Series Analysis

ANIL BHUIMALI* & SIDHARTHA SANKAR LAHA•

Abstract

Since independence and especially since 1950-51 India has been pursuing economic polices aimed at maximising the well-being of its every citizen. International trade, like many other aspects of the economy, may contribute a lot to the growth of the economy. The present paper tries to examine, as Robertson asserts, how trade has contributed to the growth of the Indian economy in terms of export performance, employment generation, foreign exchange earning and so on in the context of liberalised trade regime. The paper specifically tries to evaluate India's intra-industry trade (IIT), intensity of IIT across sections in multilateral trade, and what is more to measure India's overall IIT with the help of time series analysis.

Key Words: IIT, Engine of Growth, SITC, International Trade Statistics

* Professor, Department of Economics, North Bengal University.

• Lecturer, DACEEFO, North Bengal University.

Introduction

India is vast and multi-faceted country. Since 1950-51, it has been pursuing a course of economic development aimed at universalising material affluence among its population. Its economic performance can be assessed in terms of its agricultural, industrial or trade and service sector development. International trade contributes to the growth and development of a country in many respects. Firstly, it boosts output and income by enabling greater employment of domestic resources, both natural and human. Secondly, it helps the country to streamline production portfolio by specialising in the production of goods for which it enjoys a natural, comparative advantages over other producing nations. Trade based on comparative cost advantages increases the general availability of capital or consumer goods and services that would otherwise be either costlier or impossible to produce domestically. Thus, each country, in theory is able to obtain more goods than it can actually produce by itself.

India's foreign trade has undergone significant changes in terms of volume, composition and direction and there is empirical evidence that it has contributed in some measure to the country's development effort by making available to its indispensable raw materials and capital goods key to infrastructural and technological improvement .Robertson considers foreign trade to be an engine of economic growth. The validity of this assertion with respect to India can be tested by scrutinizing India's performance and experience in the field of international trade (Shoney, 1972).

Recent studies on intra-industry trade (IIT) have brought to light rapid increases in vertical IIT, i.e. intra-industry trade where goods are differentiated by quality. As Falvey (1981) pointed out in his seminal theoretical paper, commodities of the same statistical group but of different quality may be produced using different mixes of factor inputs. Moreover, developed economies may export physical and human capital-intensive products of high-quality and import unskilled labor-intensive products of low-quality from developing economies. Through this mechanism, an increase in vertical IIT may have a larger impact on factor demands and factors of production.

Methodology

The traditional measure of intra-industry trade is the Grubel-Lloyd Index (1975). Before Grubel-Lloyd index Bela Balassa developed an index in 1966 that measures the degree of the trade overlap-simultaneous import and export of goods within an industry. This is shown in equation (1) below.

$$B_{ij} = \frac{|X_i - M_i|}{(X_i + M_i)} \quad \text{.................} (1)$$

Where i = Commodity within industry j. This index is the ratio of net trade to gross trade, ranges from 0 to 1, with 0 representing "Perfect" trade overlap, and therefore pure intra-industry trade, while 1 represents pure inter-industry trade. In order to calculate the degree of intra-industry trade for all industries (country level), Balassa took an unweighted average for each B_{ij}, i.e.,

$$B = \frac{1}{n}\sum B_{ij} \quad \text{.......................} (2)$$

Where n = number of industries. This can be generalized to be a weighted index, i.e.,

$$B = \sum_{j=1}^{n} w_j B_{ij} \quad \text{.......................}(3)$$

Where w_j = industry j's share of total trade.

Though the essence of this index has remained intact to this day, an index that measured intra-industry trade gave pure intra-industry trade a value of zero was not intuitively appealing. Grubel and Lloyd (1975) proposed an alternative index as follows:

$$GL = \frac{(X_i + M_i) - |X_i - M_i|}{(X_i + M_i)} = 1 - \frac{|X_i - M_i|}{(X_i + M_i)} = 1 - B_{ij} \quad \text{.........}(4)$$

Where i = commodity within industry j, that assigned pure intra-industry trade a value of 1 and pure inter-industry trade a value of 0. As with the Balassa index and the Grubel-Lloyd index has been calculated as an unweighted average to measure the degree of intra-industry trade at the country level.

Evidence of Intra-Industry Trade in India

The study by Havrylyshyn and Civan (1985) shows that IIT of India with the world, using Grubel Lloyd index, was 37.41 percent in 1978 [Havrylyshyn and Civan (1985)]. Havrylyshyn and Civan (1983), in a cross-country regression analysis, have shown that IIT levels across counties are strongly correlated with level of per-capita GNP, and product diversity of an IIT with the developed countries and newly industrialised countries. Their calculation was based on U.N. trade data.

Empirical estimates of IIT for the individual lessdeveloped countries are relatively scare. However, some work at the country group level focused on developed countries IIT with LDCs [See Balassa (1985), Balassa nad Bauwens (1987), Culem and Lundberg (1986), Dixion and Menon (1995), Harylyshyn and Civan (1983,1985), Tharakan (1984, 1989), Loertscher and Wolter (1980), Ocampo (1986), Bergstrand (1983)]. According to Havrylyshyn and Civan (1985), India's IIT with the newly industrialising economies was 15.1 percent in 1978 as compared to 17.0 percent in 1968. Thus the importance of IIT in India's trade is evident. Table 1 presents the IIT indices (as calculated by Havrylyshyn and Civan, (1985)] by country for 1978. It is evident from the table that like other developing countries, there have been changes in India's trade pattern during 1968-1978.

Table 1
Intra-Industry Trade Indices by Country in 1978.

(Percentage of Total Trade)

Developing Countries	*Intra-Industry Trade Indices*
Chile	10
Colombia	20
Kenya	13.9
Malawi	6.6
Malaysia	3.4
Pakistan	14.8
Peru	10.3
Philippines	15
Developed Countries	*Intra-Industry Trade Indices*
Thailand	14.3
Yugoslavia	50.7
Tunisia	17.4
Turkey	7.9
Portugal	32.8
Argentina	42.3
Brazil	37.8
Greece	21.1
Hongkong	40.8
Korean Rep.	24.9
India	37.4
Israel	61.9
Mexico	31.9
Singapore	66.9
Australia	5.3
Austria	74.1
Canada	66.9
France	80.3
Germany	0.7
Italy	59
Japan	26
New Zealand	25.9
Sweden	68.3
Switzerland	59.5
U.K.	81
U.S.A.	59.4

Source: Havrylyshyn and Civan (1985), *Journal of Development Economics*, Volume 18.

The share in the increase of IIT can be accounted for by giving a closer look at India's export performance. According to Nayyar (1988 pp. 217-252), "the share of primary commodities in total exports declined from 47 percent in 1970-71 to 41 percent in 1977-78. It stayed at this level until 1980-81 but returned to its earlier level of 47 percent in 1984-85 as the share of fuels rose to 15 percent. The share of manufactured product in total exports registered a corresponding increase from 53 percent in 1970-71 to 59 percent in 1977-78, thus sustaining the repaid growth of exports during this period; it stayed at this level until 1980-81, but dropped to 53 percent again in 1984-85". A steady increase in the share of manufacturers in non-fuel exports was observed. Nayyar (1988) also identified exports. According to him the share of resource based manufactures remained at the same level of 40 percent. India's principal exports in this category are jute manufactures, cotton textiles, leather and leather manufactures, metal manufactures, iron and steel and gems and jewellery. As against this, the share of miscellaneous manufactured articles in export registered a gradually increasing share from 5 percent in 1970-71 to more than 12 percent in 1984-85. The share of manufactured articles in India's non-fuel exports was recorded in his study at 14.7 percent in 1984-85.

According to Veeramani (March 2001), "The IIT a phenomenon being observed largely in the context of advanced industrialized countries, is also found to be significant in India's international trade". He also argued that, the growth of IIT in response to economic liberalisation is often seen as a manifestation of the process of resource reallocation taking place within the industry as opposed between the industries.

Table 2: Intensity of IIT across Sections in Multilateral Trade

Section	*GL 1995*	*Growth of Exports (in US \$) 1998-99*	*Share of Exports to total (in percentage)*	
Group A			*1998*	*1999*
1. Live Animals	1.12 (1.67)	12.09	5.21	4.27
2. Vegetable Products	25.02 (1.68)	7.25	16.67	9.71
3. Fats & Oil	14.69 (1.40)	29.62	0.28	0.50
4. Beverage & Tobacco	6.45 (1.42)	15.60	3.98	4.38
5. Mineral Products	13.88 (1.38)	1.40	9.13	3.44
8. Hides, Skin & Leather	10.96 (1.69)	6.73	5.18	3.88
9. Wooden Cork	9.28 (1.47)	12.60	0.16	0.01
11. Textiles.	7.06 (1.38)	13.01	23.74	26.85
12. Footwear, Umbrellas	7.19 (2.02)	6.73	2.52	1.59
Group B				
6. Chemical	27.82 (0.78)	17.87	3.95	9.44
7. Plastics & Rubber	32.45 (0.83)	25.73	0.85	2.08
10. Paper	21.68(0.82)	20.94	0.21	0.33
13. Stone & Cement	21.48(0.83)	27.29	0.29	0.94
14. Gems and Jewellery	47.98(1.30)	10.08	16.78	15.31
15. Base Metals	32.69(0.85)	22.96	1.96	6.31
16. Machinery	37.66(0.66)	12.74	4.74	5.82
17. Transport Equipments	21.43(1.35)	18.78	1.56	2.66
18. Instruments & Apparatus	21.33(1.19)	6.97	0.55	0.45
20. Misc. Manufactures	32.29(0.86)	19.12	0.31	0.49

Source: Veenamani C, Working paper No. 313, ICSSR, March 2001, New Delhi.

Table 2 shows that the coefficients of variations are substantially less compared to the former. Regarding export, the growths in most of the sections during 1988-99 are above the average (10.61). The higher growth is also reflected in the shares which have improved significantly in most of the commodity sections, the combined share having increased from 31.2 percent to 43.8 percent.

Table 3 shows that there is in general an upward trend in the level of multilateral IIT during 1988, 1995 and 1999. Regarding the overall level of IIT the GL index increased by more than 11 percentage point in 1995 over 1988 and about 6.5 percentage point in 1999 over 1995. This trend is observed in most of the individual commodity sections with the notable exception of gems and jewellery and instruments and apparatus.

Table 3: Levels of Multilateral IIT Across Sections

Sections	*1988*	*1995*	*1999*
6. Chemical	24.30	32.45	32.90
7. Plastics & Rubber	13.95	21.68	25.73
10. Paper	8.42	21.48	20.61
13. Stone and Cement	19.16	47.98	26.69
14. Gems & Jewellery	86.88	32.69	50.95
15. Base Metals	15.15	37.66	39.43
16. Machinery	28.80	21.43	41.40
17. Transport Equipments	30.22	21.23	37.99
18. Instruments and Apparatus	30.11	32.23	22.99
20. Mis Manufactured	23.69	32.29	44.97
Total	23.61	35.02	41.53

Source: Veeramani C, Working Paper No. 313, ICSSR, March, 2001.

A.R. Kemal (2000) pointed out that, intra-industry trade plays an important role in bolstering economic and trade restrictions within the SAARC region. This is because intra-industry trade can take place even in situations where the trade and production structure of the trading partners lack strong complementarities, as observed in the case of South Asian countries. The low intensity of intra-trade in region (See table 4) indicates the potential for widening the scope of this type of trade is largely driven by product differentiation and increasing returns to scale. Therefore, an increased level of intra-industry trade in the region can only be achieved if the regional countries are able to develop the technological capacity to produce different product varieties at selling average cost.

Table 4: Average Bilateral GL Indices Matrix of Intra-Industry Trade: 1995

Countries	*Bangladesh*	*India*	*Nepal*	*Pakistan*	*Sri Lanka*
Bangladesh	-	0.010	0.000	0.008	.001
India	-	-	0.140	0.083	0.017
Nepal	-	-	-	0.000	0.017
Pakistan	-	-	-	-	0.393
Sri Lanka	-	-	-	-	0.068

Source: A. R. Kemal, 2000.

Measuring India's Overall IIT

This section deals with measuring the sensitivity of our IIT index for 1975-2003 with the 2-digit level of disaggregation. For our purpose, we have used GNP and GDP figures for various years at 1980-81 prices (in crore of Rs),GNP and GDP have been taken at factor cost as they represent aggregate income of the residents as opposed to expenditure approach. The GNP/GDP figures are converted to $US by dividing the average exchange rate (rupee per unit of $US) of base year 1980-81 which is 7.91.

Per capita GNP (PCGNP) be the ratio of GNP figures (in million US dollar) and population (in million).

The share of exports of manufactured products in 2-digit as a percentage of total exports in all commodities is calculated by dividing the sum of exports with the world by total exports of all commodities. This gives the share of manufactured exports (SME) as a proportion of overall exports.

The share of manufactured goods trade (SMT) as a proportion of total trade is obtained by dividing the sum of exports and imports in 2-digit with world by total trade (i.e. exports plus imports) in all commodities.

The trade concentration ratio (TCONC) as a proxy of trade orientation is measured as the ratio of sum of exports and imports of all commodities (Sum of total trade in all commodities) to GDP. This is a measure of trade policy in intervention.

In the time series regression analysis, the variables SME, TCONG, GNP, and PCGNP are the explanatory variables and the dependent variable is India's intra-industry trade in total trade with the world (IW) calculated at 2-digit ITC level.

Here we first measure, using Grubel Lloyd IIT index, India's IIT share with the world as a whole (IW) in value terms. Table 5 presents our calculation of overall IIT for India with the world over 1975-2003. As per table 5 the lowest value of the index, recorded in 1982-83, is 0.31 and the highest value recorded in 2001-02 ,is 0.67, rise of about 116.12 percent over 1982-83 value. This increase, however, has been achieved with fluctuations with one major downturn in 1979-80 (-20.45 percent). In fact, the value has increased in the terminal years by 4.48 percent. Taking the initial year and terminal year, the value has grown by 93.94 percent.

Table 5: India's Intra-Industry Trade (1975-2003) at 2-Digit Classification

Year	*Volume of Intra-Industry Index (IW)*	*Percentage change over Previous Years*
1975-76	0.33	-
1976-77	0.41	(+24.24)
1977-78	0.40	(-2.44)
1978-79	0.44	(+10.00)
1979-80	0.35	(-20.45)

1980-81	0.36	(2.80)
1981-82	0.32	(-11.11)
1982-83	0.31	(-3.12)
1983-84	0.39	(+25.81)
1984-85	0.36	(-7.70)
1985-86	0.35	(-2.78)
1986-87	0.34	(-2.85)
1987-88	0.39	(+14.76)
1988-89	0.40	(+2.56)
1989-90	0.45	(+12.5)
1990-91	0.43	(+12.5)
1991-92	0.44	(-4.44)
1992-93	0.46	(+2.33)
1993-94	0.45	(+4.55)
1994-95	0.49	(-2.17)
1995-96	0.61	(+12.86)
1996-97	0.58	(+4.91)
1997-98	0.63	(+7.94)
1998-99	0.60	(+5.00)
1999-00	0.59	(-1.67)
2000-01	0.61	(+3.27)
2001-02	0.67	(+9.84)
2002-03	0.64	(+4.48)

Source: Calculated from International Trade Statistics Year Book, U.N. (various years).

Figure 1: Volume of Intra-Industry Trade Index (IW)

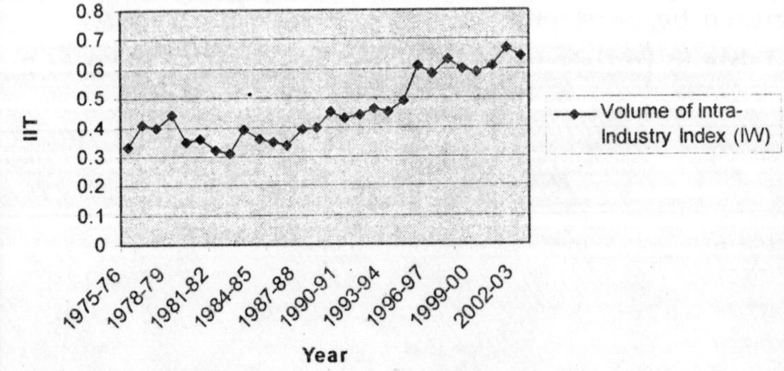

The trend of IIT of India has been increasing. It is important to note that the value of index might be highly responsive to the level of aggregation used for classification of industries. We have chosen 2-digit levels of SITC (Standard International Trade Classification). At a more disaggregated level, the "imperfect" close substitutes might be categorized in separate product groups or firms without any clear trend of pattern.

From table 6, it is evident that from 1986-87 to 2002-2003 the value of index (IW) has increased from 0.34 to 0.64. This is a consistent rise except for the year 1990-91 (-4.44 percent), 1994-95 (-2.17 percent) for developed countries (ID), developing countries (IG) and world (IW) at 2- digit level of SITC over the period 1986-2003.

Table 6: India's Intra-Industry Trade with Different Country Groups (1986-2003)

Year	*ID*	*IG*	*IW*
1986-87	0.27	0.33	0.34
1987-88	0.35	0.32	0.39
1988-89	0.43	0.30	0.40
1989-90	0.42	0.35	0.45
1990-91	0.40	0.38	0.43
1991-92	0.44	0.31	0.44
1992-93	0.43	0.37	0.46
1993-94	0.44	0.39	0.45
1994-95	0.46	0.51	0.49
1995-96	0.43	0.52	0.61
1996-97	0.46	0.57	0.58
1997-98	0.42	0.52	0.63
1998-99	0.51	0.49	0.60
1999-2000	0.53	0.54	0.59
2000-01	0.49	0.61	0.61
2001-02	0.54	0.57	0.67
2002-03	0.56	0.59	0.64

Source: U.N. Commodity Trade Statistics, Statistical Paper, Series D. Vol. 1 (Various Issues).

Figure 2: India's Intra-Industry Trade with Different Country Groups

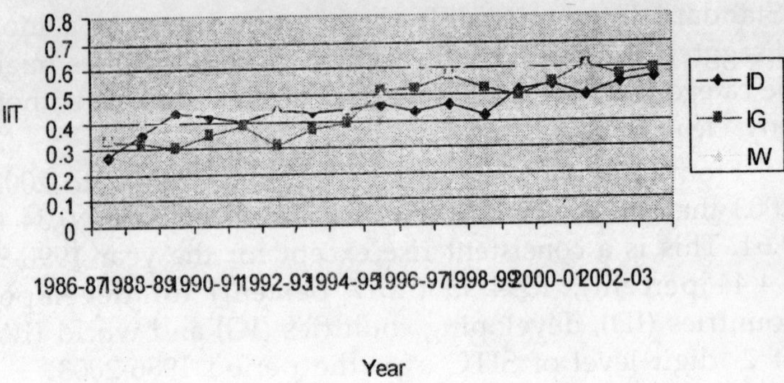

Using 2-digit SITC, IW has registered an increase of 88.24 percent over the period 1986-2003. ID has registered an increase of 107.41 percent from initial year 1986 to 1992 for 2 digit levels whereas for IG, it is 78.79 percent.

The analysis suggests growing importance of intra-industry trade flows in total trade in India. The annual compound growth rate of intra-industry trade of India with world (calculated at 2-digit level) is around 3.4 percent and the annual average growth rate is approximately 4 percent.

The share of manufactured exports has increased over the years from 50 percent in 1975 to 91 percent in 2003 for Standard Industrial Trade Classification 2-digit and the share of manufactured trade as a percent of total trade in all commodities has also increased from 48 percent to 73 percent. This is represented in table 7.

Table 7

Share of Trade in Total Trade (SMT) and Share of Export in Total Export (SME) of India (1975-2003)

(In percent)

Year	*SMT*	*SME*
1975	48	50
1976	49	57
1977	52	58
1978	57	62
1979	54	59
1980	48	80
1981	48	50
1982	49	51
1983	51	53
1984	52	59
1985	58	63
1986	67	67
1987	61	71
1988	64	71
1989	66	71
1990	61	73
1991	62	74
1992	62	75
1993	63	76
1994	68	72
1995	72	71
1996	70	84
1997	71	83
1998	74	89
1999	68	90
2000	69	89
2001	70	89
2002	71	88
2003	72	91

Source: Calculated from International Trade Statistics Year Book Vol. 1 and 2,U.N. Publication, (Various Issues) and U.N. Commodity Trade Statistics, Statistical Papers, Series, D, Vol. XL (various issues).

Upward trend in intra-industry trade might be attributable to higher level of per capita GNP. Intertemporally, India's GNP and per capita GNP have grown by around 3.5 to 4 percent per annum (Economic Survey of India). This has a positive influence on demand for variety and can be analysed in the light of India's experience of industrialisation.

The paper has specifically been devoted to study the following aspects:

(i) The growth of average levels of IIT will be directly related to the growth of percapita GNP (PCGNP) [Dixit and Norman(1980)].

(ii) The share of IIT in total trade is a positive function of market size(proxied by GNP/GDP) [Linder(1961), Lancaster(1980)].

(iii) The impact of Trade Concentration Variable (TCONC) will be directly related to the level of IIT [Dollar(1992)].

The present paper is based on the secondary data. The pattern of IIT indices with world and basic indicators for India over 1975-2003 are presented-

The Posited relationship is

$$IW_t = \int[GNP_t(MarketSize), PCGNP, SME_t TCONC_t]$$

Where t- denotes time horizon. IW_t is value of IIT index over t where t = 1975-2003.

Estimation and Empirical Results

Using Ordinary Least Square (OLS) estimation method, the simple regression model takes the following form:

$$IW_t = B_{1t} + B_{2t}\ GNP_t + B_{3t}\ SME_t + B_{4t}\ TCONC_t + U_t$$

Where B_{1t} is the constant term, B_{2t}, B_{3t}, B_{4t} are all parameters coefficient to be estimated.

The result of the estimation is presented below in table 8. Overall fit is 65 percent and these are no serial correlation in the OLS estimation.

Table 8: Regression Result with OLS Estimation (Dependent Variable, IW_t)

Variable	*Coefficient*	*t. Statistics*	*Two-Tail Significance*
Constant (B_{1t})	-0.4862	-1.3396	0.203
$PCGNP_t$	0.005126	2.2623	0.072
GNP_t	-3.5E 0.8	-1.9235	0.135
SMEt	0.3492	1.8062	1.253
$TCPMC_t$	-0.4983	-0.5962	0.792
D.W. Statistics	2.251	-	-
R^2	0.652	-	-

The result shows that GNP and TCONC have negative coefficients and other variables PCGNP and SME have expected positive sign. The coefficient being very small, the negative effect is very negligible. Since the values of GNP, PCGNP are very high as compared to values of IW, as shown in table 9, the variables become highly significant if expressed in logarithmic terms, which compress the outline and reduce the variability of them which is quite large compared to the variability of IWt. The coefficient of determination has also increased to 0.69.

Table 9

Regression Result with Logarithmic Transformation of Variables (Dependent Variable, IW_t)

Variable	*Coefficient*	*t. Statistics*	*Two-Tail Significance*
Constant (B_{1t})	0.7932	0.6978	0.520
Log ($PCGNP_t$)	1.5846	2.8102	0.063
Log (GNP_t)	-0.7241	-25761	0.061
SME_t	0.3642	1.7203	0.189
$TCONC_t$	-0.3946	-0.4827	0.892
D.W. Statistics	2.842	-	-
R^2	0.69	-	-

Conclusion

Findings show that PCGNP has a strong positive impact on IW confirming Linder's hypothesis (1961). PCGNP, as a proxy for development, implies higher stage or level of development with higher values and as such increases the value of IW through demand pull factor. In our analysis, GNP is not significant with negative small country effect on IIT. This is explained in terms of vertical specialisation of intra-industry trade.

Another variable TCONC (ratio of total trade to GDP) has an adverse impact on IW. Although the coefficients are negative, it is not statistically significant in explaining the upward trend of IW. If the coefficient of TCONC is high this indicates that India has been adopting an export promotion policy.

REFERENCES

Aggaral, N. (2004):"Corporate Travel to India Takes off", *The Straits Times,* Singapore, February.

Asher, M.G., R. Sen and S. Srivastava (2003): ASEAN-India: Emerging Economic Opportunities' in *Beyond the Rhetoric: The Economics of India's Look-East Policy* edited by F. Gare and A. Mattoo, Manohar Publications, New Delhi, India, pp. 45-79.

Bhattacharya, B. and M. Ariff. (2002): Study on AFTA-India Linkages for the Enhancement of Trade and Investment, a report submitted to the government of India and the ASEAN Secretariat, May.

Asian Development Outlook. (2002).The Asian Development Bank, Philippines. EIU, 2001. USA Country Report, New York.

Das, R.U. (2004): "Economic Philosophy of SAFTA", *The Financial Express,* February 2.

Datt, P.T.J.(2004): "Global Bodies Endorse Indian Companies", *Business Line* (India), April 8.

Balassa, B. (1985): "Intra-Industry Specialization: A Cross Country Analysis", *European Economic Review,* 30, No. 1-3, pp. 27-42.

Balassa, B. and Lue Bauwens (1987):"Intra-Industry Specialization in a Multi-Country and Multi-Industry Framework", *The Economic Journal,* Vol. 97, No. 388. pp. 923-939.

Bergstrand, J.H. (1983):"Measurement and Determinants of Intra-International Trade", in P.K.M. Tharakan (ed) *Intra-Industry Trade: Empirical and Methodological Aspects*. Amsterdam: North-Holland, pp. 281-300.

Culem, C. and L. Lundberg(1986):"The products Pattern of Intra-Industry Trade: Stability Among Countries and Over Time", *Review of World Economics* (Weltwirtschaftliches Archiv), Band 122, pp. 113-130.

Dixit, A.K. and V. Norman (1980): *Theory of International Trade*, Cambridge University, Press.

Dixon, P.B. and J. Menon.(1995):"Measures of Intra-industry trade as Indicators of Factor Market Disruption." *Economic Record*. Vol. 73. pp. 233-237.

Dollar, D. (1992):"Outward-Oriented Developing Economic Do Grow More Rapidly: Evidence from 95 LDCs, 1976-85". *Economic Development and Cultural Changes*, 40 (3), pp. 523-44.

Das, Gouranga Gopal.(2005):"Growth and Pattern of Intra-Industry Trade in Manufactures in India's overall Trade: A Quantitative Analysis" Vol.4, No.4,pp.161-184

Greenaway, D. (1983):"Intra-Industry Trade and Inter-Industry Trade in Switzerland".

Gujarati, D.N. (1988): *Basic Econometrics*, 2nd Edition, McGraw Hill.

Gartner, Research (2002): "Comparison: Indian and Chinese Software Services Markets", *Gartner Research*, M-16-1762, May.

Goodman, P.S. (2004) "China Boosts Regional Trade: Dependence on Export Leaves Southeast Asia Vulnerable", *The Asian Wall Street Journal*, February 6-8.

Gaur, S (2004): "ASEAN-India Ties Entering a New Phase", *Business Times*, Singapore, October 8.

Goswami, O.(2001):"India 2003-2010: Economic and Political Scenarios", Confederation of Indian Industry (CII), April.

Gartner, Research (2002): "Comparison: Indian and Chinese Software Services Markets", *Gartner Research*, M-16-1762, May.

Goodman, P S.(2004) "China Boosts Regional Trade: Dependence on Export Leaves Southeast Asia Vulnerable", *The Asian Wall Street Journal*, February 6-8.

Lancaster, K. (1980): "Intra-Industry Trade under Perfect Monopolistic Competition", *Journal of International Economics*, Vol. 10, pp. 151-170.

Loertscher, R. and Wolter, F. (1980): "Determinants of Intra-Industry Trade among countries and Across industries", *Review of World Economics* (Weltwirtschaftliches Archiv), 116, pp. 281-293.

International Monetary Fund (IMF) (2001): *International Financial Statistics Yearbook.*

Financial Times (2004):"India Awakes", Special Report on India Released at the World Economic Forum at Davos, Switzerland, January.

Milner, C. and D. Greenaway (1987):"Intra-Industry Trade: Current Perspectives and Unresolved Issues", *Review of World Economics* (Weltwirtschartliches Archiv), Band 123, Heft 1, pp. 109-119.

Nayyar, D. (1988): "India's Export Performances: 1970-85", in R.E.B. Lucas and G.F. Papanek (eds.), *The Indian Economy: Recent Developments and Future Prospects,* Oxford University Press, 1988, pp. 217-252.

Sarma, A. and P.K. Mehta. (2002): *Exploring Indo-ASEAN Economic Partnership in Globalizing World,* New Delhi: Bookwell.

Sen, R., Asher, M. G and R. Rajan. (2004): "ASEAN-India Economic Relations: Current Trends and Future Prospects", *Economic and Political Weekly,* Vol. XXXIX no. 29, pp. 3297-3309.

Srivastava, S. (2003):"What is the True Level of FDI Flows to India?", *Economic and Political Weekly,* 38, February 15, 2003, pp. 608-611.

Stibora, J. J and De Vaal, A. (1995): Services and Services trade: A Theoretical Inquiry, Tinbergen Institute Research series; 97, Thesis publishers, Amsterdam, 273 p.

Veermamani,C.(2001): Working Paper, No.313, ICSSR, New Delhi.

Vollrath, L.T. (1991):"A Theoretical Evaluation of Alternative Trade Intensity Measures of Revealed Comparative Advantage", *Review of World Economic* (Weltwirtschaftliches Archiv), Band 130, Heft 4, pp. 265-279.

Vona, S. (1991): "On the Measurement of Intra-Industry Trade: Some Further Thoughts", *Review of World Economics* (Weltwirtschaftliches Archiv), Band 127, Heft 4, pp. 678-700.

6

ARIMA Forecasting for Exchange Rate (INR/NR) Quoted in Indo-Nepal Trade: A Study with Box-Jenkins Methodology

C.K.MUKHOPADHYAY* & SHYAM CHARAN BARMA**

Abstract

Univariate model for exchange rate (INR/NR) has been estimated and used for making one-period ahead forecast. Box-Jenkins Methodology is adopted for building ARIMA model. Quarterly data for the study cover the period ranging from the first quarter of 1973 to the second quarter 2006. ARIMA(1,1,2) is found to constitute the univariate process for the series. The forecasting based on this structure is efficient since the forecast errors are white noise.

Key Words: Exchange Rate Forecasting, ARIMA, Box-Jenkins Methodology, White Noise, Forecast Errors.

Introduction

The ultimate purpose of any forecasting exercise is to aid decision making, while the decision making environment influences the methodology and evaluation of forecast. The decision making environment could vary so widely following variation in sales management, production planning, central banking practices, traffic management and even military operations. So the search for an ideal and universally applicable forecasting strategy is an impossible task.

Exchange rate can be forecasted in broad ways by using a multivariate approach in which exchange rate of a country maintains a relationship with other macroeconomic variables like money supply, output, inflation, interest rate, balance of payment etc.

This structural methodology has several limitations which make it less valuable in the field of finance. One such reason is that data for these macroeconomic variables are available at the most quarterly. On the other hand, special class of time series models are ARIMA models which are often associated with Box and Jenkins (1976) for their efforts to systematize the whole methodology for estimating, checking and forecasting models.

AR and MA Structures for Any Series and Relevent Correlogram

An autoregressive model is one where the current value of a variable can be explained in terms of values of the variable taken in the past plus an error term. An autoregressive model of order p, AR(p) is explained as:

$$y_t = a + \beta_1 y_{t-1} + \beta_2 y_{t-2} + \ldots\ldots\ldots\ldots + \beta_p y_{t-p} + ut \qquad (1)$$

where ut is a white noise disturbance term. In the lag operator form equation (1) can be written as

$$\beta(L)y_t = \alpha + u_t$$

where $\beta(L) = (1 - \beta_1 L - \beta_2 L^2 - \ldots\ldots\ldots\ldots - \beta_p L_p)$

A moving average processes assumes that the current value of a variable can be explained in terms of sum of a constant term plus a moving average of current and past white noise disturbance terms. A moving average of order q, MA(q) is explained as:

$Y_t = \alpha + u_t + \gamma_1 u_{t-1} + \gamma_2 u_{t-2} + \ldots\ldots\ldots + \gamma_q u_{t-q}$ (2)

In the lag operator form equation (2) can be written as

$Y_t = \alpha + \gamma(L)\, u_t$

where, $\gamma(L) = 1 + \gamma_1 L + \gamma_2 L_2 + \ldots\ldots\ldots\ldots + \gamma_q L_q$

ARIMA(p,q) process is a combination of AR(p) and MA(q) models. In the lag operator from this model is written as:

$B(L)yt = \alpha + \gamma(L)\, u_t$ ....(3)

ARIMA process shows a combination of the characteristics of AR and MA process. AR process has a geometrically declining ACF (Autocorrelation Function) and a number of non-zero points in PACF (Partial Autocorrelation Function), while MA process has a number of non-zero points in ACF and a geometrically declining PACF. ARMA process will be having both geometrically declining ACF and PACF. One very essential condition of the time series analysis is that underlying series must be stationary. So for the stationary conversion of the series, one more letter(I) is added to the ARMA process, which shows the number of the times underlying series is differenced for making it stationary. On account of this transformation, ARMA process is also referred to as ARIMA process.

Identification and Estimation of ARIMA (p,d,q) Model

Let the estimable ARIMA (p,d,q) model be

$\Phi(B)\Delta^d y_t = \Phi(B)\omega_t = \theta B(\varepsilon_t)$..................................(4)

with $\Phi(B) = 1 - \Phi_1 B - \Phi_2 B_2 - \ldots\ldots\ldots - \Phi_p B_p$ and

$\theta(B) = 1 - \theta_1 B - \theta_2 B_2 - \ldots\ldots\ldots \theta_q B_q$.

We seek to estimate p autoregressive parameters $\Phi_1 \ldots \Phi_p$ and q moving average parameters $\theta_1, \ldots\ldots\ldots\ldots, \theta_q$. The parameters will be so chosen as to minimize the sum of squared differences between the actual time series $\omega t = \Delta^d y_t$ and the fitted time series $\hat{\omega}_t$.

Eqn (4) in terms of the error series,

$\varepsilon_t = \theta^{-1}(B)\, \Phi(B)\, \omega_t$ ....(5)

Consequently, estimation consists in finding a set of autoregressive parameters ($\Phi_1 \ldots \Phi_p$) and a set of moving average parameters ($\theta_1, \theta_2 \ldots\ldots \theta_q$) that minimize the sum of squared errors

$$S(\Phi_1,\ldots\ldots,\Phi_p, \theta_1,\ldots\ldots\ldots,\theta_q) = \Sigma\varepsilon^2_t \ldots\ldots\ldots\ldots\ldots\ldots\ldots\ldots\ldots\ldots(6)$$

Let the parameters which minimize Eqn(6) be $(\phi_1 \ldots\ldots \phi_p)$ and and the residuals associated with the parameters values be ε_t so that

$$\hat{\varepsilon}_t = \hat{\theta}^{-1}(B)\hat{\theta}(B)\omega_t$$

Thus $(\hat{\theta}_1, \ldots\ldots\ldots \hat{\theta}_p ; (\hat{\theta}_1, \ldots\ldots\ldots \theta_q) = \sum \hat{\varepsilon}_t^2$

The residual $\hat{\varepsilon}_t$, t = 1,……, T, are expected to resemble the true errors ε_t which, by assumption, are uncorrelated. So the diagnostic check involves examining if residuals are uncorrelated. If the residuals are white noise such that the residuals are free from any ARMA structure, the identification and estimation of the model is taken to be valid.

Forecasting: Methodological Issues

Let the ARIMA (p,d,q) be

$$\Phi(B)\,\Delta^d y_t = \theta(B)\,\omega_t = \theta(B)\varepsilon_t \ldots\ldots\ldots\ldots\ldots\ldots\ldots\ldots\ldots\ldots(7)$$

Eqn (7) can be written as

$$\Phi(B)\,(1-B)^d\, y_t = \theta(B)\,\varepsilon_t \ldots\ldots\ldots\ldots\ldots\ldots\ldots\ldots\ldots\ldots\ldots(8)$$

Since $\Delta = 1 - B$,

$$y_t = \Phi^{-1}(B)\ (1-B)^{-d}\ \theta(B)\varepsilon_t = \psi(B)\varepsilon_t = \sum_{j=0}^{\infty}\psi_j\varepsilon_{t-j} \quad (9)$$

Eqn (9) presents the ARIMA model as a purely moving average process of infinite order. Then

$$y_{T+L} = \psi_0\varepsilon_{T+l} + \psi_1\varepsilon_{T+l-1} + \ldots\ldots + \psi_L\varepsilon_t + \psi_{L+1}\,\varepsilon_{T-1} + \ldots$$
$$= \psi_0\varepsilon_{T+L} + \psi_1\varepsilon_{T+l-1} + \ldots\ldots\ldots + \psi_{L-1}\,\varepsilon_{T+1} + \Sigma\psi_{L+j}\,\varepsilon_{T-j} \ldots(10)$$

Eqn (10) describes information up to and including the time period T. Consequently, the forecast $\hat{y}_t(1)$ can be based only on information available up to time T.

This allows us to compare this forecast with the actual value y_{T+L} as expressed in Equation (10).

The forecast can be written as a weighted sum of the estimable error terms, ε_T , ε_{T-1},......... Then the desired forecast is

$$\hat{y}_t\ (1) = \sum_{j=0}^{\alpha} \psi^*_{L+j}\ t_{T-j} \qquad (11)$$

where, the weights ψ^*_{L+j} are to be chosen optimally to minimize the mean squared forecast error.

From Eqn (10) and (11) we have the forecast error, $e_T(l)$ as

$$e_T(1) = y_{T+1} - \hat{y}T(1) = \psi_0 \varepsilon_{T+1} + \psi_1 \varepsilon_{T+l-1} + \psi_{L-1} \varepsilon_{T+1} + \sum_{j=0}^{\alpha} (\psi_{L+j} - \psi^*_{L+j}) \varepsilon_{T-j} \qquad (12)$$

Assuming $E(\varepsilon i \varepsilon j) = 0$ for i=j , the mean-square forecast error is

$$E[e^2_T(L)] = (\psi^2_0 + \psi^2_1 + \ldots\ldots + \psi^2_{L-1})\sigma^2_t + \sum_{j=0}^{\alpha} (\psi_{L+j} - \psi^*_{L+j})^2 \sigma^2 \varepsilon \qquad (13)$$

$E[e^2_T(L)]$ is minimized by setting the 'optimum' weights ψ^*_{L+j} equal to the true weights ψ_{L+j},
j= 0, 1, ...

Then the optimum forecast $\hat{y}T(1)$ becomes the conditional expectation of y_{T+l}.

Let us take the conditional expectation of y_{t+l} in eqn (13). Then the expected values of ε_{T+l} , ...ε_{T+1} are all 0 (Zero) while the expected values of ε_T, ε_{T-1}, ... are just the residuals from the estimated equation. Thus we have,

$$\hat{y}T(1) = \sum_{j=0}^{\alpha} \Psi_{L+j}\ \hat{\varepsilon}_{T-j}$$

$$= E[y_{T+l} / y_T, \ldots\ldots, y_1] \ \ldots\ldots (14)$$

Data

The study uses quarterly data for nominal exchange rate of Indian rupee (INR) with respect to Nepalese currency (NR). Data cover the period ranging from first quarter of 1976 to second quarter of 2006. There are overall 122 observations in the dataset.

Non-Stationary and Order of Integration

The ACF and PACF of the Log E(Exchange rate) dataset are given by the Figure 1. The ACF describes a gradually dying out pattern for the autocorrelation coefficients with a singular significant spike at lag 1 in the PACF. This testifies for the non-stationarity of the series.

The Figure 2 presents the ACF and PACF of the differenced Log E dataset. The ACF and PACF of the series testify for the statonarity of the series. Consequently, Log E series is I(1).

Figure 1

Correlogram of LOGE

Included observations: 122 Sample: 1976:1 2006:2

Autocorrelation | Partial Correlation

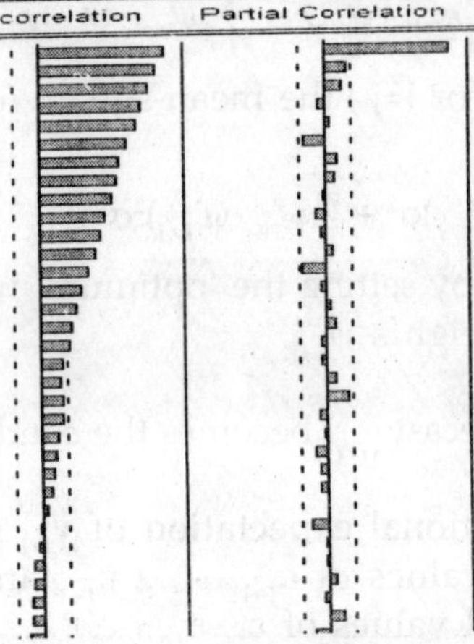

	AC	PAC	Q-Stat	Prob
1	0.894	0.894	99.820	0.000
2	0.829	0.154	186.53	0.000
3	0.789	0.123	265.62	0.000
4	0.732	-0.050	334.34	0.000
5	0.689	0.031	395.65	0.000
6	0.619	-0.151	445.56	0.000
7	0.582	0.098	490.07	0.000
8	0.557	0.060	531.25	0.000
9	0.517	-0.015	567.01	0.000
10	0.475	-0.060	597.46	0.000
11	0.431	-0.035	622.83	0.000
12	0.408	0.046	645.74	0.000
13	0.348	-0.179	662.57	0.000
14	0.291	-0.041	674.43	0.000
15	0.256	0.026	683.68	0.000
16	0.229	0.070	691.18	0.000
17	0.200	-0.029	696.96	0.000
18	0.160	-0.029	700.67	0.000
19	0.145	0.061	703.74	0.000
20	0.161	0.152	707.58	0.000
21	0.149	-0.048	710.90	0.000
22	0.131	-0.024	713.50	0.000
23	0.105	-0.084	715.20	0.000
24	0.085	-0.051	716.33	0.000
25	0.063	-0.046	716.95	0.000
26	0.030	-0.004	717.09	0.000
27	-0.014	-0.126	717.12	0.000
28	-0.039	-0.010	717.36	0.000
29	-0.058	-0.009	717.91	0.000
30	-0.076	0.053	718.86	0.000
31	-0.096	-0.039	720.38	0.000
32	-0.086	0.108	721.63	0.000

Figure 2

Correlogram of DLOGE

Included observations: 121 Sample: 1976:1 2006:2

Autocorrelation | Partial Correlation

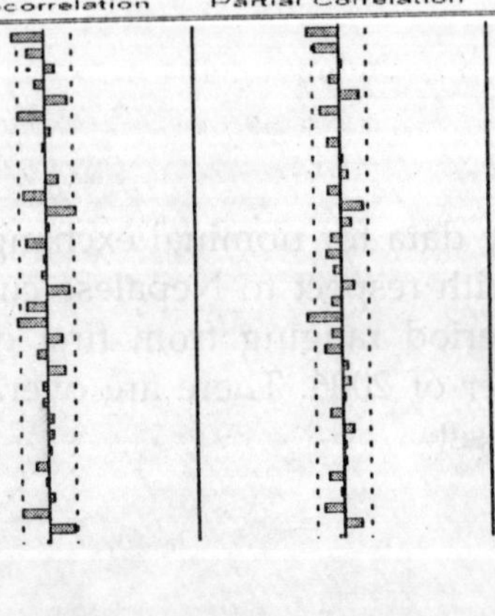

	AC	PAC	Q-Stat	Prob
1	-0.234	-0.234	6.7982	0.009
2	-0.115	-0.180	8.4580	0.015
3	0.082	0.008	9.2960	0.026
4	-0.065	-0.067	9.8362	0.043
5	0.151	0.145	12.761	0.026
6	-0.182	-0.140	17.051	0.009
7	0.030	0.000	17.171	0.016
8	-0.013	-0.082	17.193	0.028
9	0.004	0.022	17.195	0.046
10	0.093	0.057	18.345	0.049
11	-0.163	-0.086	21.939	0.025
12	0.208	0.162	27.828	0.006
13	0.018	0.077	27.874	0.009
14	-0.136	-0.064	30.461	0.007
15	-0.021	-0.114	30.521	0.010
16	-0.039	-0.054	30.742	0.015
17	0.161	0.083	34.433	0.007
18	-0.145	-0.067	37.484	0.005
19	-0.218	-0.264	44.447	0.001
20	0.107	-0.065	46.119	0.001
21	-0.063	-0.120	46.712	0.001
22	0.119	0.040	48.829	0.001
23	-0.034	0.041	49.003	0.001
24	-0.030	0.023	49.139	0.002
25	0.027	-0.084	49.248	0.003
26	0.037	0.075	49.464	0.004
27	0.024	0.022	49.557	0.005
28	-0.087	0.016	50.766	0.005
29	-0.018	-0.108	50.817	0.007
30	0.036	-0.009	51.029	0.010
31	-0.183	-0.134	55.541	0.003
32	0.172	0.128	61.498	0.001

Identification of AR(1) Structure

The ACF and PACF of the dlogEt series contain one significant spike at lag one. This is indicative of the AR(1) process for dlogEt series. Consequently, the estimable model becomes

$$\text{dlog Et} = \alpha + \beta \text{dlogE}_{t-1} + v_t \quad (15)$$

The estimated equation is given by the Table-1. The Table 1 shows that the coefficient of dlog E_{t-1} is significant at 1% level. DW statistic (2.07) implies that the equation is free from autocorrelation.

Table 1: Estimation of the Equation (15)

Dependent Variable: D LogE_t

Sample(adjusted): 1976:3 2006:2

Included observations: 120 after adjusting endpoints

Variable	*Coefficient*	*Std. Error*	*t-Statistic*	*Prob.*
DLogE_{t-1}	-0.235614	0.089763	-2.624849	0.0098
C	-0.000744	0.000959	-0.775464	0.4396

R^2	0.055167	Mean dependent var	-0.000619
Adjusted R^2	0.047160	S.D. dependent var	0.010749
S.E. of regression	0.010492	AIC	-6.259794
SSR	0.012991	SIC	-6.213336
Log likelihood	377.5877	F-statistic	6.889830
DW-stat	2.072407	Prob(F-statistic)	0.009816

Figure 3

Correlogram of residual (dloge&ar1)

Included observations: 120 Sample: 1976:1 2006:2

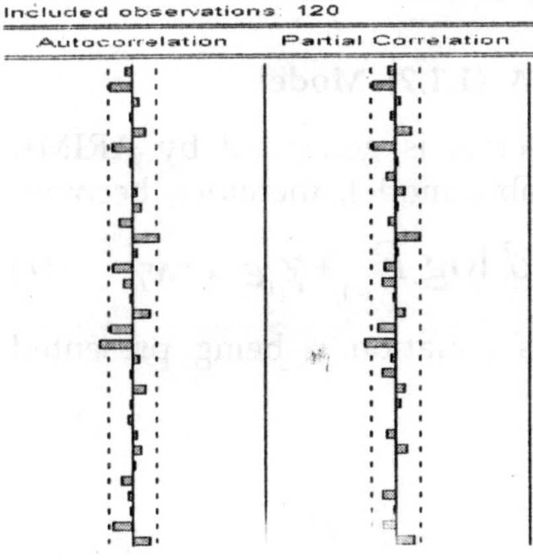

	AC	PAC	Q-Stat	Prob
1	-0.041	-0.041	0.2096	0.647
2	-0.166	-0.168	3.6213	0.164
3	0.045	0.031	3.8795	0.275
4	-0.015	-0.040	3.9064	0.419
5	0.103	0.122	5.3877	0.370
6	-0.155	-0.164	8.4630	0.206
7	-0.019	0.016	8.5077	0.290
8	-0.006	-0.080	8.5121	0.385
9	0.029	0.057	8.6247	0.473
10	0.060	0.022	9.1013	0.523
11	-0.107	-0.053	10.642	0.474
12	0.198	0.194	15.954	0.193
13	0.038	0.017	16.150	0.241
14	-0.153	-0.096	19.382	0.151
15	-0.069	-0.106	20.045	0.170
16	-0.009	-0.010	20.055	0.218
17	0.133	0.069	22.565	0.164
18	-0.177	-0.145	27.062	0.078
19	-0.255	-0.239	36.524	0.009
20	0.046	-0.038	36.838	0.012
21	-0.013	-0.104	36.863	0.017
22	0.109	0.073	38.640	0.016
23	-0.017	0.030	38.683	0.021
24	-0.037	-0.004	38.886	0.028
25	0.031	-0.067	39.031	0.037
26	0.058	0.097	39.546	0.043
27	0.014	0.007	39.577	0.056
28	-0.095	-0.008	41.022	0.053
29	-0.031	-0.107	41.179	0.066
30	-0.010	-0.013	41.196	0.084
31	-0.152	-0.101	44.974	0.050
32	0.145	0.145	48.457	0.031

Identification and Estimation of MA Structure

The ACF and PACF of the residuals of the estimated equation is given by the Figure 3. The significant spike at lag 2 in the ACF and PACF of the residuals is indicative of the MA(2) structure of the residuals. Consequently, the estimable equation is

$$e_t = \delta + \gamma e_{t-2} + v_t \quad (16)$$

The estimated equation is given by the Table 2. The coefficient of e_{t-2} is found to be significant at 10% level.

Table 2: Estimation of the Equation-16

Dependent Variable: e_t

Sample(adjusted): 1977:1 2006:2

Included observations: 118 after adjusting endpoints

Variable	*Coefficient*	*Std. Error*	*t-Statistic*	*Prob.*
e_{t-2}	-0.167217	0.091612	-1.825273	0.0705
C	4.90E-05	0.000957	0.051233	0.9592

R^2	0.027919	Mean dependent var	4.92E-05
Adjusted R^2	0.019539	S.D. dependent var	0.010501
S.E. of regression	0.010398	AIC	-6.277563
SSR	0.012542	SIC	-6.230602
Log likelihood	372.3762	F-statistic	3.331621
DW-stat	2.072443	Prob(F-statistic)	0.070533

Estimation of the ARIMA (1,1,2) Model

We observe that log E_t series is generated by ARIMA (1,1,2) process. The estimable model, therefore, becomes

$$d\log E_t = \alpha_1 + \beta_1 d\log E_{t-1} + \gamma_1 e_{t-2} + v_t \quad (17)$$

The estimation of this equation is being presented through the Table 3.

Table 3: Estimation of the Equation 17

Dependent Variable: D Log E_t

Sample (adjusted): 1977:1 2006:2

Included observations: 118 after adjusting endpoints

Variable	*Coefficient*	*Std. Error*	*t-Statistic*	*Prob.*
DLog E_{t-1}	-0.279091	0.092879	-3.004884	0.0033
e_{t-2}	-0.179068	0.095345	-1.878112	0.0629
C	-0.000715	0.000961	-0.743419	0.4587
R^2	0.082090	Mean dependent var		-0.000586
Adj R^2	0.066126	S.D. dependent var		0.010796
S.E. of regression	0.010433	AIC		-6.262517
SSR	0.012518	SIC		-6.192076
Log likelihood	372.4885	F-statistic		5.142302
DW- stat.	1.987048	Prob(F-statistic)		0.007261

The Table 3 shows that

(i) AR(1) coefficient is significant at 1% level

(ii) MA(2) coefficient is significant at about 5% level

These coefficients indicate that the identification of ARIMA (1,1,2) structure for Log E series is appropriate.

Forecasts

The fitted values of log E_t (Log $\hat{E}_T$) have been calculated. These constitute the forecast values for log E_t (t=1,2,..........). The time plots of Log E_t and the corresponding forecast have been presented through the Figure 4.

Figure 4 :Time Plots of Log E_t & the Forecast

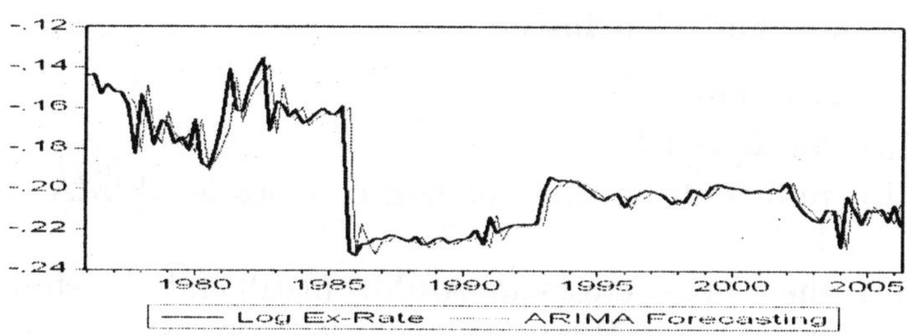

Efficiency of Forecast

The residuals of the estimated equation (17) constitute the forecast errors. Forecasting is efficient if there exists no scope of improving upon forecasting through adaptation of further information from the forecast errors. In other words, efficiency of forecast depends on the nature of the forecast errors. If forecast errors are white noise such that these depict ARIMA (0,0,0) structure, then these error do not provide any deterministic information for forecast anymore.

The ACF and PACF of the residuals of the forecast errors are given by the Figure 5. The ACF and PACF are free from any significant spike at any lag. This indicates that forecast errors are white noise and therefore, forecasting is efficient.

Figure 5

Correlogram of residual (dloge,itslag1&ma2)

Included observations 118 Sample: 1976:1 2006.2

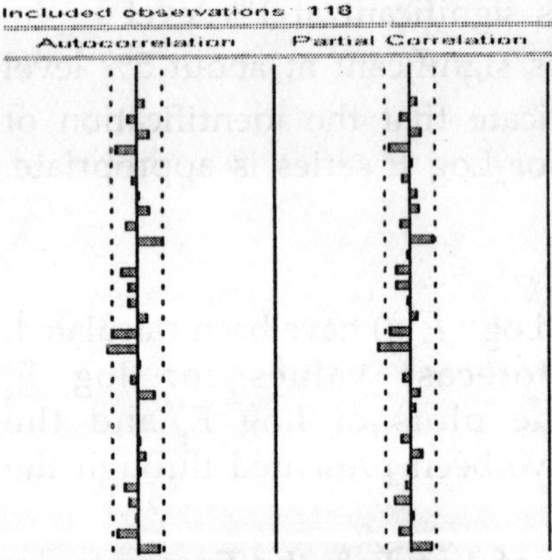

	AC	PAC	Q-Stat	Prob
1	0 004	0 004	0 0015	0 969
2	-0.008	-0.008	0.0091	0.995
3	0.055	0.055	0.3848	0.943
4	-0.064	-0.065	0.8908	0.926
5	0 088	0 090	1 8642	0 868
6	-0.148	-0.156	4.6172	0.594
7	-0.004	0.011	4.6196	0.706
8	-0.034	-0.066	4.7671	0.782
9	0 016	0 052	4 8024	0 851
10	0.098	0.068	6 0583	0.810
11	-0.097	-0.089	7.3042	0.774
12	0 194	0.179	12.318	0.420
13	0 005	-0 014	12 321	0 502
14	-0.118	-0.111	14.213	0.434
15	-0.064	-0.104	14.768	0.468
16	-0.070	-0.012	15.445	0.492
17	0.076	0.044	16.263	0.505
18	-0.186	-0.154	21.142	0.272
19	-0.234	-0.242	28.962	0.067
20	0.017	0.006	29.001	0.088
21	-0.056	-0.056	29.457	0 103
22	0.121	0.075	31.604	0.084
23	-0.004	0.029	31.606	0.109
24	0.006	0.001	31.611	0.137
25	0.009	-0.073	31.625	0.169
26	0.046	0.092	31.952	0.195
27	0.012	-0.008	31.973	0.233
28	-0.099	-0.026	33.511	0.217
29	-0.059	-0.128	34.072	0.237
30	-0.016	0.014	34.112	0.276
31	-0.155	-0.096	38.018	0.180
32	0.153	0.150	41.861	0.114

Summary and Conclusion

The study shows that

(i) $\log E_t$ is I(1)

(ii) univariate process for Log E_t series is ARIMA (1, 1, 2).

(iii) the forecast errors are ARIMA (0,0,0) and, therefore, white noise. This signifies efficient forecasting based on the ARIMA (1,1,2) structure of the log E_t series.

The forecasting can be extended to $t=_{T+1}$ .... periods. These may represent one-step ahead forecasting. Efficiency of ARIMA(1,1,2) forecasting is also implicitly expected to generate efficient one-step ahead forecasting for the extended periods.

REFERENCES

An Sing Chen and Mark T. Leun,(2003) 'A Bayesian Vector Error Correction Model for Forecasting Exchange Rates', *Computers & Computers & Operations Research* Vol. 30, pp. 887–900.

A Sing Chen and Mark T. Leun, (2004) 'Regression Neural Network for Error Correction in Foreign Exchange Forecasting and Trading', *Computers & Computers & Operation Research*, Vol. 31, pp. 1049 -1068.

___ (1984), 'Bayesian Forecasting', in *The Forecasting Accuracy of Major Time Series Methods*, New York: John Wiley, pp. 221-238.

Box, G.E.P., and Jenkins, G.M. (1976), *Time Series Analysis, Forecasting and Control* (2nd ed), San Francisco: Holden-Day.

Brown, R.G. (1982), 'The Balance of Effort in Forecasting,' *Journal of Forecasting*, Vol. 1, pp. 49-53.

Rao., Garcia Jurado I.,(1995) Gonzalez Monteiga W., Prada Sanchez J.M. and Febrero- Bande M., 'Predicting Using Box-Jenkins, Non-Parametric and Bootstrap Techniques', *Technometrics*, Vol. 37, pp. 303-310.

Fildes, R. (1983), 'An Evaluation of Bayesian Forecasting,' *Journal of Forecasting*, Vol. 2, pp. 137-150.

____ (1989), *Forecasting Structural Time Series Model and the Kalman Filter*, New York: Cambridge University Press.

Harald Reinton and Steven Ongena, (1999) 'Out-of-sample Forecasting Performance of Single Equation Monetary Exchange Rate Models in Norwegian Currency Market', *Applied Financial Economics*, 1999, Vol. 9, pp. 545-550.

Harvey, A.C., (1984), 'A Unified View of Statistical Forecasting Procedures', *Journal of Forecasting*, Vol. 3, pp. 245-283.

Harvey, A.C., and Durbin, J. (1986), 'The Effects of Seat Belt Legislation on British Road Causalities: A Case Study in Structural Time Series Modelling', *Journal of the Royal Statistical Society*, Ser. A. 149, 187-227.

Harvey, A.C., and Koopman, S.J. (1992), 'Diagnostic Checking of Unbiased-Components Time Series Models,' *Journal of Business & Economic Statistics,* Vol. 10, pp. 377-389.

Harvey, A.C., and Peters, S. (1990), 'Estimation Procedures for Structural Time Series Models,' *Journal of Forecasting,* Vol. 9, pp.89-108.

Harvey, A.C., and Todd, P.H.J. (1983), 'Forecasting Economic Time Series with Structural and Box-Jenkins Models: A Case Study', *Journal of Business & Economic Statistics,*Vol. 1, pp. 299-315.

Holt, C.C. (1957), *Forecasting Seasonal and Trends by Exponentially Weighted Moving Averages,* Pittsburgh, PA: Carnegie Institute of Technology.

Jenkins, G.M. (1982), 'Some Practical Aspects of Forecasting in Organizations,' *Journal of Forecasting,* Vol. 1, pp. 3-21.

Kahl, D.R., and Ledolter, J.(1983), 'A Recursive Kalman Filter Forecasting Approach,' *Management Science,* Vol. 29, pp. 1325-1333.

Lindsay I. Hogan, 'A Comparison of Alternative Exchange Rate Forecasting Models', Bureau of Agricultural Economics, Canberra ACT 2601.

Lutz Lillian and Mark P. Taylor, (2003) 'Why It is So Difficult to Beat Random Walk Forecast of Exchange Rate?', *Journal of International Economics,* Vol. 60, pp. 85-107.

Makridakis, S., and Wheelwright, S.C. (1979), 'Forecasting the Future and the Future of Forecasting,' in *TIMS Studies in the Management Sciences* (Vol.12) eds. S. Makridakis and S.C. Wheelwright, Amsterdam: North-Holland, pp. 329-352.

Mary E. Gerlow and Scott H. Irwin, (1991) 'The Performance of Exchange Rate Forecasting Models: An Economic Evaluation', *Applied Economics,* Vol. 23, pp. 133-142.

7

India Under Free Trade Regime

ANIL BHUIMALI* & TULIKA KAR**

Abstract

India at present is on a high growth path in terms of its trade performance. Growth effect of trade is phenomenal. This has been reflected in the growth of exports, imports and the well-being of the economic agents. The phenomenal growth of India's trade and commerce has been noticed especially since the adoption of new trade policy in 1991. The present paper analyses, among others, the main features of new trade policy, our trade policy changes under globalisation perspective, liberalisation of exchange rate regime and EXIM Policy, export performance, composition of exports, impact of import liberalisation on export performance and so on. .

Key Words: Open General License (OGL), Export Processing Zone (EPZ), Outward Looking, QRs.

* Professor, Department of Economics, University of North Bengal.

** Lecturer (Part time), Kalipada Ghosh Tarai Mahavidyalaya, Bagdogra.

The Context

There have been a remarkable changes in the volume and direction of our exports and imports especially since 1990s. The so-called reform in trade has in fact integrated the Indian economy with the World economy more intensively. Before adopting new economic policy India's foreign exchange reserve was at its lowest position. Its share of exports to total world exports was just over 0.5 percent, with a huge trade deficit due mainly to cumulative effect in pushing up imports. The factors responsible for increasing imports were larger outflow of foreign exchange owing to rise in POL prices in 1970s and 1980s, severe shortages on account of the unprecedented drought of 1987, and the growing pressure of demand accompanied with the stepping up of the real growth of the economy. The present paper highlights, among others, the main features of new trade policy, globalisation and our policy changes on trade and trade related matters, liberalisation of exchange rate regime and EXIM policy (2002-2007), export performance, composition of exports, impact of import liberalisation on export performance and the exposition of volume of exports and imports in the post reformed regime.

Main Elements

In the pre-reformed period there were various types and ways of importing and import licenses. The importers were of three categories i.e. actual users for industrial products and non-industrial products, exporters and other import licenses. Other import licenses were sub-divided into open general license (OGL), automatic license, supplementary import license and import through government owned canalised agencies. The coverage of OGL has been extended and the restricted list has been cut drastically. On March 31, 1996, the tariff line-wise import policy was first announced and 6,161 tariff lines were made free. Additional 1,905 tariff lines were freed in March, 2000. Quantitative restrictions on 714 items were lifted from April, 2000 and the remaining 715 items were also lifted by April,1, 2001. Following Chelliah Committee's recommendation (1993) the Government of India announced substantial cut in import duties in 1993-94 and 1994-95 budgets (reducing the duty on goods from 110% to 85 % in 1993-94, from 85 to 65% in 1994-95 from 65 % to 50 % in 1995-96 and from 50 % to 40 % in 1998-99). The 2000-2001 budget reduced the peak rate of basic custom duty rates of 35%. Now there are only four customs duty rates of 35%, 25%, 15% and 5 percent. But a surcharge of 10% has been levied for revenue consideration.

Before the adjustment of new trade policy a large numbers of exportables and importables used to be canalised . After a thorough review of the system 16 export items and 20 import items were decanalised in August 13, 1991. During 1992-1997 a number of import goods such as newsprint, non-ferrous metals, natural rubber, intermediates and raw materials for fertilizers were decanalised. Due to the policy of decanalisation the proportion of canalised items in total imports declined from 27% to 19% between 1988 and 1998.

The major decision on liberalising our exchange rate policy has been taken especially since 1993 although the Govt. announced the liberalised exchange rate mechanism system in the budget of 1992-1993 through partial convertibility of Indian rupee. Under this system a dual exchange rate was fixed in which 40 percent of foreign exchange earnings were to be surrendered at the official exchange rate and the remaining were to be converted at a prevailing market rate. Full convertibility of rupee on trade account was introduced in 1993-94 in which the ratios were extended to 100 percent conversion. The conversion was extended to almost the entire merchandise trade transaction and on all receipts but not on all payments. The RBI, in 1994, further liberalised invisible payment and accepted obligations under Article - VIII of the IMF.

We achieved full convertibility on current account under which we are committed to forsake the use of exchange restrictions on current international transaction as an instrument of managing the balance of payments. During 1995-1996, 1996-1997, and 1997-1998 other relaxations of restrictions on current transactions such as on exchange control, more liberal indicative ceilings for release of foreign exchange by authorised dealer, basic travel quota, studies abroad, media expenses, casual remittance, donations, release of exchange for persons proceeding on employment abroad and greater flexibility in the Exchange Earner Foreign Currency (EEFC) etc. were announced.

For the purpose of promoting imports and exports export houses and trading houses were set up with the provision of benefit of self-certification under the advance license system. This permits duty free imports for promoting exports. For increasing export trading houses were set up with 51 percent foreign equity.

Export Processing Zones (EPZs), Electronic Hardware Technology Park (EHTP), Software Technology Park (STP), and Export Oriented Units (EOUs) were set up for producing goods solely for export purposes. Recent changes in those schemes include extending tax holiday from five years to ten years, higher domestic access, rationalisation of minimum 'Net Foreign Exchange Earning' as percentage of exports and minimum export performance, enlargement of the scope of private warehouses in EPZs to include procurement of indigenous goods for export, and undertaking of job work on behalf of domestic units for direct exports in certain sectors etc.

The setting up of Free Trade Zones (FTZs) was proposed in 1999. But due to a number of factors this could not be implemented. However, to increase the level of our export over the provision of Special Economical Zones (SEZs) was created in 2000 with full flexibility of operations. The SEZs are also able to import capital goods and raw materials duty free and to access the same for

Domestic Tariff Area without payment of terminal excise duty. The first such SEZs operating successfully are at Piparav in Gujarat and Tuticorin in Tamil Nadu. For the purpose of enhancing the export-oriented production infrastructural facilities were provided in 1994 and centrally sponsored scheme "Export Promotion Industrial Park" was started. For this purpose State governments were provided with 75% of capital expenditure towards creation of infrastructure facilities. During the entire decade of 1990s many tax benefits and exemption were announced to liberalise imports and promote export-import policy.

Exim Policy 2002-2007

Since the beginning of the present decade restictions on designated items were lifted to increase export of agro and agro- based products. Non–actionable sudsidies have been granted for exporting fruits, vegetables, horticulture, poultry and dairy products. The EXIM policy 2002-2007 provides a package of incentives to cottage, small-scale and handicraft sector to improve upon their productivity and export competitiveness. The incentives include Export Promotion Capital Goods (EPCG) scheme, permission to achieve a lower threshold level for achieving the Export House Status, preferential access to Market Access Initiative Funds and duty free access to trimming and embellishment for achieving value added exports.

In order to remove restrictions on textile products by 2005 under the Agreement on Textile and Clothing, the EXIM Policy focused on measures to encourage value added exports in the garment sector.

Electronics Hardware Technology Park (EHTP) scheme was modified, during 2002-2007 to enable hardware sector to face the zero duty regime under Information Technology Agreement –1. Schemes introduced in gems and jewellery include abolition of the licensing regime for the import of rough diamonds, reduction in the value addition norms for export of jewellety and permitting personal carriage of jewellery.

Procedural simplifications have been made in the EXIM policy to further reduce transation costs covering DG of Foreign Trade, Customs and Banks. These include adoption of 8 digit commodity classification of import which would eliminate the classification disputes, reduction of maximum free limit for electronic filing from Rs. 1.5 lakh to 1 lakh, introducing of some day licensing new norms for reduction in percentage of physical examination of export cargo, introduction of the simplified brand rate of drawback scheme and EXIM Policy 2002-2007 including widening of the scope of the Scope of the Market Access Initiative Scheme to include activities considered necessary for a focused market promotion of exports, settings up of 'Business Centre' in India mission abroad for visiting Indian exporters/businessmen for ensuring a facilitator environment for exports, transport subsidy for exports to units located in the North East, Sikkim and Jammu and Kashmir and introduction of 'Focus Africa' with 'Focus Commonwealth' of Independent States to follow to diversify market.

Trade Performance

There has been a phenomenal change in out trade performance in terms of growth rate in the balance of payments and their ratios (table 1 and 2). Table 1 shows that both the trade and invisible accounts are much more resilient than in the 1980s and merchandise trade has increased significantly to an average of more than 20 percent of the GDP in the post crisis period. Between pre-crisis to post-crisis periods, the proportion of the imports financed by exports has increased from 0.59 to 0.74% (see table-1). The growth of custom exports (in US$) has increased from 8.1% to 10.9 % during pre-crisis and post–crisis period (see table 2) This is due to increase in the volume of exports (from about 5.4 % in the first period to 10.2% in the second period per annum).

Table 1: Balance of Payment (US $ million) Growth Rates (Percent)

	1970-79 *Seventies*	*1980-89* *Per Crisis*	*1992-00* *Post Crisis*	*1990-99* *Nineties*
Exchange rate (ER)				
Real Effective	-2.1	2.0	0.0	-1.9
Standard Deviation	5.8	4.6	6.4	7.4
Normal Effective	0.4	-3.0	-4.6	-6.579
Standard Deviation	2.2	4.8	6.5	-2.0
REER Calendar Year	-3.9	-1.7	-0.7	7.9
Inflation (WPI)	8.5	7.2	6.7	3.6
Standard Deviation	9.4	3.9	3.3	17.3
Money Supply	17.5	17.2	17.4	14.4
Bank Credit, net	17.2	18.5	14.0	14.3
Commercial	18.9	17.2	14.6	14.3
Government	15.0	20.4	13.4	14.5
RBI Credit to Govt.	14.5	20.0	5.6	7.1
Payment (BOP)				
Exports, fob	17.3	80.3	10.8	8.6
Imports, cif	20.6	7.8	12.7	9.7
Foreign Investment	-	-	11.4	10.2
FDI	-	-	4.9	5.2
Customs Export Total ($)	16.6	8.1	10.9	8.6
Quantam Index	6.9	5.4	10.2	10.6
Unit value Index	10.2	10.3	7.7	9.5
Manufacture($)	18.4	10.4	10.9	9.7
Primary	14.9	2.4	8.9	6.2
Oil	20.3	109.6	-11.9	-14.5
Customs import Tools ($)	21.9	7.2	11.4	9.6
Quantum index	7.1	7.5	16.3	12.7
Unit value index	16.3	8.0	4.2	6.9
Manufacture($)	18.7	11.1	14.5	8.5
Machinery and equipment	14.2	13.4	4.9	1.7
Primary	15.8	4.6	19.5	12.5
Oil	54.1	3.3	5.5	15.8
Net exports (US$ million)	493	-2136	1894	1809
Non-oil				
Manufacture	-207	-2686	-1220	-1131
Primary	648	1026	2594	2477

Oil	-1487	-3944	-7211	-6810
World Merchandise Export Growth Value ($)	20.2	6.6	6.1	-
Volume	6.0	3.7	6.7	-
Unit Value	13.4	2.7	-0.7	-

Source: Hand Book of Statistic on the Indian Economy, Reserve Bank of India, World Trade Ogranisation, World Merchandise Trade Data.

Table 2: Balance of Payment is Ratios

	1970-79 Seventies	*1980-89 Per Crisis*	*1992-00 Post Crisis*	*1990-99 Nineties*
Fiscal deficit (center)	3.6	6.6	5.2	5.5
Fiscal deficit (center and state)	8.1	7.2	7.4	7.3
current Account Deficit	0.1	1.8	1.1	1.3
Goods and Services deficit	1.5	3.7	3.1	3.0
Trade deficit	1.2	3.2	3.1	2.9
Export fob	4.4	4.7	8.5	8.0
Imports, cif	5.6	7.9	11.6	10.9
Export-Import Ratio	0.80	0.59	0.74	0.74
Non-customs imports	0.3	0.7	1.8	1.6
Invisibles, net	1.1	1.4	2.0	1.6
Non factor services	0.3	0.4	0.4	0.3
Private Transfers	0.6	1.1	2.5	2.2
Official transfers	0.6	0.2	0.1	0.1
Income (including interest)	-0.3	-0.4	-1.0	-1.1
Capital inflow (adjusted)	0.9	1.6	2.4	2.2
Foreign Investment	0.0	0.0	1.1	0.9
FDI	-	-	0.5	0.5
Protfolio	-	-	0.6	0.5
External assistance	0.7	0.6	0.4	0.5
Private/market	0.2	0.9	0.9	0.9
NRI deposists, net	0.1	0.4	0.4	0.4
Rupee debit Service	0.0	0.0	-0.2	-0.3
Reserves (increase is negative and decrease is positive)	-0.5	0.2	-1.1	-1.0
Customs data				
Total imports	5.3	7.2	9.8	9.3

Oil imports	1.1	2.0	2.2	2.1
Non-oil imports	4.0	5.2	7.6	7.2
Manufactures imports	2.7	4.1	6.6	6.3
Total export	4.5	4.6	8.4	7.8
Manufactures exports	2.7	2.8	6.3	5.9
Other Ratios				
Export/import ratio	0.87	0.64	0.86	0.85
Manufactured exports ratio to total	55.7	60.7	76.1	75.4
To registered manufacturing	7.2	6.4	13.2	12.4
Net imports of manufactured goods ratio to manufacturing GDP	1.8	8.9	2.5	2.3
Machinery & equipment import share in manufacture imports	26.0	29.0	29.6	29.7

Sources: RBI, Handbook of Statistics on the Indian Economy, Directorate General of Commercial Intelligence and Statistics 2000.

Manufacturing sector responded well to the trade reform and increased from an average of 60.77 % in the 1980 to an average of 76.11% of total exports after the crisis. (see table 2)

Oil and non-oil imports followed a significantly different path in the import side. After the crisis, Oil imports increased marginally by 0.2% of the GDP while the non-oil imports jumped from 5.2% in the per-crisis period to 7.6% of the GDP to the post-crisis period. The value of new imports of manufactured products had fallen dramatically from a pre-crisis average of 8.9% to a post-crisis average of 2.5% of the GDP (table 2). The real effective exchange rate averaged the same in the pre-crisis and post-crisis periods. However, the real effective exchange rate depreciated by an average of 1.9% per annum in the 1990s because of depreciation of 15.1% in 1991-1992 and 11.1% in 1992-1993. The real depreciation rate was only 0.1% per annum slower than in the 1980s and 0.2 % per annum slower than in the 1970s. As a result, from 1990 to 2000 our share in the world exports continued to increase from 0.52 % to 0.67%. Because of QRS and reduction in customs tariffs this increase was higher than in the previous decade.

In the post-reform period the mean growth of GDP was 6.0 percent but the mean growth of import was 23 percent (see table 3). In the post-reform period the growth rate of exports as well as import is inconsistent. However, exports have increased steadily during the period due to openness of trade. The data show that during 1990-1991 the share of the exports as percentage of GDP was 4.7 percent which increased to 19.9 percent in 2003-2004, the mean growth in export rate being 16.5 percent. Between 1990-1991 and 2003-2004 the share of manufacturing goods increased from 71.6 to 77.8 percent (see tables 4 and 5). Table 5 also shows that export growth has been consistent during the post-reform period. It is observed that the negative growth rate is registered in primary products as compared to manufacturing exports.

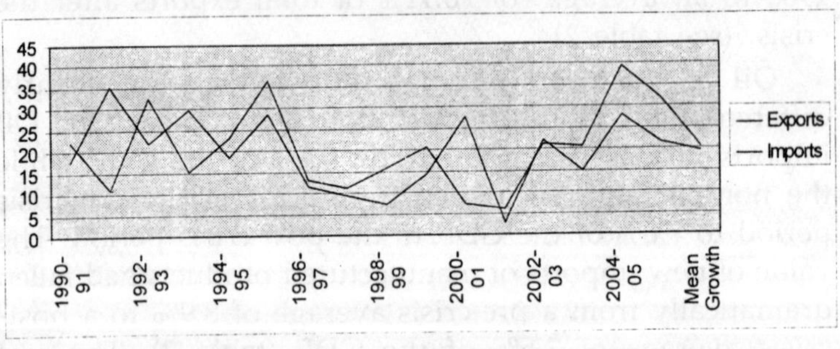

Table 3: Trade Openness and GDP in India 1990-2006

Year	Growth Rate Exports	Growth Rate Import	Growth Rate GDP	As a percentage of GDP Export	As a percentage of GDP Import	Trade Openness	EEX/Im
1990-91	17.7	22.3	5.6	4.7	6.2	10.9	0.75
1991-92	35.3	10.8	1.3	6.3	6.8	13.0	0.92
1992-93	21.9	32.4	5.1	7.3	8.6	15.8	0.84
1993-94	29.9	15.3	5.9	8.9	9.3	18.3	0.95
1994-95	18.5	23.1	7.3	9.8	10.7	20.6	0.92
1995-96	28.6	36.4	7.3	11.8	13.6	25.5	0.87
1996-97	11.7	13.2	7.88	12.2	14.3	26.6	0.85
1997-98	9.5	11.2	4.8	12.8	15.2	27.9	0.84
1998-99	7.4	15.7	6.5	12.9	16.5	29.4	0.78
1999-00	14.2	20.7	6.1	13.8	18.7	32.6	0.74
2000-01	27.6	7.3	4.0	17.1	19.3	36.4	0.88
2001-02	2.7	6.2	6.0	16.5	19.3	35.8	0.85
2002-03	22.1	21.2	4.2	19.5	22.5	46.5	0.87
2003-04	15.0	20.8	8.5	19.9	24.3	44.2	0.82
2004-05	27.9	39.5	7.5	12.2*	17.1*	29.3*	0.71*
2005-06	21.6	31.8	9	13.1	19.5	32.6	0.67
Mean Growth	19.47	20.5	6.6	13.6	15.1	27.8	0.82

Source: Economic Survey, Government of India, various issues. *Economic Survey, Government of India 2006-07

Table 4: Exports of Principal Commodities

Year of Commodities	Primary Products	Manufactured goods	Petroleum Products	Other	Total
1990-91	4324	12996	522	302	18145
1991-92	4132	13148	414	170	17865
1992-93	3873	14038	476	148	18537
1993-94	4915	16656	397	268	22238
1994-95	5214	20404	416	294	26330
1995-96	7256	23747	453	583	31794
1996-97	8035	24613	481	339	33469
1997-98	7687	26546	352	419	35006
1998-99	6927	25791	89	409	33218
1999-00	6524	29714	38	544	36822

2000-01	7126	34335	1869	1229	44560
2001-02	6146	33792	3177	712	43827
2002-03	6962	41070	4275	412	52719
2003-04	7888	49671	5666	618	3843

Source: Economic Survey (Various issues), Govt. of India

Table 5: Percentage Share of Broad Groups of Exports to Total Exports

Year of commodities	*Primary Products*	*Manufactured goods*	*Petroleum Products*	*Others*
1990-91	23.8	71.7	2.9	1.6
1991-92	23.1	73.6	2.3	0.9
1992-93	20.8	75.7	2.5	0.9
1993-94	22.2	74.9	1.8	1.2
1994-95	19.8	77.5	1.6	1.1
1995-96	22.8	74.7	1.4	1.1
1996-97	24.0	73.5	1.4	1.1
1997-98	21.9	75.8	1.0	1.3
1998-99	20.8	77.6	0.3	1.3
1999-00	17.7	80.7	0.1	1.5
2000-01	16.0	77.0	4.2	2.8
2001-02	14.0	77.1	7.2	1.7
2002-03	13.2	77.9	8.1	0.8
2003-04	12.4	77.8	8.9	0.9

Source: Economic Survey (Various issues), Govt. of India.

Import Liberalisation on Export Performance

Our trade share in the total world trade was improved from 0.57 % in 1980 to 0.6% in 1990 and to 0.7% in 2000. This is reflected in the improvement of our ranking in trade performance. Our position was 43 in 1980 which was improved to 33 in 1990 and to 27 in 2000. Our import rank was slightly better and export rank was slightly lower than the trade rank.

Studies conducted by many economists show that due to import liberalisation, import intensity of exports has increased sharply. New trade policy has abandoned inward-looking policy and adopted outward-looking policy. India's volume of exports and imports is shown in terms of unit value index, volume index and terms of trade (see table 6). During 1990-1991 and 1998-1999 India's export to OECD countries rose from 53.5 % to 57.9 %. To the OPEC it came down from 27.5 % to 26 % .During the same period of time India's exports to the US rose from 14.7 % to 21.8 %. But it came down drastically from 17.9 % to 3 % to east Europe. The share has gone up from 8 % to 32.4 % in the developing countries other than the OPEC. The export performance as percentage of GDP has been represented in table 7 below. Table 7 shows that India is on a growth path in terms of our trade performance.

Table 6: Unit Value Index, Volume Index and Terms of Trade

	Unit Value Index		*Volume Index*		*Terms of Trade*		
	Export	*Import*	*Export*	*Import*	*Gross*	*Net*	*Income*
1984-85	169.8	161.7	120.8	156.1	129.2	105.0	126.8
1985-86	170.8	158.8	111.3	182.3	163.8	107.6	119.8
1986-87	179.4	139.4	121.3	212.3	175.0	128.6	156.0
1987-88	195.4	160.0	140.0	204.8	146.3	122.1	170.9
1988-89	232.2	185.5	152.1	224.2	147.4	125.2	190.4
1989-90	276.6	228.4	174.9	227.8	130.2	121.1	211.8
1990-91	292.5	267.7	194.1	237.7	122.5	109.3	212.2
1991-92	369.5	309.1	208.6	228.0	109.3	119.5	249.3
1992-93	421.5	331.0	222.9	282.0	126.5	127.3	283.8
1993-94	474.1	327.2	251.5	329.1	127.8	144.9	373.1
1994-95	494.6	324.6	292.7	408.3	139.5	152.4	446.0
1995-96	484.2	351.0	384.3	514.8	134.0	137.9	530.0
1996-97	504.7	399.8	411.8	511.8	124.3	126.2	519.7
1997-98	589.4	404.2	386.0	562.1	145.6	145.8	562.8
1998-99	611.7	407.8	399.2	644.2	161.4	150.0	598.8
1999-00	604.5	450.5	461.0	704.8	152.9	134.2	618.7
2000-01	624.3	487.5	571.4	697.7	122.6	128.1	732.0

2001-02	618.0	492.9	592.7	732.8	123.6	125.4	743.2
2002-03	619.6	545.6	721.6	802.4	111.2	113.4	819.7
2003-04	672.4	545.1	764.6	907.4	126.9	123.4	943.5
2004-05	732.0	663.0	899.0	1113.0	110.0	124.0	991.0
2005-06	881.0	988.0	1307.0	1095.0	67.0	90.0	662.0

Source: Economic Survey 2006-07, Govt. of India.

Table 7: Export as % of GDP

Year	*% (at current prices)*
1990-1991	5.8
2000-2001	9.9
2001-2002	9.4
2002-2003	10.6
2003-2004	11.0
2004-2005	12.2
2005-2006	13.9

Source: Economic Survey, GDI, 2006-2007.

India's volume of exports during 1990-1991 to 2003-2004 has been shown in table 8.

Table 8: India's Exports During 1990-2003

Year	*Volume of Export (in us $ Million)*	*Export as % of GDP at MP*	*India's share in world trade*	*% change in Export*
1990-1991	18477.00	6.2	0.53	9.2
1991-1992	18266.00	6.7	0.53	1.5
1992-1993	18869.00	9.1	0.52	3.8
1993-1994	22683.00	8.3	0.57	20.0
1994-1995	26855.00	8.1	0.59	18.4
1995-1996	32311.00	8.9	0.60	20.7
1996-1997	31133.00	8.6	0.62	5.3
1997-1998	34849.00	8.3	0.62	1.5
1998-1999	16634.00	-	0.62	29.0
1999-2000	41543.00	-	0.70	-
2002-2003	63028.00	10.6	0.86	-
2003-2004	79846.00	11.0	0.90	-

Source: Economic Survey 2006-07, GDI.

India's share in the world trade, its total volume of exports and imports, trade balance have been represented in tables 9, 10 and 11. Data represented in tables 7, 8, 9, 10 and 11 show that economic reforms has led to increase in India's exports as percent of GDP, its volume of exports and imports and its share in world trade. At the outset of economic reforms it was expected that due to liberalisation exports would increase and this would improve balance of trade. But trade deficit in 1997-1998 rose to US $ 6398 million form US $ 1546 in 1991-1992.

Table 9: Trends in India's Volume of Export 1990-91 to 2003-04

Year	*Volume of Export (in us $ Million)*	*Export as % of GDP at MP*	*India's share in world trade*	*% change in Export*
1990-91	18477.00	6.2	0.53	9.2
1991-92	18266.00	6.7	0.53	1.5
1992-93	18869.00	9.1	0.52	3.8
1993-94	22683.00	8.3	0.57	20.0
1994-95	26855.00	8.1	0.59	18.4
1995-96	32311.00	8.9	0.60	20.7
1996-97	34133.00	8.6	0.62	5.3
1997-98	34849.00	8.3	0.62	1.5
1998-99	16634.00	-	0.62	2.9
1999-00	41543.00	-	0.70	-
2002-03	63028.00	10.6	0.86	-
2003-04	79846.00	11.0	0.90	-

Source: Economic Survey 2006-07, Govt. of India.

Table 10: India's Share in the World Trade

	1993	*1994*	*1995*	*1996*	*1997*	*2000*
India	0.57	0.59	0.6	0.62	0.61	0.7
China	3.63	3.37	3.41	3.42	3.45	3.9
Malaysia	1.26	1.38	1.46	1.48	NA	1.5
Indonesia	0.98	0.94	0.9	0.94	NA	1.0
Singapore	1.98	2.28	2.32	2.37	2.29	2.2
Thailand	0.98	1.06	1.11	1.05	NA	1.1
U.S.A.	12.46	12.08	11.5	11.84	12.62	13.0
Developing Countries	30.73	31.48	31.91	32.68	33.45	37.1

	2001	*2002*	*2003*	*2004*	*2005*	*2006*
India	0.7	36.8	0.8	0.8	1.0	1.0
China	4.3	5.1	5.9	6.6	7.4	7.8
Malaysia	1.4	1.5	1.3	1.4	1.4	1.4
Indonesia	0.9	0.9	0.8	0.8	0.8	0.9
Singapore	2.0	2.0	2.0	2.0	8.8	2.3
Thailand	1.1	1.1	1.1	1.1	1.1	1.1
U.S.A.	NA	13.4	11.6	10.7	10.6	10.3
Developing Countries	0.8	37.8	38.8	40.7	43.8	44.8

Source: Computed from International financial statistics, May 1998, p-60 and Economic Survey, Government of India 2006-07.

Table 11: Imports and Exports

(in US $ Million)

Year	*Import*	*Export*
1996-97	39132	33470
1997-98	41484	35006
1998-99	42389	33218
1999-00	496.71	36822
2000-01	50536	44566
2001-02	51413	43827
2002-03	61412	52719
2003-04	78150	63843
2004-05	111518	83536
2005-06	149166	103091

Source: Economic Survey, Government of India 2006-07.

This was due to *(i)* adoption of advanced technology in the production of export goods, *(ii)* rise in FDI inflow, *(iii)* reduction in import duties, and *(iv)* relaxation of regulations on the importation of capital goods. Upto 1996-1997 there was a spectacular growth in the volume of exports, but it remained stagnant afterwards. Since 1998 share of agriculture and allied products in total exports declined sharply but at the same time the share of gems and jewellery increased. Exports of machinery, transport and metal manufactured also increased. The exports of software was phenomenal during 1992-1993 and 1996-1997 (from US $ 22.5 million to US $ 1085 million). The growth of imports was larger during 1990-2005 (see table 11) than exports. A serious hindrance is that majority of our exports is accounted for by small-scale sector. This sector faced in accessing working capital and export finances. On the other hand the contribution of organised sector was not significant. Even the top companies share of India's exports was 5 % though their imports intensity was high. So for a majority of these domestic market occupies the top priority and this market is vast and thus profitable. When the home demand is met, the producers look upon exports as a residual activity. The commodity basket is also narrow. During the last few years, India has registered high growth in the export of services such as software services, business services, financial services and communication services. We have bright future in the world trade of fish, livestock and poultry product which have maximum possible employment creating capacity.

Conclusion

The well-being of a nation much depends on its involvement in international trade and commerce which in effect determines the well-being of its population. Since our adoption of new trade policy in 1991 our industries have become more competitive in the global market and we have moved forward with traditional macroeconomic tools to handle balance of payments, deficits and inflation. To improve our trade cover in terms of expansion of both exports and imports the licensing system has been dismantled. Due to this, remarkable achievements have taken place in boosting up the growth of information technology and its exports have covered a wide range in agricultural and industrial sector as also engineering goods, ores and minerals, chemicals and related products gems and jewellery and petroleum products. Out imports also have increased due to lifting of QRs especially since 2001. This is a sign of overall growth of trade and also the growth of the economy benefiting both the consumer and producer.

REFERENCE

Agarwala, R. (2003), "Towards a Multipolar World of International Finance", *Indian Economic Journal,* Vol 51, No. 2 July – Sept.

Baldev, Raj (2001), "Opening up and Openness of Indian Economy," *Economic and Political weekly,* 3529-3537, Sept.15. Prof,

Baldev, Raj (2001), *Globalisation and Nationalisation,* Sage Publications, New Delhi.

Basam, A. L. (1997), *The World that was India,* Rupa and Co., Calcutta PP 226-231.

Bhagwati, J. N. and T.N. Srinivasan (1975), *Foreign Trade Regimes and Economic Development: India,* National Bureau of Economic Research, New York, Columbia University Press.

Bokare, M. G. (1993), *Hindu Economics* (External Economic Order) Janaki Prakasan, New Delhi.

Brahmananda, P.R. (1997), "Factor Mobility, Globalisation, multi - National Corporations, Convergence and the Consequent Revolution in Internation Trade Theory": *The Indian Economic Journal;* Vol. 44, No. 3.

Dholakia, R.H. and Deepak Kapur (2001), "Economic Reforms and Trade Performance, Private Corporate Sector in India", *Economic and Political Weekly,* December 8.

Dholakia, Ravindra (1994), "Special Dimensions of the Acceleration of Economic Growth in India", *Economic and Political Weekly,* Vol. 29, No. 35, pp. 2303-2309.

Diwan, Romesh (1996), "Economic Reforms-Alternative Policy Package," *The Statesman,* Feb 21.

Dutta, Bhabatosh, *Indian Planning at the Cross-road.*

Government of India, *Economic Survey* (Various Issues).

Government of India (1999), Export-Import Policy Statement, July.

Jalan, Bimal (2001-02), "India and the Challenge of Globalisation" *The Indian Economic Journal,* Vol. 49, No. 3, 9-12.

Jaffrelot, C. (2001-2002), "Is India Globalisable", *Indian Horizon,* Vol. 48, Oct-2001-March 2002, 134-140

Jayashankar, Mitu (2004), "India Today, The World Tomorrow", *Business World,* Vol. 23.

Jha, L.K. (1987), "Indian Economy in Eighties and Nineties" *Mainstream* (Republic Day), 26.

Kalamkar, Shrikants (2003), "Liberalisation and India's Horticulture Export," *Economic Affairs*, Vol. 48, No 4,199-210, Dec.

Kapoor, R.S. (2005), "Integrating with Global Economy," *Yojana* 43-46, May

Karnar, N.G. (2005), "Paradigm Change", *The Hindu Survey of Indian Industry*, 197-201.

Kapila, Uma (2001), *Understanding the Problems of Indian Economy*, Academic Foundation (New Delhi).

Kent, George (2004), "What is Free Trade? Where is Free Trade?", *UN Chronicle*, No. 3, 34

Khartik, S.K. (2003), "Globalisation and Post Reforms Scenario at Global Economy: Some Issues", *The Indian Journal of Commerce*, Vol. 56, No.4 77-82, Oct-Dec.

Khusro, A.M. (1992), "Myths and Misconceptions," *Financial Express* March 12.

Lekhi, R.K., *The Economics of Development and Planning*, Kalyani Publishers.

Mehta, Rajesh (2000), "Removal of QRs and Impact on India's Import," *Economic and Political Weekly*, 1667-1671, May 6.

Memorandum of Economic Policy from 1991-92 to 1992-93, submitted by Finance Minister to I.M.F, August 27, 1991.

Michael, Kideran, *Foreign Investment in India*.

Moore, Mike (2003), *A World without Walls, Freedom, Development, Free Trade and Global Governance*.

Nanda, Nitya (2003), "WTO and Trade Facilitation Some Implications", *Economic and Political Weekly*, 2622-2625.

Narula, M. (2003), "Looking ahead", *Business India*, 47-48, May 26-June 8,

Nayyar, Deepak (1996), "Globalisation: The Past and the Present". *Indian Economic Journal*, Vol-43 Jan-Mar.

Panchamukhi, V. R. (2000), *Indian Classical Thoughts on Economic Development and Management*, Bookwell Publications, New Delhi.

Planning Commission (2000), "India's 1990-91 Crisis: Myths Reform and Paradoxes," Working Paper No. 4.

Raj, K.N. (1985), "New Economic Policy Engine to Growth", *Economic Times*, December 21.

Rajput, Jyotsna (2001), "Globalisation and Emerging Trends in Industrial Development", *Yojana,* March.

Rao, C.N. (1989). "Trade Related Aspects of Intellectual Property Rights", *Economic and Political Weekly,* 1053-1057, May 13.

Ravindra (2004), "WTO and Tariff Preferences", *Economic and Political Weekly,* May.

Rostow, W.W., *The World Economy, History and Prospect.*

Sen, R.K. (2003-04), "Globalisation and Indian Economic Thinking in the Past and their Relevance in the Present and Future", *The Indian Economic Journal,* Vol. 51, No. 2, 2003-04.

Sen, R.K. and Ratan Lal Basu (2004), *Economics in Arthashastra* (Forthcoming), Deep and Deep Publications, New Delhi.

Shandilya, T. K. (2003), "Globalisation, Challenges Ahead and Implications for India", *Economic Affairs,* Vol. 48, Qr. 4, December.

Singh, P.N. (1995), "Globalisationing Indian Economy : The Environment", an article publishing in *India's Economic Reform and Beyond,* edited by R.K. Sinha, Anamika Publishers, Delhi, 1995, p. 31.

Singh, T. (2001), "Balance of Trade, Exchange Rate and Trade Policy Regimes in India: Some Issues and Policy Perspective", *The Indian Economic Journal,* Vol. 48, No. 1.

Tasswing, F.W., *Free Trade Tariff and Reciprocity.*

Virmani, A. (2003), "India's External Reforms; Modest Globalisation, Significant Gains", *Economic and Political Weekly,* August 9.

Virmani, A. (1991), "Trade Policy Reform: De-licensing, Tariff Reform and Exchange Rates": Development Policy Research Planning Commission, New Delhi, September.

Vyas, V.S. (2002), "Globalisation: Hopes, Realities and Coping Strategy", *Economic and Political Weekly,* March 23.

World Bank (2000), *Finance for Growth,* Oxford University Press.

8

Structural Changes in the Causal Relationship Between Money and Price Level in the Economy of Nepal—A Recursive Estimation Study

CHANDAN KUMAR MUKHOPADHYAY* & SHYAM CHARAN BARMA•

ABSTRACT

The paper examines the stability of the causal relationship between consumer price level and money (M_1 and M_2) supplies over the period 1987:1-2005:1. Structural changes in such relationships have been identified through Recursive Residual Tests. Causal relationships between consumer price level and money (M_1 and M_2) supplies have been found to vary in two different sub-periods. Moreover, such observed causal relationships are different from those obtained from the historical dataset.

* Professor, Department of Economics, University of North Bengal.

• Rajiv Gandhi Scholar (Doctoral), Department of Economics, University of North Bengal.

Key Words: Stationarity, Co-integration, Granger Causality, Recursive Residuals

I

Introduction

Robert E. Lucas (1976) analyzes the uses and abuses of existing econometric works for policy evaluation. He argues that, without a reliance on rules and models that can handle them, it is virtually impossible to do any sophisticated policy analysis. Lucas arrives at this dramatic conclusion by examining the nature of the equations used in typical econometric models. Current practice, he argues, is to estimate an econometric relationship and then use this relationship in formulating economic policy prescriptions. An implicit assumption in this type of exercise is that the econometric relationship will remain stable under different scenarios. Lucas argues that dynamic economic theories hold that this assumption is false. Consequently, we would expect the behavioral equations in the model to change as the scenarios change.

The substance of this analysis is that the relationship among macro-economic variables estimated by using the historical dataset may not represent the dynamic nature of the relationship. The relationship among the variables undergo changes following structural changes in the economy. The data used for econometric analysis embody the outcome of structural changes and, therefore, the consequent changes in the macroeconomic relationship. In the event of the presence of structural changes, the estimated econometric relationship among macro-economics variables fail to represent the true economic relationship.

It, therefore, becomes pertinent for any researcher to identify structural charges in the historical dataset. In that case, some definite sub-periods will be identified in which econometric relationship among macroeconomic variables remain stable over the period concerned.

Objective of the Study

This paper is devoted to examining the existence of any causal relationship between consumer price level and money supply in the economy of Nepal. Besides, we seek to examine the nature and direction of causality.

The study further examines if such causal relationship underwent significant changes over the period concerned. More specifically, we have sought to identify structural changes in the causal relationship between money supply and price level in Nepal.

Organization of the Paper

The section II deals with the methodological issues. The section III is being devoted to the study of 'Stationarity' of the macroeconomic variables concerned while the section IV presents the 'Co-integration Analysis'. Section V deals with Granger Causality between variables concerned. Section VI presents the study on 'Structural Changes' in the observed Granger Causality in different sub-periods. Section VII presents the summary and conclusion.

II

METHODOLOGY ISSUES

Relevance of Granger Causality

The study of co-integration relates to examining if the variables are related or not. The co-integration procedure stresses upon estimating distributed lag relationship along with the error correction structure. However, the auto-regressive structure does not play any significant role in the study of co-integration between variables concerned.

This particular feature of the co-integration equations accounts for the inability of the equation to explain if the variables concerned are 'exogenous' or 'endogenous'.

Engel, Hendry and Richard (1983) define a set of a variable X_t in a parameterized model to be 'weakly exogenous' if the full model can be written in terms of a marginal probability distribution of X_t and a conditional distribution of Y_t/X_t such that estimation of the parameters of the conditional distribution is no less efficient than estimation of the full set of parameters of the joint distribution. With reference to time series applications, variable X_t is said to be predetermined in the model if X_t is independent of all subsequent structural disturbances ε_{t-s} for s>0. Variables that are predetermined in the model can be treated, at least asymptotically, as if they were exogenous in the sense that consistent estimates can be obtained when they appear as regressors.

Causality

Study of co-integration indicates a long run equilibrium relationship between the variables concerned. However, co-integration results do not indicate the direction of causation. Co-integration tests simply rule out the possibility of 'no causation' between variables and imply that there should be at least one way of causation between the variables concerned. Further tests like Granger Causality Test and /or Sim Test are needed to establish the direction of causation.

Granger Causality: The Methodology

Let us consider a jointly covariance stationary stochastic process y_t, x_t with $E(x_t) = E(y_t) = 0$ and with a covariance generating function gx(z), gy(z) and gxy(z). It is assumed that x possesses an autoregressive representation and that both y and x are linearly indeterministic. Then the projection of xt on past values of x and past values of z is given by

$$X_t = \sum_{j=1}^{\infty} h_j \, x_{t-j} + \sum_{j=1}^{\infty} v_{t-j} \, y_{t-j} + u_t \quad (2.1)$$

where the least square residual u_t obeys the orthogonality condition

$$E(u_t\ x_{t-\beta}) = E(u_t\ y_{t-\beta}) = 0 \text{ for } \beta = 1, 2, \ldots\ldots\ldots\ldots$$

Solving (2.1) for u_t permits the orthogonality condition to assume the form of normal equations

$$E\{(xt - \textstyle\sum_{j=1}^{\infty} h_j\ x_{t-j} - \sum_{j=1}^{\infty} v_j\ y_{t-j})\ x\ t\text{-}\beta\} = 0, \quad (2.2)$$
$$\beta = 1,2, \ldots\ldots\ldots\ldots$$

$$E\{(xt - \textstyle\sum_{j=1}^{\infty} h_j\ x_{t-j} - \sum_{j=1}^{\infty} v_j\ y_{t-j})\ y\ t\text{-}\beta\} = 0, \quad (2.3)$$
$$\beta = 1,2, \ldots\ldots\ldots\ldots$$

These equations can be written as

$$Cx(\beta) = \textstyle\sum_{j=1}^{\infty} h_j\ c_x\ (\beta-j) + \sum_{j=1}^{\infty} v_j\ c_{yx}\ (\beta-j) \quad (2.4)$$

$$Cx(\beta) = \textstyle\sum_{j=1}^{\infty} h_j\ c_{xy}\ (\beta - j) + \sum_{j=1}^{\infty} v_j\ c_y\ (\beta-j) \quad (2.5)$$

These equations hold only for positive integer

$$\beta = 1,2,\ldots\ldots\ldots\ldots$$

Multiplying both sides of equations (2.4) and (2.5) by z^{β} and summing over all β, we get the following equations in terms of z transformation

$$g_x\ (z) + m(z) = h(z)\ g_x(z) + v(z)\ g_{yx}\ (z) \quad (2.6)$$

$$g_{xy}\ (z) + n(z) = h(z)g_{xy}(z)+v(z)\ g_y(z) \quad (2.7)$$

where m(z) and n(z) are each unknown series in non-positive power of z only. That m(z) and n(z) series are non-positive powers of z is equivalent with equations (2.4) and (2.5) holding only for $\beta > 1$. Equations (2.6) and

(2.7) are the normal equations for h(z) and v(z).

Following Weiner, Granger (1969) has proposed that "y causes x" whenever $v(z) \neq 0$. That is, y is said to cause x if, given all past values of x, past values of y help predict x. The conditions under which v(z) does or does not equal to zero turn out to be of substantial interest to econometrician and macro-economists.

Let us consider the projection of y_t on the entire x process

$$y_t = \sum_{j=1}^{\infty} b_j \; x_{t-j} + e_t \tag{2.8}$$

where $E(\varepsilon t \; x_{t-j}) = 0$ for all j

Let x_t have the 'Wold Moving Average' presentation such that

$$X_t = d(L)\,\eta_t$$

$$\eta_t = xt - P[\,x_t / x_{t-1}, x_{t-2}, \ldots\ldots\ldots\ldots\ldots\ldots]$$

$$\sum_{j=1}^{\infty} d^2_j < \infty$$

$$\text{Then } g_x(z) = \sigma^2_n d(z) d(z^{-1}) \tag{2.9}$$

It is assumed that x possesses an autoregressive representation so that $[d(z_{-1})]$ is one sided square summable in non-negative power of z. It is always possible to uniquely factor the cross covariance generating function as

$$g_{yx}(z) = \alpha(z)\,\varphi\,(z^{-1}) \tag{2.10}$$

where $\alpha(z)$ and $\varphi(z)$ are one sided in non-negative power of z.

Substituting (2.9) and (2.10) into the usual relation

$$b(z) = g_{yx}(z) / g_x(z) \tag{2.11}$$

we have

$$b(z) = \alpha(z)\ \varphi(z^{-1}) / \sigma^2\eta d(z)\ d(Z^{-1}) \tag{2.12}$$

Evidently, b(z) is one sided in non-negative powers of z if and only if $\varphi(z^{-1}) = kd(z^{-1})$, where k is a constant. Under this condition equation (2.11) becomes

$$b(z) = k\ \alpha(z) / \sigma^2\eta d(z) \tag{2.13}$$

Here $\alpha(z)$ has an inverse that is one sided in non-negative power of z.

Now, if b(z) is one sided in non-negative power of z, the equations (2.6) and (2.7) are both satisfied with v(z) = 0 and

$$h(z) = z\ [d(z) / z] + d(z^{-1}) \tag{2.14}$$

Consequently, equation (2.7) becomes

$$\Phi(z)\ \alpha(z^{-1})\ n(z) = z\ [d(z)/z] + 1/d(z)\ \alpha(z^{-1})\varphi(z) \tag{2.15}$$

Dividing both sides of equation (2.15) by $z\alpha(z^{-1})$ gives

$$\Phi(z)/z + n(z)/z\alpha(z^{-1}) = [d(z)/z] + \varphi(z)/d(z) \tag{2.16}$$

where $n(z)/z\alpha(z^{-1})$ involves only negative powers of z. Since the right hand side involves only non-negative power of z, equation (2.16) implies

$$d(z)[\varphi(z)/z] = [d(z)/z] + \varphi(z) \tag{2.17}$$

This equation (2.17) can be satisfied if $\varphi(z) = kd(z)$ where k is a constant.

Now let (x_t, y_t) be a jointly covariance stationary, strictly indeterministic process with zero mean. Then $\{y_t\}$ fails to Granger cause $\{x_t\}$ if and only if there exists a vector moving average representation

$$\begin{bmatrix} x_t \\ y_t \end{bmatrix} = \begin{bmatrix} c(L)_{11} & 0 \\ c(L)_{21} & c(L)_{22} \end{bmatrix} \begin{bmatrix} \varepsilon_t \\ u_t \end{bmatrix} \tag{2.18}$$

where ε_t and u_t are serially uncorrelated processes with means zero and $E(\varepsilon_t\, u_s) = 0$ for all t and s, and where the one-step-ahead prediction errors $[x_t - p(x_t/x_{t-1}, \ldots\ldots, y_{t-1}, \ldots\ldots)]$ and $[y_t - p(y_t/y_{t-1}, \ldots\ldots, y_{t-1}, \ldots\ldots)]$ are each linear combination of ε_t and u_t.

Under these situations Sims (1972) explains the concept of causality through the following theorem:

"Y_t can be expressed as a distributed lag of current and past x's (with no further x's) with a disturbances process that is orthogonal to past, present and future x's if and only if y does not Granger cause x".

Consequently, the test involves estimating the following regressions:

$$y_t = \sum_{i=1}^{n} \alpha_i X_{t-j} + \sum_{j=1}^{n} \beta_j y_{t-j} + u_{1t} \tag{2.19}$$

$$x_t = \sum_{i=1}^{m} \lambda_i y_{t-j} + \sum_{j=1}^{n} \delta_j X_{t-j} + u_{2t} \tag{2.20}$$

where it is assumed that the disturbances u_{1t} and u_{2t} are uncorrelated.

Equation (2.19) postulates that current y_t is related to past values of y_t itself as well as of xt and equation (2.20) postulates a similar behavior for x_t. Four cases then can be distinguished.

Unidirectional Causality from x to y

It is indicated if the estimated coefficients on the lagged x in equation (2.19) are statistically different from zero as a group (i.e., $\Sigma\alpha_i \neq 0$) and the set of estimated coefficients on the lagged y in (2.20) is not statistically different from zero (i.e., $\Sigma\delta_j \neq 0$).

Unidirectional causality from y to x

It exists if the set of lagged x coefficients in equation (2.19) is not statistically different from zero (i.e., $\Sigma\alpha_i \neq 0$) and the set of the lagged y coefficient in equation (2.20) is statistically different from zero (i.e., $\Sigma\delta_j = 0$).

Feedback or Bilateral Causal

It is suggested when the sets of x and y coefficient are statistically significantly different from zero in both regressions.

Independence

It is suggested when the sets of x and y coefficients are not statistically significant in both the regressions.

Basic Granger Causality Test

The model for Conventional Granger causality test in our study is based on the following equations:

$$P_t = \sum_{j=1}^{m} a_j M_{t-j} + \sum_{j=1}^{m} b_j P_{t-j} + \varepsilon_t \qquad (2.21)$$

$$M_t = \sum_{j=1}^{m} a_j P_{t-j} + \sum_{j=1}^{m} b_j M_{t-j} + \eta t \qquad (2.22)$$

where M_t and P_t represents first difference of Money Supply and Price (Wholesale/Consumer) series respectively.

Structural Shift in Causal Relation

Sometimes researcher seeks to investigate the stability of the co-efficient estimates as the sample size increases. Researcher may also want to find out if the estimate will be different in enlarged samples and whether these will remain stable over time. Working with a sample, a researcher may produce a regression which is too closely tailored to his sample by experimenting with too may formulations of the model. In this case, it becomes important to know if the estimated function will perform equally well outside the sample of data which has been used for the estimation of coefficients. Furthermore, there may have occurred events which change the structure of the relationship like changes in taxation law, introduction of birth control measures and so on. If such structural changes occur, the co-efficient may not be stable. These may be sensitive to the changes in the sample compositions.

Testing for structural stability calls for the use of additional observations besides the sample that are used to estimate a given model. Procedures for testing structural stability are given by Rao (1960) and Chow (1952).

The econometric method which involves "Window Finding" uses Chow test to identify the sub-periods. Here equality between two regressions co-efficients concerning the relationship over two different periods is tested. This is done by F-test.

Window Finding of Structural Changes – The Methodology

Let us consider two samples with n1 and n2 observations respectively and the general model for data set is –

$$Y = X\beta + u \tag{2.23}$$

where
$$Y \longrightarrow n \times 1$$
$$X \longrightarrow n \times k$$
$$\beta \longrightarrow k \times 1$$
$$n \longrightarrow n_1 + n_2$$

Let us rewrite the model for these two individual samples such as

$$Y_1 = \begin{pmatrix} Z_1 & W_1 \end{pmatrix} \begin{pmatrix} \gamma_1 \\ \delta_1 \end{pmatrix} + u_1 \tag{2.24}$$

$$Y_2 = \begin{pmatrix} Z_2 & W_2 \end{pmatrix} \begin{pmatrix} \gamma_2 \\ \delta_2 \end{pmatrix} + u_2 \tag{2.25}$$

where $Y_1 \longrightarrow n_1 \times 1$
$Y_2 \longrightarrow n_2 \times 1$
$Z_1 \longrightarrow n_1 \times 1$
$Z_2 \longrightarrow n_2 \times 1$
$W_1 \longrightarrow n_1 \times m$
$W_2 \longrightarrow n_2 \times m$
$\gamma_1 \longrightarrow 1 \times 1$
$\gamma_1 \longrightarrow 1 \times 1$
$\delta_1 \longrightarrow m \times 1$
$\delta_2 \longrightarrow m \times 1$

By combining equations (2.24) and (2.25) we have

$$\begin{pmatrix} y_1 \\ y_2 \end{pmatrix} = \begin{pmatrix} z_1 & 0 & w_1 & 0 \\ 0 & z_2 & 0 & w_2 \end{pmatrix} \begin{pmatrix} \gamma_1 \\ \gamma_2 \\ \delta_1 \\ \delta_2 \end{pmatrix} + \begin{pmatrix} u_1 \\ u_2 \end{pmatrix} \tag{2.26}$$

and the null hypothesis of interest is

$H_0 : \gamma_1 = \gamma_2$ (= β say)

Under the null hypothesis, the model is

$$\begin{pmatrix} y_1 \\ y_2 \end{pmatrix} = \begin{pmatrix} z_1 & w_1 & 0 \\ z_2 & 0 & w_2 \end{pmatrix} \begin{pmatrix} \beta \\ \delta_1 \\ \delta_2 \end{pmatrix} + \begin{pmatrix} u_1 \\ u_2 \end{pmatrix} \tag{2.27}$$

The L.S estimate of the efficient vector in equation (2.27) is

$$\begin{bmatrix} \beta \\ \delta_1 \\ \delta_2 \end{bmatrix} = [\begin{pmatrix} z_1 & w_1 & 0 \\ z_2 & 0 & w_2 \end{pmatrix}' \begin{pmatrix} z_1 & w_1 & 0 \\ z_2 & 0 & w_2 \end{pmatrix}]^{-1} [\begin{pmatrix} z_1 & w_1 & 0 \\ z_2 & 0 & w_2 \end{pmatrix}'] \begin{pmatrix} u_1 \\ u_2 \end{pmatrix} \tag{2.28}$$

If we fit equations (2.24) and (2.25) individually, their LS estimates of the coefficients will be

$$\begin{pmatrix} c_1 \\ d_2 \end{pmatrix} = [(z_1 \; w_1)' (z_1 \; w_1)]^{-1} (z_1 \; w_1)' \, y_1 \tag{2.29}$$

$$\begin{pmatrix} c_1 \\ d_2 \end{pmatrix} = [(z_1 \; w_1)' (z_1 \; w_1)]^{-1} (z_1 \; w_1)' \, y_1 \tag{2.30}$$

where ci is the estimate of γ_i. The sum of squares

necessary for computing test statistics can then be obtained by using the results in equations (2.28), (2.29) and (2.30). The sum of squares measures the distance of individual observations from the common regression plane is

$$Q_1 = \left[\begin{pmatrix} y_1 \\ y_2 \end{pmatrix} - \begin{pmatrix} z_1 & w_1 & 0 \\ z_2 & 0 & w_2 \end{pmatrix}\begin{pmatrix} b \\ \delta_1 \\ \delta_2 \end{pmatrix}\right]' \left[\begin{pmatrix} y_1 \\ y_2 \end{pmatrix} - \begin{pmatrix} z_1 & w_1 & 0 \\ z_2 & 0 & w_2 \end{pmatrix}\begin{pmatrix} b \\ \delta_1 \\ \delta_2 \end{pmatrix}\right] \quad (2.31)$$

Here Q_1 / δ2 has χ^2 distribution with (n-2m-1) degrees of freedom where we assume that u_1 and u_2 have a common variance δ_2. Now Q_1 can be decomposed into two sum squares Q_2 and Q_3. Q_2 will measure the distances of observations from the individual estimated regression planes, and Q_3 measures the distance of the individual estimated plane from the common regression plane. Thus,

$$Q_2 = \left[y_1 - (z_1 \;\; w_1)\begin{pmatrix} c_1 \\ \delta_1 \end{pmatrix}\right]' y_1 - (z_1 \;\; w_1)\begin{bmatrix} c_1 \\ \delta_1 \end{bmatrix}$$

$$+\left[y_2 - (z_2 \;\; w_2)\begin{pmatrix} c_2 \\ \delta_2 \end{pmatrix}\right]' y_2 - (z_2 \;\; w_2)\begin{bmatrix} c_2 \\ \delta_2 \end{bmatrix} \quad (2.32)$$

and $Q_3 = Q_1 - Q_2$. Here Q_2/δ_2 has a χ^2 distribution with (n-2m -1) degrees of freedom.

Again,

$$Q_3 = \left[(z_1 \;\; w_1)\begin{pmatrix} c_1 \\ \delta_1 \end{pmatrix} - (z_1 \;\; w_1)\right]' \left[(z_1 \;\; w_1)\begin{pmatrix} c_1 \\ \delta_1 \end{pmatrix} - (z_1 \;\; w_1)\begin{pmatrix} b \\ \delta_1 \end{pmatrix}\right.$$

$$+ \left[(z_2 \;\; w_2)\begin{pmatrix} c_2 \\ d_2 \end{pmatrix} - (z_2 \;\; w_2)\begin{bmatrix} b \\ d_2 \end{bmatrix}\right]' \left[(z_2 \;\; w_2)\begin{pmatrix} c_2 \\ d_2 \end{pmatrix} - (z_2 \;\; w_2)\begin{bmatrix} b \\ d_2 \end{bmatrix}\right]$$

It may be noted that c_1 is the estimate of γ_1 obtained from the first regression and that δ_2 is the estimate of δ_2 , obtained from pooled regression plane. So the ratio is

$$F = \frac{\frac{Q_3}{1}}{\frac{Q_2}{(n-2m-2l)}} \quad (2.33)$$

So, we have an F-distribution with (l, n-2m-2l) degress

of freedom. Here Q_3 is the restricted sum of squares and that Q_2 is the unrestricted sum of squares.

If, however, the new observations n2 are fewer than the number of parameters in the function we may proceed as follows. First, from the augmented sample we obtain the regression equation.

$$\hat{Y} = \beta_0 + \beta_1 + \dots\dots\dots\dots\dots\dots \beta_k X_k \quad (2.34)$$

From which we calculate the residual sum of squares

$$\Sigma e^2 = \Sigma y^2 - \Sigma y^2 \quad (2.35)$$

with $(n_1 + n_2 - k)$ degrees of freedom. Second from the original sample of size n_1 we have

$$Y_1 = \hat{\beta}_0 + \beta_1 + \beta_k X_k \quad (2.36)$$

from which the unexplained sum of squares is

$$\Sigma e_1^2 = \Sigma y_1^2 - \Sigma y_1^2 \quad (2.37)$$

with n_1 - k degrees of freedom.

Third, subtracting the two sums of residuals we find

$$\Sigma e^2 = \Sigma e_1^2 \quad (2.38)$$

with $(n_1+n_2-k) - (n - k) = n_2$ degrees of freedom, where n_2 are the additional observations.

Further, we form F* ratio where

$$F^* = \frac{\Sigma e^2 - \Sigma e_{12} / n_2}{\Sigma e_{12} / (n_1 - k)} \quad (2.39)$$

The null hypotheses are

H_0: b_i = β_i (i =0,1,2...........................,k)

H_0: b_i $\neq$ β_i

The F* ratio is compared with the theoretical value of F obtained from the F- table with $v_i = n_2$ and v_2 = (n – k) degrees of freedom.

If F* ratio exceeds the table value of F, we reject the null hypothesis i.e, we accept that the structural coefficients are unstable. This indicates that their values are changing in extended sample period.

III

STATIONARITY

The Data

The Consumer price index is used for the study and the base period is 2000. Two measures of money supply are available for Nepal. One is narrow money (M_1) which includes currency held by non-bank public and demand deposits held by commercial bank. M_2 consists of M_1 and time deposits held by commercial banks. Both types of money supply have been used in the present study in order to investigate into their effects on price level. The data have been collected from different issues of International Financial Statistics (IFS). Again quarterly data have been used in the study. The data range from first quarter of 1987 through the first quarter of 2005.

Correlogram Analysis for Stationarity

The stationarity of the variables has been examined through the study of their Auto-Correlation Functions (ACFs) and Partial Auto-correlation Functions (PACFs).

Figure 1-3 present the ACFs and PACFs of the consumer price, M_1 and M_2 money supplies respectively.

It is observed from the Figures 1-3 that

i. ACF of each variable contains a dying out pattern of spikes and,

ii. PACF of each variable is marked by the presence of a singular significant (at 1% level) spike at lag one while spikes at all other lags are highly insignificant (even at 10% level)

All these observations indicate non-stationarity of the Con-price, M_1 and M_2 series at levels.

The series for M_1, M_2 and Consumer price level are non-stationary and, therefore, these contain unit roots.

The ACFs and PACFs of the first differenced series of the variables concerned are being presented through the figures 4-6 which show that

i. the ACF of each variable is free from any dying out pattern of spikes

ii. the PACF of such variable does not contain any singular significant spike at lag 1. All these observations testify stationarity for the series concerned upon first differencing.

Figure 1

Correlogram of Log Con-Price

ncluded observations: 73 Sample: 1987:1 2005:1

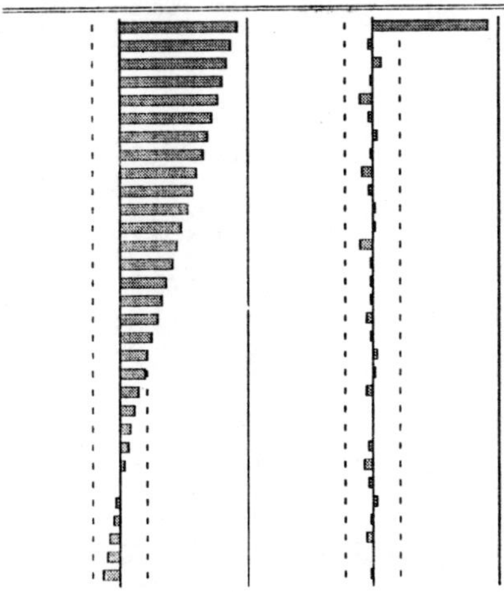

	AC	PAC	Q-Stat	Prob
1	0.956	0.956	69.556	0.000
2	0.912	-0.027	133.75	0.000
3	0.876	0.070	193.81	0.000
4	0.841	-0.014	249.90	0.000
5	0.798	-0.102	301.11	0.000
6	0.753	-0.031	347.51	0.000
7	0.715	0.025	389.91	0.000
8	0.678	-0.013	428.57	0.000
9	0.634	-0.082	462.93	0.000
10	0.589	-0.028	493.12	0.000
11	0.551	0.021	519.91	0.000
12	0.515	0.009	543.76	0.000
13	0.471	-0.106	564.04	0.000
14	0.428	-0.017	581.01	0.000
15	0.388	-0.011	595.20	0.000
16	0.349	-0.022	606.91	0.000
17	0.306	-0.057	616.07	0.000
18	0.263	-0.019	622.97	0.000
19	0.228	0.034	628.26	0.000
20	0.197	0.008	632.26	0.000
21	0.161	-0.053	634.98	0.000
22	0.126	-0.007	636.68	0.000
23	0.096	0.006	637.69	0.000
24	0.067	-0.036	638.19	0.000
25	0.032	-0.062	638.31	0.000
26	-0.003	-0.037	638.32	0.000
27	-0.030	0.034	638.42	0.000
28	-0.055	-0.009	638.78	0.000
29	-0.084	-0.056	639.67	0.000
30	-0.112	0.006	641.27	0.000
31	-0.135	-0.013	643.65	0.000

Figure 2

Correlogram of Log M_1

Included observations: 73 Sample: 1987:1 2005:1

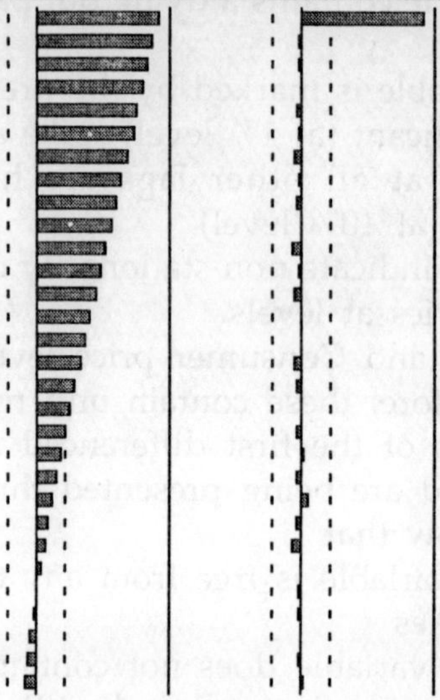

Autocorrelation	Partial Correlation		AC	PAC	Q-Stat	Prob
		1	0.957	0.957	69.715	0.000
		2	0.916	-0.009	134.42	0.000
		3	0.875	-0.018	194.29	0.000
		4	0.835	-0.003	249.65	0.000
		5	0.795	-0.030	300.51	0.000
		6	0.755	-0.014	347.11	0.000
		7	0.713	-0.056	389.24	0.000
		8	0.671	-0.011	427.20	0.000
		9	0.629	-0.035	461.06	0.000
		10	0.589	0.001	491.24	0.000
		11	0.547	-0.059	517.61	0.000
		12	0.505	-0.016	540.49	0.000
		13	0.462	-0.046	559.92	0.000
		14	0.421	0.001	576.37	0.000
		15	0.383	0.003	590.20	0.000
		16	0.343	-0.049	601.51	0.000
		17	0.302	-0.038	610.45	0.000
		18	0.264	0.000	617.40	0.000
		19	0.226	-0.033	622.58	0.000
		20	0.191	0.009	626.36	0.000
		21	0.156	-0.030	628.93	0.000
		22	0.127	0.045	630.67	0.000
		23	0.098	-0.034	631.72	0.000
		24	0.066	-0.057	632.20	0.000
		25	0.036	0.004	632.35	0.000
		26	0.008	-0.021	632.36	0.000
		27	-0.020	-0.021	632.40	0.000
		28	-0.045	-0.008	632.65	0.000
		29	-0.070	-0.011	633.26	0.000
		30	-0.090	0.019	634.30	0.000

Figure 3

Correlogram of LOGM_2

Included observations: 73 Sample: 1987:1 2005:1

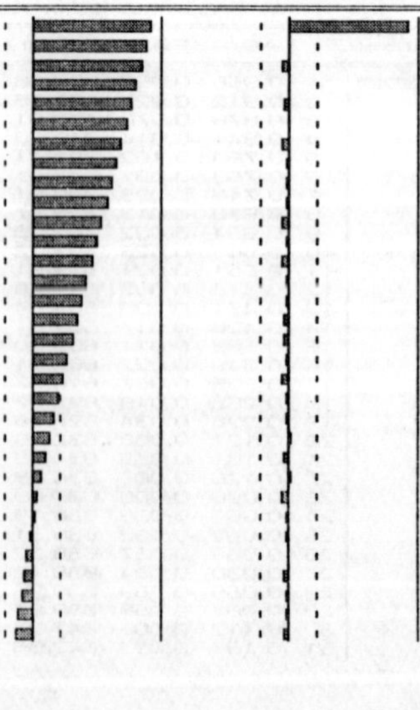

Autocorrelation	Partial Correlation		AC	PAC	Q-Stat	Prob
		1	0.960	0.960	70.009	0.000
		2	0.920	-0.008	135.28	0.000
		3	0.879	-0.042	195.68	0.000
		4	0.839	0.004	251.55	0.000
		5	0.799	-0.028	302.91	0.000
		6	0.760	-0.006	350.08	0.000
		7	0.719	-0.042	392.98	0.000
		8	0.679	-0.015	431.85	0.000
		9	0.639	-0.022	466.82	0.000
		10	0.601	-0.009	498.20	0.000
		11	0.561	-0.043	525.96	0.000
		12	0.522	-0.012	550.40	0.000
		13	0.481	-0.047	571.52	0.000
		14	0.441	0.020	589.56	0.000
		15	0.401	-0.019	604.76	0.000
		16	0.362	-0.028	617.34	0.000
		17	0.322	-0.033	627.47	0.000
		18	0.284	-0.010	635.49	0.000
		19	0.244	-0.047	641.53	0.000
		20	0.206	-0.010	645.92	0.000
		21	0.169	-0.018	648.95	0.000
		22	0.136	0.013	650.94	0.000
		23	0.102	-0.039	652.00	0.000
		24	0.072	0.023	652.66	0.000
		25	0.040	-0.053	652.85	0.000
		26	0.009	-0.023	652.86	0.000
		27	-0.020	-0.013	652.91	0.000
		28	-0.047	0.008	653.17	0.000
		29	-0.073	-0.026	653.84	0.000
		30	-0.098	-0.015	655.07	0.000
		31	-0.122	-0.018	657.02	0.000
		32	-0.146	-0.028	659.89	0.000

Figure 4

Correlogram of D Log Con-Price

Included observations: 72 Sample: 1987:1 2005:1

Autocorrelation | Partial Correlation

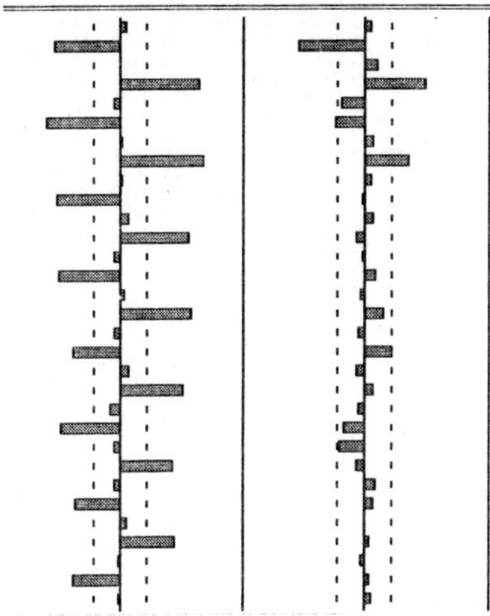

	AC	PAC	Q-Stat	Prob
1	0.044	0.044	0.1431	0.705
2	-0.562	-0.565	24.209	0.000
3	0.008	0.105	24.214	0.000
4	0.674	0.516	59.790	0.000
5	-0.043	-0.184	59.937	0.000
6	-0.616	-0.254	90.539	0.000
7	0.020	0.061	90.573	0.000
8	0.706	0.369	132.12	0.000
9	0.012	0.047	132.13	0.000
10	-0.548	-0.009	157.94	0.000
11	0.064	0.068	158.30	0.000
12	0.587	-0.062	188.86	0.000
13	-0.049	-0.022	189.08	0.000
14	-0.532	0.088	215.06	0.000
15	0.035	-0.031	215.17	0.000
16	0.612	0.162	250.80	0.000
17	-0.045	-0.051	250.99	0.000
18	-0.406	0.223	267.28	0.000
19	0.065	-0.067	267.70	0.000
20	0.546	0.073	298.22	0.000
21	-0.087	-0.054	299.01	0.000
22	-0.502	-0.180	325.82	0.000
23	-0.042	-0.201	326.02	0.000
24	0.449	-0.073	348.41	0.000
25	-0.048	0.083	348.67	0.000
26	-0.387	0.073	366.00	0.000
27	0.049	-0.003	366.29	0.000
28	0.465	0.035	392.51	0.000
29	-0.009	-0.032	392.52	0.000
30	-0.395	0.033	412.30	0.000
31	-0.009	0.047	412.31	0.000

Figure 5

Correlogram of DLog M_1

ncluded observations: 72 Sample: 1987:1 2005 1

Autocorrelation | Partial Correlation

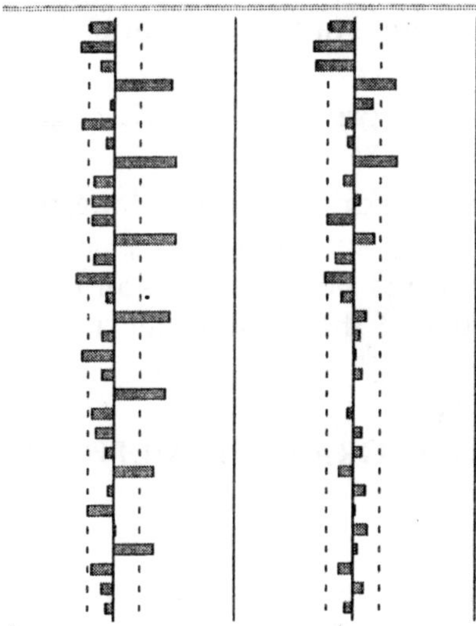

	AC	PAC	Q-Stat	Prob
1	-0.210	-0.210	3.3031	0.069
2	-0.287	-0.347	9.5938	0.008
3	-0.117	-0.322	10.653	0.014
4	0.506	0.353	30.697	0.000
5	-0.032	0.148	30.781	0.000
6	-0.287	-0.062	37.417	0.000
7	-0.074	-0.047	37.861	0.000
8	0.541	0.376	62.206	0.000
9	-0.179	-0.094	64.909	0.000
10	-0.183	0.047	67.799	0.000
11	-0.195	-0.222	71.116	0.000
12	0.544	0.173	97.353	0.000
13	-0.178	-0.163	100.22	0.000
14	-0.325	-0.240	109.94	0.000
15	-0.063	-0.114	110.31	0.000
16	0.493	0.112	133.39	0.000
17	-0.111	0.044	134.58	0.000
18	-0.280	0.018	142.30	0.000
19	-0.112	0.067	143.56	0.000
20	0.455	0.005	164.82	0.000
21	-0.185	-0.052	168.40	0.000
22	-0.161	0.071	171.15	0.000
23	-0.064	0.068	171.60	0.000
24	0.356	-0.128	185.70	0.000
25	-0.057	0.099	186.06	0.000
26	-0.223	0.020	191.81	0.000
27	0.011	0.120	191.82	0.000
28	0.357	0.027	207.25	0.000
29	-0.196	-0.115	212.01	0.000
30	-0.106	0.097	213.43	0.000
31	-0.073	-0.080	214.13	0.000

Figure 6

Correlogram of D Log M_2

ncluded observations: 72 Sample: 1987:1 2005:1

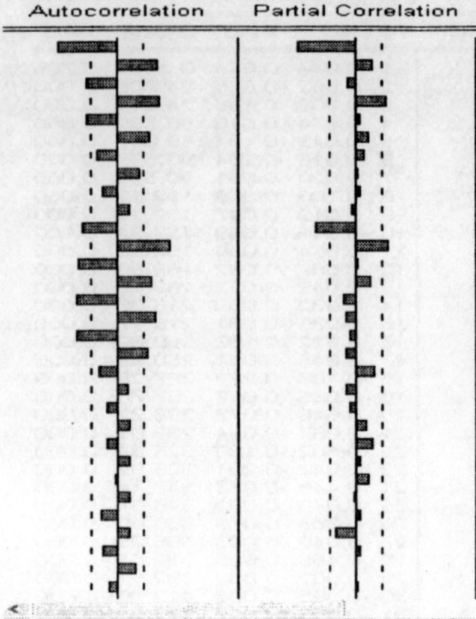

	AC	PAC	Q-Stat	Prob
1	-0.501	-0.501	18.816	0.000
2	0.355	0.139	28.395	0.000
3	-0.267	-0.060	33.897	0.000
4	0.375	0.263	44.940	0.000
5	-0.268	0.031	50.637	0.000
6	0.285	0.108	57.175	0.000
7	-0.167	0.071	59.473	0.000
8	0.181	0.014	62.193	0.000
9	-0.116	0.032	63.327	0.000
10	0.112	-0.035	64.397	0.000
11	-0.297	-0.342	72.103	0.000
12	0.447	0.283	89.862	0.000
13	-0.320	0.015	99.132	0.000
14	0.300	0.122	107.40	0.000
15	-0.355	-0.100	119.20	0.000
16	0.328	-0.086	129.45	0.000
17	-0.338	-0.056	140.54	0.000
18	0.266	-0.084	147.50	0.000
19	-0.154	0.158	149.89	0.000
20	0.083	-0.097	150.59	0.000
21	-0.096	-0.048	151.56	0.000
22	0.107	0.098	152.79	0.000
23	-0.096	0.131	153.78	0.000
24	0.104	0.036	154.99	0.000
25	-0.021	0.102	155.04	0.000
26	0.115	-0.021	156.56	0.000
27	-0.132	0.028	158.63	0.000
28	0.109	-0.168	160.06	0.000
29	-0.125	0.037	162.00	0.000
30	0.156	0.001	165.08	0.000
31	-0.059	0.019	165.54	0.000

Implications of the Findings

It is, therefore, observed that

i. consumer price, M1 and M2 money supplies are non-stationarity at level and these are I(1)

ii. these variables become stationary upon first differencing

iii. first differenced consumer price, M1 and M2 money supply series are I(0)

iv. study of co-integration for examining long-run relationship between M1 and consumer price, or M2 and consumer price is possible since all these variable are integrated of the same order, I(1).

IV
COINTEGRATION: ENGLE GRANGER METHOD

Introduction

Co-integration is the study concerning the stability of long run equilibrium relationships among variables. The study allows for the researcher to describe the existence of an equilibrium or stationary relationship among two or more time series, each of which is individually non-stationary. According to Engle and Granger (1987) the variables will be co-integrated when the linear combination of the non-stationary variables is stationary. Co-integration provides a method for elimination of the cost of differencing by rationalizing terms in levels but only in linear combinations, which are stationary.

The Model

The model for the Co-integration Study is as follows:

$$\text{Log Con-price}_t = \alpha_1 + \beta \text{Log} M_{1t} + \mu_{1t} \quad (4.1)$$

$$\text{or,} \quad \mu_{1t} = \text{Log Con-price}_t - \alpha_1 - \beta \text{Log} M_{1t}$$

$$\text{Log Con-price}_t = \alpha_2 + \beta \text{Log} M_{2t} + \mu_{2t} \quad (4.2)$$

$$\text{or,} \quad \mu_{2t} = \text{Log Con-price}_t - \alpha_2 - \beta \text{Log} M_{2t}$$

where, Con-Price = Consumer Price ,

M_{1t} = Narrow money supply,

M_{2t} = Broad money supply

μ_{1t} & μ_{2t} are residual terms.

Estimated Model

The Estimated equations are given below:

$$\text{Log Con-Price} = 1.0574 + 0.5282 \text{Log } M_{1t} \quad (4.3)$$

S.E. (0.0140) (0.0092)

t-stat. [75.3084] [57.5072]

$R^2 = 0.9790$ Adj. $R^2 = 0.9787$

D-W stat. = 0.7194

$$\text{Log Con-Price} = 0.9674 + 0.4592 \text{ Log} M_{2t} \quad (4.4)$$

S.E. (0.0143) (0.0073)

t-stat. [67.7065] [62.6839]

$R^2 = 0.9822$ Adj. $R^2 = 0.9820$

D-W stat. = 0.4292

Stationarity of the Residuals: Correlogram Study

The ACFs and PACFs of the residuals and are given by the Figures 7 and 8 respectively.

Figure 7

Correlogram of Resi (Log Con-Price & Log M_1)

ncluded observations: 73 Sample: 1987:1 2005:1

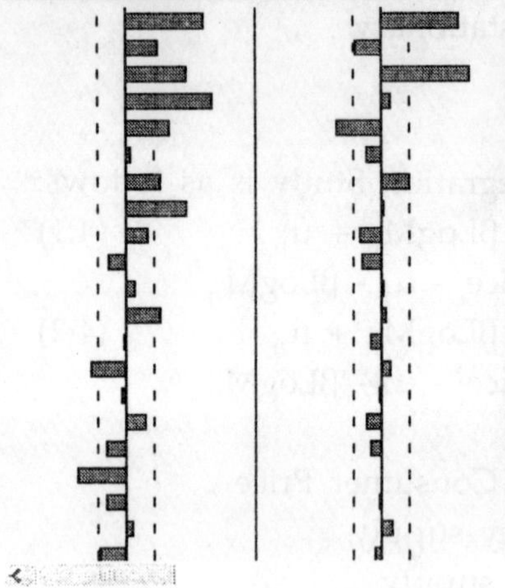

Autocorrelation	Partial Correlation		AC	PAC	Q-Stat	Prob
		1	0.619	0.619	29.144	0.000
		2	0.260	-0.201	34.337	0.000
		3	0.490	0.712	53.103	0.000
		4	0.704	0.063	92.392	0.000
		5	0.360	-0.367	102.80	0.000
		6	0.037	-0.119	102.91	0.000
		7	0.277	0.231	109.29	0.000
		8	0.494	0.022	129.84	0.000
		9	0.168	-0.173	132.26	0.000
		10	-0.144	-0.154	134.06	0.000
		11	0.073	0.017	134.54	0.000
		12	0.286	0.036	141.87	0.000
		13	-0.019	-0.096	141.90	0.000
		14	-0.278	0.060	149.09	0.000
		15	-0.038	-0.013	149.22	0.000
		16	0.148	-0.119	151.33	0.000
		17	-0.152	-0.093	153.59	0.000
		18	-0.391	-0.008	168.80	0.000
		19	-0.155	-0.021	171.24	0.000
		20	0.048	0.087	171.47	0.000
		21	-0.209	-0.044	176.08	0.000

Figure 8

Correlogram of Resi (Log Price & Log M_2)

Included observations: 73 Sample: 1987:1 2005:1

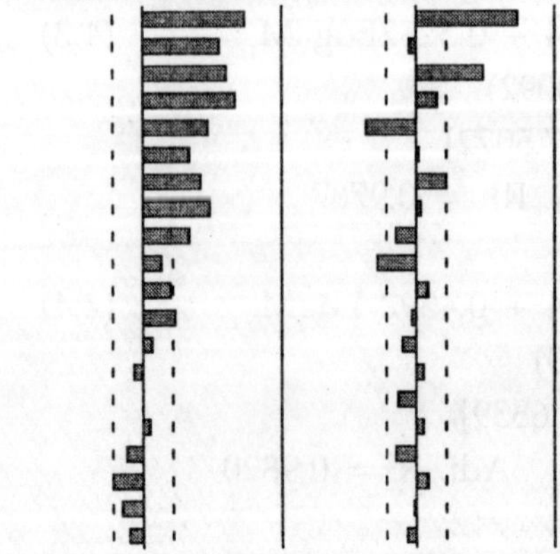

Autocorrelation	Partial Correlation		AC	PAC	Q-Stat	Prob
		1	0.765	0.765	44.451	0.000
		2	0.567	-0.042	69.240	0.000
		3	0.627	0.500	99.978	0.000
		4	0.694	0.156	138.17	0.000
		5	0.493	-0.387	157.77	0.000
		6	0.339	0.018	167.18	0.000
		7	0.441	0.237	183.29	0.000
		8	0.510	0.025	205.19	0.000
		9	0.336	-0.150	214.85	0.000
		10	0.146	-0.293	216.71	0.000
		11	0.215	0.087	220.79	0.000
		12	0.253	-0.040	226.55	0.000
		13	0.071	-0.110	227.01	0.000
		14	-0.068	0.042	227.44	0.000
		15	-0.004	-0.143	227.44	0.000
		16	0.051	0.055	227.69	0.000
		17	-0.124	-0.148	229.20	0.000
		18	-0.227	0.097	234.32	0.000
		19	-0.153	-0.017	236.68	0.000
		20	-0.106	-0.068	237.84	0.000

Findings

It is observed from the Figures 7 and 8 that

i. ACFs of residuals are marked by the presence of ladder like pattern of spikes

ii. PACFs are marked by significant spike at lag one.

It, therefore, follows that

(i) Consumer price and M1 are not co-integrated at level, and

(ii) Consumer price and M1 are also not co-integrated at level.

These necessitate for examining the co integration with differenced dataset.

Co-Integration with Differenced Datasets

In this case the estimable equations are

$$\Delta \text{Log Con-Price}_t = \alpha_1 + \beta_1 \, \Delta \text{LogM}_{1t} + u_t \qquad (4.5)$$

$$\text{or } u_t = \Delta \text{Log Con-Price}_t - \alpha_1 - \beta_1 \Delta \text{LogM}_{1t}$$

$$\text{Again } \Delta \text{Log Con-Price}_t = \alpha_2 + \beta 2 \Delta \text{LogM}_{2t} + v_t \qquad (4.6)$$

$$\text{or } v_t = \Delta \text{Log Con-Price}_t - \alpha_2 - \beta_2 \Delta \text{LogM}_{2t}$$

Estimated Equations

The estimated equations (4.7) and (4.8) are given below.

$$\Delta \text{Log Con-Price}_t = 0.0120 - 0.2598 \, \Delta \text{LogM}_{1t} \qquad (4.7)$$

S.E (0.0018) (0.0655)

t- Stat. [6.7399] [-3.9643]

$R^2 = 0.1833$ Adj $R^2 = 0.1717$

RSS = 0.0109 D-W Stat. = 2.0448

$$\Delta \text{Log Con-Price}_t = 0.0069 + 0.0645 \Delta \text{LogM}_{2t} \qquad (4.8)$$

S.E (0.0022) (0.0911)

t.Stat. [3.0569] [0.7098]

$R^2 = 0.0071$ Adj $R^2 = -0.0070$

RSS = 0.0138 D.W Stat. = 1.9080

Stationarity of the Residuals in Equations (4.7) and (4.8)

The stationarity residuals of the equations (4.7) and (4.8) have been examined through the corresponding ACFs and PACFs which are presented through the Figures (9-10). The ACF and PACF plots indicate that

i. ACFs are free from any dying out pattern of spikes, and
ii. PACFs are not market by the existence of a significant spike at lag one

All these observations testify for the stationarity of residuals concerned. It, therefore, follows that

i. Consumer Price and M_1 are I(1) Co-integrated i.e. CI(1)
ii. Consumer Price and M_2 are also I(1) Co-integrated i.e. CI(1).

Figure 9

Correlogram of Resi (D Log Price &DLog M'$_1$)

ncluded observations: 72 Sample: 1987:1 2005:1

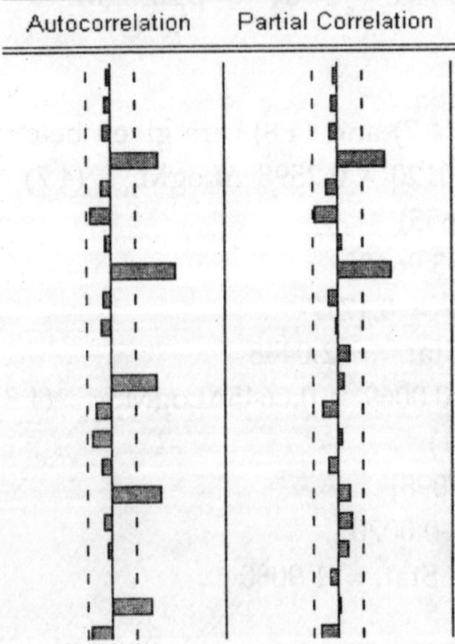

Lag	AC	PAC	Q-Stat	Prob
1	-0.026	-0.026	0.0503	0.822
2	-0.044	-0.045	0.1971	0.906
3	-0.078	-0.080	0.6659	0.881
4	0.442	0.439	15.958	0.003
5	-0.092	-0.109	16.624	0.005
6	-0.188	-0.199	19.465	0.003
7	-0.043	0.038	19.618	0.006
8	0.583	0.499	47.914	0.000
9	-0.074	-0.087	48.378	0.000
10	-0.082	-0.019	48.956	0.000
11	0.000	0.107	48.956	0.000
12	0.417	0.050	64.382	0.000
13	-0.144	-0.135	66.262	0.000
14	-0.169	0.035	68.899	0.000
15	-0.084	-0.090	69.554	0.000
16	0.455	0.108	89.266	0.000
17	-0.071	0.121	89.755	0.000
18	-0.028	0.093	89.833	0.000
19	0.004	-0.058	89.835	0.000
20	0.372	0.012	103.99	0.000
21	-0.195	-0.151	107.98	0.000

Figure 10

Correlogram of Resi (D Log Price & DLog M_2)

ncluded observations: 72 Sample: 1987:1 2005:1

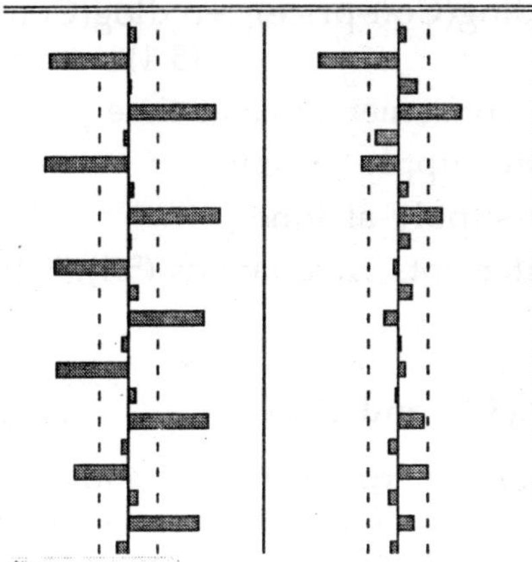

	AC	PAC	Q-Stat	Prob
1	0.044	0.044	0.1482	0.700
2	-0.600	-0.603	27.524	0.000
3	0.014	0.132	27.539	0.000
4	0.671	0.473	62.774	0.000
5	-0.040	-0.165	62.903	0.000
6	-0.644	-0.272	96.399	0.000
7	0.035	0.080	96.502	0.000
8	0.695	0.320	136.74	0.000
9	0.024	0.097	136.78	0.000
10	-0.579	-0.036	165.61	0.000
11	0.081	0.100	166.19	0.000
12	0.568	-0.101	194.87	0.000
13	-0.042	0.011	195.03	0.000
14	-0.556	0.054	223.40	0.000
15	0.048	-0.020	223.62	0.000
16	0.609	0.187	258.93	0.000
17	-0.046	-0.076	259.13	0.000
18	-0.423	0.234	276.75	0.000
19	0.074	-0.076	277.30	0.000
20	0.548	0.115	308.06	0.000
21	-0.085	-0.045	308.81	0.000

V
GRANGER CAUSALITY: THE ESTIMABLE MODELS

The 'Granger- Approach to Causality' uses the past information of both variables. To conduct the causality test between money and price, we have used the following two equations both for narrow money as well as for broad money.

$dlog(Con\text{-}price)_t = \alpha_1+\beta_1 dlog(Con\text{-}price)_{t-1} +\beta_2\, dlog(Con\text{-}price)_{t-2} + \beta_3\, dlog(Con\text{-}price)_{t-3} + \beta_4\, dlog(Con\text{-}price)_{t-4} + \gamma_1 dlogM_{1t-1}+\gamma_2 dlogM_{1t-2}+\gamma_3 dlogM_{1t-3}+\gamma_4 dlogM_{1t-4}+u_{1t}$ (5.1)

And $dlogM_{1t} = \alpha_2+\delta_1 dlogM_{1t-1}+\delta_2 dlogM_{1t-2}+\delta_3 dlogM_{1t-3}+ \delta_4 dlogM_{1t-4}+ \pi_1\, dlog(Con\text{-}price)_{t-1} + \pi_2 dlog(Con\text{-}price)_{t-2} + \pi_3 dlog(Con\text{-}price)_{t-3} +\pi_4 dlog(Con\text{-}price)_{t-4}+u_{2t}$ (5.2)

Similarly, the other equations used for the Granger Causality tests are

$dlog(Con\text{-}price)_t= \alpha_3+ \Phi_1 dlog(Con\text{-}price)_{t-1} + \Phi_2 dlog(Con\text{-}price)_{t-2} + \Phi_3 dlog(Con\text{-}price)_{t-3} + \Phi_4 dlog(Con\text{-}price)_{t-4} + \Phi_1 dlogM_{2t-1}+ \Phi_2 dlogM_{2t-2} + \Phi_3 dlogM_{2t-3} +$

$\Phi_4 dlogM_{2t-4} + u_{3t}$ (5.3)

And $dlogM_{2t} = \alpha 4 + \psi_1 dlog\ M_{2t-1} + \psi_2 dlogM_{2t-2} + \psi_3 dlogM_{2t-3} + \psi_4 dlogM_{2t-4} + \rho_1 dlog(Con\text{-}price)_{t-1} + \rho_2 dlog(Con\text{-}price)_{t-2} + \rho_3 dlog(Con\text{-}price)_{t-3} + \rho_4 dlog(Con\text{-}price)_{t-4} + u_{4t}$ (5.4)

where, Con-Price $_t$ = Consumer price at time $_t$

M_{1t} = Narrow money supply at time $_t$

M_{2t} = Broad money supply at time $_t$

$\alpha 1, \alpha 2, \alpha 3$ and $\alpha 4$ are intercepts of equations (5.1),(5.2), (5.3) and (5.4).

Estimation of Equations (5.1) and (5.2)

The results of estimation of the equations (5.1) and (5.2) with different lags are being presented through the Table 5.1 below.

Table 5.1: Granger Causality Test on Consumer Price & M1 Money Supply

Null Hypothesis	*Observation*	*Lag*	*F-stat.*	*Prob*
dLogM1 does not Granger Cause dLog Con-Price	71	1	0.0703	0.7917
dLog Con-Price does not Granger Cause dLog M_1	71	1	0.9589	0.3309
dLogM1 does not Granger Cause dLog Con-Price	70	2	20.3880	1.3E-07
dLog Con-Price does not Granger Cause dLog M_1	70	2	26.2050	4.5E-09
dLogM1 does not Granger Cause dLog Con-Price	69	3	13.0077	1.1E-06
dLog Con-Price does not Granger Cause dLog M_1	69	3	13.9292	4.8E-07
dLogM1 does not Granger Cause dLog Con-Price	68	4	4.1146	0.0052***
dLog Con-Price does not Granger Cause dLog M_1	68	4	7.2592	8.0E-05

*,**,*** Indicates statistically significance at the 10%,5%,1% level respectively.

Results of the Test

It is observed from the Table 5.1 that

(i) Consumer Price Granger Causes M_1 money supply since the coefficients of dLog con-price$_{t-2}$, dLog con-price$_{t-3}$, and dLog con-price$_{t-4}$ in the equation for dLogM1t are significant at 5% level.

(ii) M1t also Granger Causes Consumer Price level since coefficients of dLogM_{1t-2} dLogM_{1t-3} and dLogM_{1t-4} in the equation for dLog con-pricet are significant at 1% level.

(iii) there exists bidirectional causality between money supply and price level.

Estimation of Eqn (5.3) and (5.4)

The results of estimation of equations (5.3) and (5.4) with different lags are being presented through the Table-5.2

Table 5.2: Granger Causality Test on Con -price & M_2 (Nepal)

Null Hypothesis	*Observation*	*Lag*	*F-stat.*	*Prob*
dLogM_1 does not Granger Cause dLog Con-Price	71	1	3.3185	0.0729*
dLog Con-Price does not Granger Cause dLog M_1	71	1	4.0363	0.0485**
dLogM_1 does not Granger Cause dLog Con-Price	70	2	3.8151	0.0271**
dLog Con-Price does not Granger Cause dLog M_1	70	2	7.5240	0.0011***
dLogM_1 does not Granger Cause dLog Con-Price	69	3	2.8052	0.0470
dLog Con-Price does not Granger Cause dLog M_1	69	3	4.6523	0.0053***
dLogM_1 does not Granger Cause dLog Con-Price	68	4	0.3942	0.8120
dLog Con-Price does not Granger Cause dLog M_1	68	4	3.3680	0.0150***

*,**,*** Indicates statistically significance at the 10%,5%,1% level respectively.

Findings

It is observed from the Table 5.2 that

i. Con-price appears to Granger Cause M_2 money supply level since the coefficients of d log con-pricet-i (i=1...4) in dlogM_{2t} equation (5.4) are statistically (at least at 5% level) are significant.

ii. M_2 also appears to Granger Cause consumer price since the coefficients of dlogM_{2t-i} (i=1,2) in d log Con-price equation (5.3) are statistically significant at least at 10% level.

Economic Interpretation

These findings indicate that variations in consumer price level in Nepal over the period of study was Granger caused by those in M_1 and M_2 money supplies. Rise in M_1 and M_2 money supplies raised the purchasing capacity of the people but failed to raise output level accordingly. This resulted in price level variations. So money supplies were inflationary by nature in Nepal over the period of study. Again Consumer price level Granger caused both M_1 and M_2 money supply.

VI
IDENTIFICATION OF SUB-PERIODS

Sub-periods in the historical datasets have been identified through the 'Chow Break-Point Test' which is basically a 'Recursive Estimation Procedure' with historical dataset. Table-6 presents the F-statistics corresponding to recursive residuals obtained from the recursive estimation of the relation between consumer price and M_1 money supply. Again the Table 7 shows the test results with M_2 money supply. The Table 6 presents the ratios of the 'Normalized' Residual sum of squares obtained from the 'Recursive Estimations' of the Equation

$$\text{dLog Con-Price}_t = \alpha + \beta \, \text{dLogM}_{1t} + u_t$$

The Table 7 presents the corresponding F-statistic for the 'Recursive Estimations' of the equation

$$dLog\ Con\text{-}Price_{t} = \delta + \gamma dLogM_{2t} + v_{t}$$

It is observed from the Table 6 that

i. there exist structural change in the relationship between consumer price level and M1 money supply over the period 1987:q_2 – 2005:q_2.

ii. two distinct sub-periods exist in this historical dataset.

iii. the first sub-period ranges over 1987:q_2 – 2000:q_1

iv. the second sub-period covers the period 2002:q_2 to 2005:q_1

Again the Table 7 shows that

i. there exist some definite structural changes in the relationship between consumer price level and M_2 money supply in the economy of Nepal

ii. two distinct sub-periods have been identified

iii. the first sub-period ranges over 1987:q_2 – 1999:q_1

iv. the Second sub-period extends from 1999:q_2 – 2005:q_1.

Table 6: Chow Break Point Test on Equation
[Δ log (Con-Price) = a+β Δ Log M_{1t})+u_t]

Year	*F-Statistic*	*Probability*
1988:1	2.128552	0.126872
1988:2	2.318150	0.106188
1988:3	2.192021	0.119522
1988:4	0.762122	0.470619
1989:1	0.805380	0.451135
1989:2	0.800867	0.453128
1989:3	0.735542	0.483019
1989:4	0.656833	0.521749
1990:1	1.071802	0.348103
1990:2	0.486360	0.616983
1990:3	0.619113	0.541429
1990:4	0.816035	0.446464
1991:1	0.753493	0.474608

1991:2	0.625866	0.537850
1991:3	0.898012	0.412154
1991:4	2.385365	0.099718
1992:1	2.972168	0.057881
1992:2	2.685387	0.075425
1992:3	4.629208	0.013036
1992:4	4.649147	0.012809
1993:1	4.083070	0.021154
1993:2	2.843416	0.065170
1993:3	3.067983	0.053005
1993:4	3.705383	0.029687
1994:1	4.060067	0.021593
1994:2	2.864542	0.063912
1994:3	3.823742	0.026686
1994:4	4.051568	0.021758
1995:1	4.317408	0.017172
1995:2	2.994710	0.056694
1995:3	3.345834	0.041120
1995:4	3.418262	0.038498
1996:1	3.682368	0.030310
1996:2	3.010026	0.055902
1996:3	3.265964	0.044225
1996:4	3.463654	0.036944
1997:1	3.422507	0.038350
1997:2	2.498785	0.089705
1997:3	2.309742	0.107028
1997:4	1.977280	0.146326
1998:1	1.896592	0.157933
1998:2	1.893075	0.158460
1998:3	2.109702	0.129143
1998:4	3.067855	0.053011
1999:1	4.134428	0.020207
1999:2	2.633105	0.079173
1999:3	3.070091	0.052903
1999:4	2.833448	0.065772
*2000:1	4.318486*	0.017155
2000:2	3.033780	0.054695
2000:3	2.810644	0.067172
2000:4	2.973045	0.057834

2001:1	2.744250	0.071424
2001:2	1.806387	0.172039
2001:3	2.051451	0.136430
2001:4	2.077934	0.133066
2002:1	1.782436	0.175997
2002:2	1.092333	0.341245
2002:3	0.962569	0.387052
2002:4	1.018615	0.366537
2003:1	0.909302	0.407646
2003:2	0.464215	0.630606
2003:3	0.816157	0.446411
2003:4	0.774835	0.464805
2004:1	0.692980	0.503580
2004:2	0.119555	0.887501
2004:3	0.094062	0.910344
2004:4	0.200544	0.818768
2005:1	-	-

* indicates structural break

Table 7: Chow Break Point Test on Equation [Δlog (Con-Price) = a +β ΔLog M_{2t})+u_t]

Year	*F-Statistic*	*Probability*
1988:1	2.443168	0.094479
1988:2	1.833732	0.167631
1988:3	1.649219	0.199794
1988:4	1.817124	0.170294
1989:1	1.489481	0.232753
1989:2	0.873662	0.422052
1989:3	0.640651	0.530100
1989:4	1.469286	0.237301
1990:1	1.575478	0.214367
1990:2	0.531116	0.590367
1990:3	0.608277	0.547223
1990:4	0.541470	0.584380
1991:1	0.580084	0.562597
1991:2	0.339470	0.713348
1991:3	0.416328	0.661134

1991:4	2.060075	0.135325
1992:1	1.980997	0.145812
1992:2	1.791983	0.174408
1992:3	1.650849	0.199484
1992:4	2.685789	0.075397
1993:1	3.194487	0.047208
1993:2	1.137311	0.326703
1993:3	1.366129	0.262004
1993:4	1.991343	0.144394
1994:1	1.920521	0.154395
1994:2	1.031896	0.361842
1994:3	1.305638	0.277706
1994:4	1.692542	0.191712
1995:1	1.750412	0.181438
1995:2	1.051462	0.355038
1995:3	1.175478	0.314864
1995:4	1.579064	0.213634
1996:1	1.577823	0.213887
1996:2	1.048557	0.356040
1996:3	1.326840	0.272095
1996:4	1.931026	0.152868
1997:1	1.822404	0.169443
1997:2	1.363011	0.262790
1997:3	1.194420	0.309153
1997:4	1.253826	0.291925
1998:1	1.120931	0.331924
1998:2	0.959637	0.388158
1998:3	1.061588	0.351568
1998:4	2.143778	0.125067
*1999:1	3.279009*	0.043701
1999:2	1.576318	0.214195
1999:3	1.740158	0.183216
1999:4	1.895873	0.158041
2000:1	1.696186	0.191048
2000:2	0.899818	0.411430
2000:3	0.815971	0.446492
2000:4	1.093519	0.340854
2001:1	0.896749	0.412662
2001:2	0.498027	0.609928

2001:3	0.521939	0.595727
2001:4	0.750087	0.476193
2002:1	0.586069	0.559297
2002:2	0.241334	0.786249
2002:3	0.233646	0.792275
2002:4	0.421237	0.657935
2003:1	0.359482	0.699357
2003:2	0.131163	0.877296
2003:3	0.396574	0.674166
2003:4	0.435043	0.649026
2004:1	0.355022	0.702450
2004:2	0.103640	0.901692
2004:3	0.093408	0.910938
2004:4	0.097421	0.907301
2005:1	-	-

*indicates the structural break

Results of Estimations of Granger Causality Equations in Different Sub-Periods

The results of estimations of Eqn (5.3) under two different sub-periods have been presented through the Tables 8 and 9. Here the 4th lags of dlog con-price and dlogM1 have been avoided.

Similarly, the Table 10-11 show the results of estimations of Eqn (5.4) [without the 4th lag of each of the variables concerned].

Table 8: Results of Estimation of The Equations (5.1) Over the Sub-Period (1987:2- 2000:1)

Equ^n for	*Regressors*	*Coefficients*	*SE*	*t-stat.*
Δlog Con-price$_t$	Constant	0.0070	0.0035	2.0100**
	Δlog Con-price $_{t-1}$	0.1282	0.1529	0.8383
	Δlog Con-price $_{t-2}$	-0.3683	0.1067	-3.4509*
	Δlog Con-price $_{t-3}$	-0.0635	0.1481	-0.4291
	Δlog M $_{1t-1}$	0.0666	0.0791	0.8491
	Δlog M $_{1t-2}$	0.3254	0.0687	4.7371*

	Δlog M $_{1t-3}$	-0.0752	0.0832	-0.9026
Δlog M_{1t}	Constant	0.0189	0.0066	2.8608*
	Δlog M $_{1t-1}$	0.3846	0.1495	-2.5723*
	Δlog M $_{1t-2}$	-0.1758	0.1298	-1.3547***
	Δlog M $_{1t-3}$	-0.2115	0.1576	-1.3423***
	Δlog Con-price $_{t-1}$	-0.0884	0.2889	-0.3662
	Δlog Con-price $_{t-2}$	1.0452	0.2017	5.1807*
	Δlog Con-price $_{t-3}$	0.1187	0.2799	0.4210

*,** and*** are significant 1%,5% and 10% level

Findings from the Table 8

It is observed from the Table-8 that in the equation for Con pricet (CP_t)

i. the coefficient of CP_{t-2} is significant at 1% level
ii. the coefficient of M_{1t-2} is significant at 1% level
iii. all other coefficients fails to be significant even at 10% level
iv. coefficient of M_{1t-2} is positive and less than one,

All these observations indicate that

i. M_1 money supply Granger causes price level over the sub-period 1987:q_2 – 2000:q_1
ii. variation in M_1 money supply over this period caused less than proportionate variation in the price level (in the same direction)
iii. monetary policy is far from being `anti-inflationary'. On the contrary, M_1 money supply stimulates the price rise.

It is observed from the Table-8 that in the equation for M_{1t}

i. the coefficient of M_{1t-i} (i = 1,2,3) are significant at least at 10% level
ii. the coefficient of CP_{t-2} is significant at 1% level
iii. all other coefficients fail to be significant even at 10% level

iv. coefficient of CP_{t-2} is positive and less than one

All these observations indicate that

i. CP_t Granger caused M_1 money supply over the sub-period 2000:q_2-2005:q_1

ii. variation in CPt over this sub-periods caused less than proportionate variation in M_1 money supply.

iii. M_{1t} is found to be affected sigficantly by the variation in two period back price level. This indicates that money supply rose to strenthen the purchasing capacity of people because rise in con-price level lowered the purchasing ability of the populace.

Table 9: Results of Estimation of Eqn (5.1) and (5.2) Over the Second Sub-period: 2000:2-2005:1

Equ^n for	*Regressors*	*Coefficients*	*SE*	*t-stat.*
Δlog Con-pricet	Constant	0.0105	0.0054	1.9521**
	Δlog Con-price $_{t-1}$	-0.0951	0.3375	-0.2819
	Δlog Con-price $_{t-2}$	-0.6229	0.2185	-2.8511*
	Δlog Con-price $_{t-3}$	-0.2343	0.2657	-0.8819
	Δlog M $_{1t-1}$	-0.1652	0.1660	-0.9955
	Δlog M $_{1t-2}$	0.2158	0.1887	1.1433
	Δlog M $_{1t-3}$	-0.2996	0-1810	-1.6560**
Δlog M_{1t}	Constant	0.0057	0.0108	0.5314
	Δlog M $_{1t-1}$	-0.0606	0.3336	-0.1818
	Δlog M $_{1t-2}$	0.0006	0.3794	0.0016
	Δlog M $_{1t-3}$	0.3590	0.3637	0.9870
	Δlog Con-price $_{t-1}$	0.4498	0.6785	-0.6629
	Δlog Con-price $_{t-2}$	0.6084	0.4392	1.3853*
	Δlog Con-price $_{t-3}$	0.2294	0.5341	0.4295

*,** and *** are significant at 1%, 5% and 10% level respectively.

Findings from the Table 9

It is observed from the Table 9 that in the sub-period 2

ranging from 2000:q_2 to 2005:q_1 in the equn (5.1) for CP_t

i. the coefficient of CP_{t-2} is significant at 1% level

ii. the coefficient of M_{1t-3} is significant at 5% level

iii. the coefficient of M_{1t-3} is is negative and less than one

iv. all other coefficients are insignificant

All these observations indicate that

i. M_1 money supply Granger caused price level over the sub-period 2000:q_2-2005:q_1

ii. the coefficient of M_{1t-3} is negative and less than one. This implies that money supply was managed so as to reduce price level. Consequently, the monetary policy was 'anti-inflationary' over this sub-period

Again the Table 9 shows that in the equ^n for M_{1t}

i. Coefficients of CP_{t-i} ; i=1,2,3 are insignificant even at 10% level

ii. Coefficients of M_{1t-i}; i=1,2,3 are also not significant even at 1% level

All these testify that price level failed to Granger cause M_1 money supply in this period.

Causality between CP_t and M_{2t} in Different Sub-Periods

The equations (5.3) and (5.4) have been estimated under different sub-periods. The Results of estimation are being presented through the Tables 10 and 11.

Table 10: Results of Estimation of Equations (5.3) and (5.4) in the First Sub-Period: 1987:$_{q2}$ – 1999:$_{q1}$

Equ^n for	*Regressors*	*Coefficients*	*SE*	*t-stat.*
Δlog Con-price$_t$	Constant	0.0125	0.0057	2.2043**
	Δlog Con-price $_{t-1}$	0.0723	0.1686	0.4289
	Δlog Con-price $_{t-2}$	-0.6509	0.1321	-4.9272*
	Δlog Con-price $_{t-3}$	-0.0493	0.1778	-0.2776
	Δlog M $_{2t-1}$	-0.0503	0.1181	-0.4263

	$\Delta\log M_{2t-2}$	0.1726	0.1346	1.2827*
	$\Delta\log M_{2t-3}$	-0.0506	0.1153	0.4387
$\Delta\log M_{2t}$	Constant	0.0279	0.0079	3.5499*
	$\Delta\log M_{2t-1}$	-0.6603	0.1629	-4.0530*
	$\Delta\log M_{2t-2}$	-0.0409	0.1856	-0.2807
	$\Delta\log M_{2t-3}$	-0.0947	0.1591	-0.5951
	$\Delta\log$ Con-price $_{t-1}$	0.3367	0.2326	1.4476*
	$\Delta\log$ Con-price $_{t-2}$	0.3766	0.1822	2.0674**
	$\Delta\log$ Con-price $_{t-3}$	-0.0103	0.2453	-0.0423

*,** and *** are significant at 1%, 5% and 10% level respectively.

Table 11: Results of Estimation of Equations (5.3) and (5.4) Over the Second Sub-Period: 1999:q_2–2005:q_1

Equ^n for	*Regressors*	*Coefficients*	*SE*	*t-stat.*
$\Delta\log$ Con-price$_t$	Constant	0.0118	0.0039	2.9954*
	$\Delta\log$ Con-price $_{t-1}$	-0.1838	0.2603	-0.7060
	$\Delta\log$ Con-price $_{t-2}$	-0.8312	0.1271	-6.5393*
	$\Delta\log$ Con-price $_{t-3}$	-01560	0.2545	-0.6129
	$\Delta\log M_{2t-1}$	-0.2457	0.1411	-1.7404
	$\Delta\log M_{2t-2}$	0.0510	0.1543	0.3305
	$\Delta\log M_{2t-3}$	-0.0118	0.1358	-0.8227
$\Delta\log$ M 2t	Constant	0.0090	0.0056	1.6030**
	$\Delta\log M_{2t-1}$	0.2426	0.2007	1.2088
	$\Delta\log M_{2t-2}$	-0.1795	0.2195	-0.8177
	$\Delta\log M_{2t-3}$	0.2668	0.1932	1.3806***
	$\Delta\log$ Con-price $_{t-1}$	-0.4462	0.3702	-1.2052
	$\Delta\log$ Con-price $_{t-2}$	0.1527	0.1807	0.8450
	$\Delta\log$ Con-price $_{t-3}$	-0.1694	0.3620	-0.4681

* ** and *** are significant at 1%, 5% and 10% level respectively.

Findings From The Table 10

It is observed from the Table 10 that in the price equation

(over the sub-period 1987:2-1999:1)

i. the coefficient of CP $_{t-2}$ is significant at 1% level

ii. the coefficient of M $_{2t-i}$; i=1,1,3 are not significant even at 10% level of significance.

All these observation imply that M_2 fails to Granger cause price level.

Again in the M_2 equation

i. the coefficient of M $_{2t-i}$; i = 2,3 are not significant even at 10% level.

ii. the coefficient of CP $_{t-2}$ is significant at 5% level.

iii. the coefficient of CP $_{t-2}$ is positive and less than unity.

These observations imply that price level Granger caused M_2 money supply in this sub-period. Again rise in price level is found to cause less than proportionate rise in M_2 money supply.

Findings From The Table 11

The Table 11 shows that in the equation for price level (over the sub-period 1999:$_{q2}$- 2005:$_{q1}$

i. the coefficient of CP $_{t-2}$ is significant at 1% level

ii. the coefficient of M $_{2t-1}$ is not significant at 10% level

All these observations testify for the fact that in this sub-period M_2 fails to Granger cause price level.

The equation for M_2 in the Table 11 shows that over the second sub-period

i. the coefficients of M $_{2t-i}$; i=1,2,3 are not significant even at 10% level

ii. the coefficients of CP $_{t-i}$; i=1,2,3 are also not significant at 10% level

All these observations indicate that, in this sub-period, price level failed to Granger cause M_2 money supply.

Summary of Findings in Sec 6.3 and Sec 6.4

A summary of these findings is being presented through the Table 12

Table 12: Summary of Findings in Sections (6.3) and (6.4)

Sub-period	*Direction of Causality*	*Nature*
1987:2-2000:1	M_1 Granger Causes price level	Positively
	Price level Granger Causes M_1 money supply	Positively
2000:2-2005:1	M_1 Granger Causes price level	Negatively
	Price level fails to Granger Causes M_1 money supply	———

Interpretation of Findings

The Table 12 indicates that

i. in the sub-period covering 1987:q_2-2000:q_1, there did exist a bi-directional causality between M_1 money supply and price level. Rise in M_1 money supply led to a rise in price level while monetary authority raised money supply following rise in the price level. This rise in money supply might be undertaken in order to maintain the purchasing ability of the populace.

ii. the sub-period ranging 2000:q_2-2005:q_1 is marked by the presence of unidirectional causality running from M_1 money supply to price level.

Summary of the Findings in Sec 6.7- 6.8

The summary of the findings in these two sub-periods have been presented through the Table 13.

Table 13

Summary of Findings in Sections (6.7) and (6.8)

Sub-period	*Direction of Causality*	*Comment*
1987:1-1999:1	M_2 failed to Granger cause price level.	There did existed Uni directional causality running from price level to M_2 money supply.
	price level Granger caused M_2 money supply.	————
1999:2-2005:1	M_2 failed to Granger cause price level.	There was no causal relation between M_2 money supply and price level.
	Price level also failed to Granger cause M_2 money supply.	Both variables are exogenous to each other.

VI
SUMMARY AND CONCLUSION

The study with the historical dataset covering the period 1987:1-2005:1 on the causal relationship between price level and M_1 or M_2 Money Supply shows that

i. there was bi-directional Granger Causality between price level and M_1 money supply in the economy of Nepal.

ii. there was uni-directional causality running from price level to M_2 money supply.

However, the 'Recursive Estimation' with historical dataset confirm structural breaks in the observed relationship over the period concerned. Two definite sub-periods were identified in causal relationship that price level maintained with M1 or M2 money supply. Consequently, the parameters estimated with historical dataset appeared to be 'unstable'.

In the first sub-period, bi-directional causality between price level and M_1 money supply was observed. This was in conformity with the findings with historical dataset.

Moreover, in the second sub-period unidirectional causality running from M_1 money supply to price level was observed. This was in striking contrast with the finding of bi-directional causality between price level and money supply with the historical dataset.

Again historical dataset is marked by the presence of uni-directional causality running from price level to M_2 money supply. This particular nature of causal relation was also confirmed in the first sub-period.

However, the second sub-period is marked by the absence of any causal relation between price level and M_2 money supply. Both appeared to be 'exogenous' to each other.

These findings confirm the instability of the estimated relationship with the historical dataset. Consequently, the estimated causal relationship with the historical dataset may not provide reliable guideline for making policy decisions. On the other hand, the estimated causal relationships under different sub-periods are stable. These may provide reliable guidelines for decision making process.

LITERATURE CITED

Bessler, David A. and John L. Kling. (1984) 'A Note On Tests of Granger Causality', *Applied Economics,* Vol. 16, June, pp. 335-42.

Box, George E.P. and D.R. Cox. (1964)'An Analysis of Transformation', *Journal of Royal Statistical Society,* Series B, Vol. 30, pp. 483-89.

Chowdhury, Abdur R. (1987) 'Are Causal Relationships Sensitive to Causality Tests?' *Applied Economics,* Vol. 19, April, pp. 459-65.

Feige, Edward L. and Douglas K. Pearce. (1979) 'The Casual Relationship Between Money and Income: Some Caveats for Time Series Analysis', *Review of Economics and Statistics,* November, pp. 521-33.

Geweke, John. (1982) 'Causality, Exogeneity and Inference', in *Advances in Econometrics,* W. Hilderbrand (eds.) , pp. 209-35. New York: Cambridge University Press.

Granger, Clive W.J. (1969) 'Investigating Causal Relationships by Econometric Models and Cross-Spectral Methods', *Econometrica* Vol. 37 July, pp. 424-38.

_____ (1980) 'Testing for Causality: A Personal Viewpoint', *Journal of Economic Dynamics and Control,* Vol .2, pp. 329-52.

_____ (1988)'Some Recent Developments in a Concept of Causality', *Journal of Econometrics,* Vol. 39 (September/October), pp. 199-211.

Granger, Clive W.J., and Poul Newblold. (1986) 'Forecasting Economic Time Series', 2d edn. San Diego: Academic Press.

Guilkey, David K., and Michael K. Salemi. (1982) 'Small Sample Properties of Three Tests for Granger- Causal Ordering in a Bivariate Stochastic System', *Review of Economics and Statistics* Vol. 64, (November), pp. 668-80.

Holland, Paul W. (1986) "Statistics and Inference", *Journal of the American Statistical Association,* Vol. 81, December, pp. 945-60.

Halmes, James M., and Patricia A. Hutton. (1988) 'A Functional-Form, Distribution-Free Alternative to Parametric Analysis of Granger Causal Model', *Advances in Econometrics* Vol. 7, pp. 211-25.

Kang, Heejoon. (1977) 'The Effects of Detrending in Granger Causality Test', *Journal of Business and Economics Statistics,* Vol. 3.

_____ 'The Characterization of Instantaneous Causality: (1979) A Comment', *Journal of Econometrics,* Vol.10 (June), pp. 257-59.

Poirier, Dale J. (1988) 'Causal Relationships and Replicability', *Journal of Econometrics* Vol. 39 (September/October), pp. 213-34.

Price, J. Michael. (1979) 'A Characterization of Instantaneous Causality: A Correction', *Journal of Econometrics,* vol.10, June, pp. 253-56.

Roberts, D.L., and Stephen Nord. (1985)'Causality Tests and Functional Form Sensitivity', *Applied Economics,* Vol.17, February, pp. 135-41.

Simon, Herbert A. (1993) 'Causal Ordering and Identifiability', in *Studies in Econometric Method* (Cowles Foundation), edited by William C. Hood and Tjalling C. Koopmans. New York: John Wiley & Sons.

Suppes, Patrick. (1971) *A Probabilistic Theory of Causality,* Amsterdam: North-Holland.

Theil, Henri. (1976) *Principles of Econometrics,* Wiley, New York.

_____ (1988) 'Causality and Causal Laws in Economics', *Journal of Econometrics* Vol. 39, September/October, pp. 7-21.

9

Impact of Tourism on Mountain Environment in Nepal

ANIL BHUIMALI* & KAMANAND DEV**

Abstract

This paper seeks to assess the impact of tourism development on mountain environment of Nepal. Tourism in Himalaya provides income and employment opportunities in remote and relatively inaccessible areas. However, it leads to over-harvesting of Himalayan resources and environmental dregradation.

Key Words: over-harvesting mountain community, socio-demographic research.

Introduction

Tourism is regarded as one of the world's biggest and fastest growing industry. It has been identified as an important source of foreign exchange earning as well as a source of employment opportunity. The World Tourism

---

* Professor, Department of Economics, University of North Bengal.

** Reader in Economics, S.M.B.M. Campus, Tribhuvan University, Nepal.

Organisation (WTO) predicts that by the year 2010 international tourism will grow to one billion visitors a year and will contribute 11.6 per cent of the global gross domestic product (GDP) (WTTC, 1999). Similarly, it is estimated that, by 2010 approximately 250 million people will be employed in the tourism industry, and 10.6% of total capital investment go to the tourism sector (WTTC, 1999). It is also assumed that 20–25% of tourism is concentrated in mountains (Mountain Agenda 1999). Thus mountain tourism represents an important aspect of national economic development in both industrialised and developing countries. In Australia, for example, tourism contributes more than 6% of the GDP and annual per capita income from tourism is roughly US$, 1,900, more than 75% per cent of the total sales in tourism is generated by the Alpine tourism industry (Smeral, 1996). The Alpine nation of Europe shares a yearly product of worth US $52 billion, or 25 per cent of the world's production in tourism, and 70 percent of the more than 12 million people in the Alps live directly or indirectly from the revenues of mountain tourism (Partsch and Zaunberger,1990, cited in Wascher, 2000). In the United State, the real-estate value of Vail, Colorado, is estimated to worth over US$ 3 billion (Buckley, et al, 2000). Similarly, tourism in Nepal is the most important earner of foreign exchange which accounts for 24 per cent of the total foreign exchange earning and it contributes 74.3 per cent of total value of merchandise export (Uprety, 2000). There is no doubt that tourism has remained on of the buoyant sectors of the Nepali economy and natural environment has remained Nepal's major tourism attraction.

Mountain Tourism in Nepal

With a per capita income of $ 250 in 2001, Nepal is one of the poorest countries in the world according to global statistics compiled by the World Bank. Mountain tourism in Nepal began in 1952 when the first ascent over an 8,000m peak was accomplished by Mourice Herzog on

Mt. Annapurna (8,091m). Another historic event involved the ascent of the highest peak on the planet, Mt. Sagarmatha or Mt. Everest (8,848m) by Tenzing Norgey and Edmund Hillary in 1953, and it received wide publicity and increased the attraction for the Nepalese mountains throughout the world. Now Nepal is well known as a mountain tourist destination in the world. Of the total land area of 147,181 sq. km., about two-thirds is occupied by hills and mountains with a congregate panoply of over 1,300 peaks and pinnacles including the world's highest mountain (Grung, 1900). Although the magnet of mountain tourism in Nepal is Mt. Everest and other high peaks, the stepping stone for all visitors still remains the capital city, Kathmandu. Its natural greenery was described as 'the widest dreams of Kew' (Kipling, quoted by D.D. Bhatt, 1964). In Nepal, Mountain tourism means trekking and mountaineering tourism; which constitutes between 20 and 25 per cent of total volume of tourism, but it is a significant income source for numerous people living in and around popular mountain destination such as the Everest and Annapurna regions (Nepal, 1999).

Trekking in Nepal is a unique mobile where one's every day trekking activity is always changed from one camp to another. In Nepal, three different categories of trekking in the mountain regions are found. They are the normal trek; controlled trek, and guided trek. Those who visit Nepal for the purpose of trekking, they do trek either through Trekking Agency (organised trek) or porters or only trekking guide from Trekking Agency (tea shop trek) or do by themselves (budget trekkers) or free individuals trekkers. The northern part of Nepal is very popular for trekking and mountaineering. The popular trekking routes are Mt. Everest area in the north east, Langtang, Helambu in the central region, Annapurna and round Annapurna and the Jomshom in North West. Trek to upper Dolpa, Lomanthang of Mustang and Jumla-Rara (Mugu) are more difficult and expensive. In each group, there should be a minimum of 4 package treks in those destinations. Trekking permits to Lamanthang are limited to 1,000 package treks annually. These limitations have been placed in order to control pollution and preserve the native culture and environment. Trek to Manaslu and Kanchanjunga are limited only to few groups and are conducted by the Trekking Agencies alone. The six new areas are recently developed by Tourism for Rural Poverty Alleviation Programme (TRPAP) namely, Taplejung in the extreme East, Dolpa in the West, Lower Everst Rupandehi in mid West, Chitwan in central region are already opned for trekking Likewise NTB's model tourist areas including Ilam Palpa, Bashantpur, Dhanushadham and Khaptad also offer immense opportunities of diversifying our tourist products. The most popular areas in the mountain regions visited by trekkers are the Annapurna Langtang, and Sagarmatha regions, which are protected areas. Trekking tourism has experienced a healthy growth.

Mountaineering is another popular feature of Himalayan tourism. There are 1300 peaks in Nepal. Out of which 293 peaks are opened for the mountaineers and 33 peaks are opened for the trekkers, In 2001, there were 112 expeditions to Nepal. Royalty to the government amounted to Rs127, 396 for the same year. A total 133 expedition teams were granted permission to climb different Himalayan peaks during 2006 out of which only 78 teams were successful in there attempts. The number of mountaineers was 986 and 4344 persons employed by the expedition team. Rcyalty to the government amounted to Rs 145,612 for the same year (NTS, 2007).

Growth Patterns

Growth of tourist arrival in Nepal during the period of 2000 to 2002 was found to decline by 5.7 to 22.7 percent respectively due to recent global events and political problems in Nepal. Although there was some improvement in 2003 and the number of tourists increased by 22.7 percent in 2003 and by 14 percent in 2004, the same growth rate could not be sustained in 2005 and the number of tourists dropped by 2.6 percent to 375,398. A slight progress was made in 2006. Accordingly 383,926 tourists visited Nepal and there was an increase of 2.3 percent in the tourists' arrival during the 10th plan period (Three Year Interim Plan, 2007-2010). Similarly, in case of trekking and mountaineering tourism, a total 118,780 in 2000; 66,931 trekkers registered in 2006. Out of total 64.52 percent in 2000; 56.62 in 2006 visited Annapurna area while those visiting the Everest and Langtang regions accounted for 22.53 percent and 9.21 percent in 2000; 30.91 percent and 6.81 percent in 2006 respectively (NTS, 2007) .

The bulk of mountain tourism in Nepal is conducted in protected areas. In some protected areas, tourism has able to bring benifits to some people. Some people from the areas like Khumbu, (Sagarmatha) Namche Bazar, parts of Annapurna and Langtang realise higher standard of living but these benefits of tourism have been confined to small pockets and therefore, only a small numbers of people have been able to reap benefits from tourism. Mountain tourism in Nepal has been essentially demand driven and the supply side section of development has been slack. The environmental resources which tourists come to enjoy have not been adequately appreciated in the host country. Without appreciation of these resources, their value cannot be realised. Neither have there been efforts to link mountain tourism development with mountain community development. Thus a host country Nepal has not been able to harness these resources to develop mountain tourism to benefits the mountain community. Policy weakness and failures have also been responsible for this performance. Although mountain people have made attempt to maximise opportunities made possible by the advent of tourism, the implication on local development as well as on conservation have not all been positive (Banskota and Sharma 1994).

Impact Assessment

Impact can be assessed from the activities of tourists and from the construction and operation of tourist facilities and services. Impacts of tourism are difficult to assess, partly because of their diversity in range and in type. Impacts may be of short or long term, direct or indirect, local, national or global, positive or negative (Hunter and Green, 1995). Mountain tourism has both negative as well as positive impact on mountain communities. But there is no denying that, despite the presence of some negative impacts, mountain tourism has had over all positive impact on mountain communities. The major impacts associated with mountain tourism are as follows.

Environmental Impact

We may present below the findings of some research works already done by the researchers.

(i) Land Use: The steady growth of tourism in mountain areas has affected agricultural practices and land use. Although the impact of tourism on land use is not well recorded, studies have noted land use changes that may be attributed to tourism. The changes in land use sited referred to changes in the crops cultivated or the cropping pattern; converting land from forestry to agricultural use; conversion of agricultural land to build lodges or tea stalls; and leaving land fallow to rent as camp grounds. Agriculture as an occupation has gradually become secondary to tourism related activities such as the operation of lodges, working as guides or kitchen boys, or working in tourism related services in Kathmandu. Households have shown preference for fruit and vegetables farming over traditional crops (Friend, 1983; CEDA 1988). Land is also left fallow to provide campgrounds replacing cultivation of traditional staple crops such as buckwheat or barley. In some areas pack animals have been substituted for milk animals, as they bring in higher cash returns to households by carrying

tourist loads. This may result in added demands for fodder and grazing demands. Also, lodge owners have purchased buffaloes for milk, and this has put pressure on surrounding forests for fodder supplies.

(ii) Litter, Garbage and Pollution: The increasing amount of littering taking place at high altitudes in the mountains is a major negative environmental impact that has received a great deal of attention in Nepal. Litter includes non-biodegradable rubbish such as plastics, glass bottles, tins, foil and batteries, improperly deposited or discarded along trails, at campsites, outside trekking lodge, and at base camps, by tourists, trekking staff, porters, trekking lodge staff and local residents; inadequately covered toilet pits and scattered toilet paper around campsites and trails are another problem (Lama and Sherpa 1994). Some trekking routes have earned the nick name `Garbage trail' as Kathmandu Lamosangu to Namche Bazar route on the way to the Everest Base Camp. There is visual pollution along the trekking routes. In Solukhumbhu area, especially from Lukla via Namche Bazar to the Everst Base Camp, the whole trail is gradually polluted, and the condition is getting worse every year. The number of tourists in this area sometimes exceeds even that of the local population.

The dimension of this problem is serious. In one study, it is estimated that an average trekking group of 15 people generate about 15kg of non-biodegradable, non-burnable garbage in 10 trekking days (Lama and Sherpa 1994). It is shown in Table 1.

Table 1: Garbage Deposited in the Mountain Environment (in kg)

Area	*Number of trekkers*	*Average deposited*	*Total deposited*
Annapurna	37,902	15	5,68,530
Khumbu	11,366	15	1,70,490
Langtang	8,423	15	1,26,345
Cumulative Total 1976 to 1993 in mt.			640mt.

Source: Lama and Sherpa 1994.

The disposal of kitchen wastes into streams and ponds is another source of water pollution. The use of water courses as a means of waste disposal by local people is yet another cause of water pollution (Grung 1990).

(iii) Forests and Firewood: Forests' degradation and deforestation is one of the most widely discussed topics on the mountain environment. The demand of firewood by tourism in the mountain areas has the most significant effect on forest, vegetation and wildlife. Every year hundred of tonnes of firewood are used for cooking and camp fire purpose by mountaineers and trekkers in addition to the local consumption. The resulting the massive deforestation is seen along the trekking routes in all region of Nepal. The destruction of scant vegetation in the Alpine Region of Nepal also leads to frequent mudslides, landslides, creep and rock fall as well as the silting of rivers. The Indian captain Kohli remembers on Everest expedition like this, 'We had about 1000 porters of which 25 stayed two months at the base camp just to collect wood everyday. The other interesting fact is that an internal German Alpine Club study revealed that as far as back 1978 tourist in the Everest Region used up to 10 percent of the local wood.

An estimate of firewood consumption by tourists is given in Table 2, which highlights the demand for firewood by tourism in some of the protected areas. In all the three areas, the seasonal demand for firewood by tourists is very high. The pressure on the forests to supply firewood is obvious. This demand has provided local people the incentive to sell firewood to the tourists. This process accentuates deforestation as sustainable yield rates are already below harvest rates.

Table 2: Estimate of Firewood Consumed by Tourism in Selected Protected Area (mt).

Year		*1980*	*1981*	*1982*	*1987*	*1988*
SNP	Group	858	747	917	1323	1671
	FITS	229	199	245	353	446
LNP	Group	466	577	514	693	955
	FITS	58	71	63	85	118

ACA	Group	456	543	628	985	1204
	FITS	261	310	359	563	688
Others	Group	748	507	436	295	863
	FITS	62	42	36	25	72
Total	Group	2528	2374	2495	3295	4693
	FITS	610	622	703	1026	1324
	Total	3138	2996	3198	4321	6017

ERL 1989, Grung 1990, Banskota and Sharma 1994.
(The estimates have been derived based on the per capita consumption figure provided in ERL1989)

Economic Impact

Economic impact of mountain tourism can be viewed in terms of how different aspects of the mountain economy are affected by tourism expenditure and tourism development. The major economic impacts depend upon seasonal employment and income earned through mountain tourism. Porters and job provided by lodges are the main forms of employment. These jobs may, however, accrue to people from outside the area due to their comparative advantage in mountain tourism. The economic impact of mountain tourism can be assessed as under.

Employment

In mountain areas, tourism generates employment opportunities for porters, cooks, kitchen boys, and guides. However the local population have not benefited in comparison of the outsiders, people outside the area reap these benefits. The bulk of employment generated in mountain areas is in the form of portering and is seasonal in nature, lasting six to seven months a year. In the thirty years of mountain tourism in Nepal, this form of employment generation has not changed for better. Table 3 provides an estimate of the total direct employment generated by mountain tourism over a period of three years.

Table 3: Estimated Direct Employment Generated by Mountain Tourism

Category		*1986*	*1987*	*1988*
	Total	19829	21337	22873
Group tourists	High	793160	853480	914920
	Low	396580	426740	457460
	Total	13780	14827	15895
FITS	High	206700	222405	238425
	Low	68900	74135	79475
Total employment	High	999860	1075885	1115345
generated	Low	465480	500875	1115345

The figure for employment generated by group tourists is the average number.

Source: Baskota and Upadhay 1989.

Since the support staffs hired by group trekkers (2 to 4) is generally higher than support staff hired by FITS (0.5 to 1.5), the former has a greater impact on direct employment than the latter. However, individual trekkers generate other indirect employment in lodges, hotels and tea stalls.

Direct employment generated by mountaineering expedition fluctuated year to year. As per the size of the number of team, the employment generation was found increase or decline in different year from 2000to 2006. For example, direct employment generated by mountaineering teams declined from 9362 persons to 636 persons in 2005 because of the decline in both the number of mountaineer teams and in number per team. Although there was an outstanding improvement in 2006 and number of employment generated by mountaineering raised to 4344 due to the increase in both the number of mountaineering team and in numbers per team. This is shown in Table 4.

Table 4

Employment Generated by Mountaineering Teams

Year	*No of Teams*	*No of Mountaineers*	*Seasonal Employment*
2000	132	773	11587
2001	112	836	6203
2002	134	913	10599
2003	152	1080	14838
2004	140	1042	9362
2005	128	940	636
2006	133	986	40344

Source: Ministry of Finance, Economic Survey (2003/2004)

Income

The generation of income through tourism-related employment (primarily portering) is the most substantial income impact of tourism in mountain areas. The impact of mountain tourism on income occurring to the private sector is significant. Group tourists have a greater impact on income because they generally hire larger support staff. The income generated by mountaineering tourism is also substantial and competes fairly closely with that generated by trekking tourism. In addition, mountaineering also generates substantial revenue in the form of royalties which however remain with the government. The total income that accrues from tourism in mountain areas is not retained locally as lodge owners are, for the most part, from outside the region, food has to be imported and income is remitted to family members living in urban areas. In general, a large proportion of the income from agency organized trekking goes to people living outside the area. Besides, over the last decade the real per capita tourist expenditure has not increased (Banskota and Sharma 1994).

Socio-Cultural Impact

The impact of tourism on local cultural traditions and values is difficult to assess. Mass tourism in mountain areas has adverse effects on the social behaviour and religious sentiments, the tradition as well as culture of Himalayan people. Some critics say that the flood of visitors is also responsible for the decline in the moral values of the local people. Change in people's behaviour, dress, life style, family and social structures, values and expectations; decline in local support for local traditions and institutions; people's preference for tourist related jobs over education; pollution of sacred places; changes in traditional architecture, and so on are generally argued to be the negative impacts of tourism on culture. Economic impacts are also important in bringing cultural changes. It is difficult to assess whether such impacts are caused by tourism, by economic factors, or by other factors. There are undoubtedly both positive as well as negative impacts of tourism on the socio-cultural practices of mountain people (Haimendorf 1984; Upadhyay 1984; Robinson 1993; Lama and Sherpa 1994). With the increase of tourism in the mountain areas, adult members often leave home for prolonged periods, which are believed to have affected Sherpa society causing family break-ups in some cases.

Impact on Women

Many women are employed in lodges and tea houses. Infact tourism has created a wide range of formal and informal employment opportunities for women in Nepal. Many mountain lodges are managed by women and perhaps, in mountain areas, more women than men are employed in this sector. Side by side women have also benefited significantly from tourism through macro-enterprise development, e.g., in the form of producing handicrafts, weaving selling honey, agro-processed products, and tea stalls.

Tourism has also helped women to undertake highly

specialised and skilful activities such as climbing Mt Everest, which undoubtedly, has improved their position in society. Women from the Sherpa community and other mountain communities have been trained as doctors and increasing numbers of women from mountain areas are enrolling in higher education. Perhaps the full impacts of tourism on women are just beginning to be seen.

Other Impacts

Tourism in Nepal has some positive impact in the economy that can be identified in the following ground:-

Poverty Alleviation

There is no doubt that tourism has been able to alleviate poverty in many areas where tourism is accruing. Running lodges and tea houses in many mountain areas has helped many household to earn better income. This is obvious if one compares areas such as Langtang, Annapurna, and Sagarmatha with similar mountain areas where tourism has not been developed.

Awareness Generation

Tourism has a positive impact on awareness generation in Nepal. Compare to other mountain region of Nepal, the level of literacy among the younger generation of the Sherpa people of Khumbu is relatively high. Among the people of Sagarmatha ,Annapurna, and Lantang regions, the awareness about language, health and hygiene is of a higher than in other mountain pockets where tourists are not frequently visited. The greater awareness about conservation of cultural sites, local monuments and nature may also be different among two groups of mountain people.

Infrastructural Development

Tourism has helped infrastructural development in some remote areas. It is most likely that airstrips, bridges, and trails would not have been developed so early if tourism had not been introduced in to these areas. Without the development of tourism the limited resources of the government and local people would not have been adequate enough to build all the infrastructures available in areas such as SNP, ACAP and LNP.

Area of Research

The area of research in Nepal is another important area that can be said to have benefited from tourism. An enormous studies have taken place in the field of anthropology, biodiversity, culture, glaciers, etc that have benefited from tourism. In many cases, tourists have either been directly involved in carrying out such studies or have founded or found financial support for Nepalese as well as foreign scholars in carrying out such studies.

International Publicity

Nepal has received a great deal of international publicity through tourism. A good number of books on Nepal have been printed. Documentary films have been televised in different countries. Many articles have been published by scholars in international journals. All of this has created awareness about Nepal, its unique natural and cultural heritage as well as the problems that need to be addressed broadly grouped as poverty alleviation, awareness generation (education, health and hygiene, conservation natural and cultural sites etc.) development (infrastructure, settlement, cottage industry, etc) socio-demographic research and publicity for Nepal.

Measures

The impact assessment studies have reflected the both negative as well as positive effects of mountain tourism in Nepal. No doubt, tourism has been a stable and a lively sector of the Nepali economy. Its growth has to be attributed to the spontaneous response of the opportunities and challenges by the private sector. The Nepali experience in the tourist shows that the private sector is both unwilling and ill suited to solve the problem of cleaning the environment. Therefore, the development of tourism can't be left to the private sector alone. It needs the adoption of integrated approach by the government, the private sector for developing the infrastructure and taking steps to protect the environment and develop productive apparatus of the area. Certain policy has to be developed in order to minimise the negative effects of tourism.

* The mountain regions need accessibility of highest order. The road net work should be planned following the counter lines so as to avoid landslides and soil erosion.
* The degradation of the mountain slopes should be checked for controlling the enhancement of waste land.
* The carrying capacity of each major trail and destination has to be determined in terms of fuel demand, garbage waste disposal problems, available accommodation, and the congestion of the tourist trial at a given period. Higher fees have to be imposed on areas with a fragile environment. Fees can also be differentiated on the basis of the seasonal.
* To relieve increasing pressure on existing destinations, new tourist destinations should be located and developed in western and extreme eastern region of Nepal where the flow of tourists is relatively low at present.
* There is a heavy demand for fuel in tourist areas of Nepal. Thus in this regions, alternative source of energy like mini and macro solar and hydro projects have to be encouraged. Again kerosene depots must be installed in appropriate locations in major trails.
* There should be provision for sanitary and toilet

facilities in major tourist destinations and a systematic collection of garbage in the site through local initiatives conservation and sanitation related education must be imparted to the tourist and the local people.

* Apart from transportation and communication linkage, the people in the mountain region should be provided with social and community facilities, i.e. health and sanitation, water supply, school and marketing facilities not only for the people living there but also to the visitors.
* The government should play a leading role in producing the man power needs in the tourist industry.

Conclusion

Tourism in the mountain region is the least eco-disturbing industry. There are certain constraints which need to be removed. The basic objective is to maintain ecological balance and at the same time harness the physical resources for the welfare of the people. As a matter of fact tourism would flourish if we could restore the ecological balance which was naturally prevalent in the pre- modern period. We should aim at such development goals which are ecologically acceptable, economically viable, socially desirable and aesthetically most satisfying.

REFERENCES

Banskota, K. and Sharma, B.(1994): 'Mountain Tourism for Local Community Development.' Kathmandu, Nepal (CREST) for International Centre for Integrated Mountain Development.

Buckley,R.C., Pickring,C.M.,Warken, J.(2000): Environmetal Management for Alpine Tourism and Resorts in Australia, in Godde,P.M.,Price ,M.F. , Zimmermann, F.M. (eds) *Tourism and Development in Mountain Region*, Cab International, Walingford.

Beniston, M. (2000): *Enviromental Change in Mountains and Uplands*, London, Arnold.

Banskota, K. and Upadhyay, M. (1989): 'A Survey of Trekking Tourists in Langtang National Park.' Kathmandu, Nepal.

Bhatt, D.D. (1964): Plant Collection in Nepal, *Madrono,* 17, 5. January.

Byers, A.C. and Banskota, K. (1992): 'Environmental Impacts of Back Country; Tourism on Three Sides of Everest.' In *World Heritage 20 years Later,* Gland Switzerland and Cambridge, U. K.; IUCN.

Centre for Economic Development and Administration (CEDA), (1991): Work Force Survey of the Accommodation and Catering Industry in Nepal. Godde, P.M., Price, Zimmerman, F.M., (eds.) (2000):Tourism and Development in Mountain Regions:CAB International, Wallingford.

Environmental Resources Ltd., (ERL) (1989): Natural Resources Management for Sustainable Development: A Study of Feasible Policies, Institution and Investment Activities in Nepal with Special Emphasis on the Hills.' Draft Final Report. London: ERL.

Friend, J. (1983): *Trek Tourism Energy and Ecologically Related Impact within the World's Deepest Value,* Tasmania, Australia: Centre for Environmental Studies, University of Tasmania.

Grung, H.B. (1990): *Environmental Management in Mountain Tourism in Nepal,* ESCAP, Bangkok.

Haimendrof, C. Von-Furer. (1984): *The Sherpas Transform: Social Change in the Buddhist Society of Nepal,* New Delhi: Sterling Publishers.

Hunter, C. and Green, H. (1995): *Tourism and Environment: A Ssustainable Relationship,* Routledge, London.

Lama, W. and Sherpa, A.(1994). Tourism Development Plan for the Makalu Base Camp Trek and the Upper Barun Valley, Revised Draft report, Makalu Barun Conservation Project, February.

Lama, W. and Sherpa, A. (1995): Tourism Management Plan for the Upper Barun Valley Report 24, The Makalu Barun National Park and Conservation Area. Department of National Parks and Wildlife Conservation and the Woodland Mountain Institute.

Lama, W. (1991): Tourism Study Arun III., Management of Basinwide Environmental Impact Study, Draft Report, King Mahendra Trust for Nature Conservation.

Mountain Agenda, (1999): Mountains of the World; Tourism and Sustainable Mountain Development, Centre for Development and Environment, University of Berne

Nepal, S.K. (1999): Tourism-Induced Environmental Changes in the Nepalese Himalayas: A Comparative Analysis of the Everest

Annapurna, and Mustang Reigons. Ph. D. Dissertation, Faculty of Natural Science, Uiversity of Berne, Switzerland.

Nepal Tourism Statistics, 2007, Government of Nepal, Ministry of Culture, Tourism and Civil Aviation, Singh Durbar, Kathmandu, Nepal.

Odell, M.J. 1998): "The Challenges for Global Conservation, Protected Area Management, Eco-Tourism and Local People" in *Sustainability in Mountain tourism:Prospective for the Himalayan Countries,* (eds.) East, P. Luger, K. Inmann, K. Book Fait India, Studien Verlag, Innsbruk.

Rabinson, D. W. (1993): Socio-cultural Impacts of Mountain Tourism on Nepal's Sagarmatha World Heritage Site: Implication for Sustainable tourism.' In *World Heritage 20 years Later,* compiled by Jim Trorsell, Gland, Switzerland and Cambridge, U.K.: IUCN.

Smeral, E. (1996): Importance and Development of Austria's Alpine Tourism Industry, In K. Weiermair (ed.) Proceedings University of Innsbruck, pp. 2–11.

Government of Nepal, National Planning Commission, Singh Durbar, Kathmandu, Nepal.

Upadhyay, M. P. (1984):.Enviromental Impact of Mountain Ecosystem by Trekkers and Mountainers: Mt. Everest Trek Route Survey Report.' Kathmandu; Nepal; NIDS.

Uprety, P. R. (2002): Impact of Tourist industry in Nepal, *Telegraph Weekly.,* Kathmandu, Nepal

World Travel and Tourism Council (WTTC), (1999): *Travel and Tourism's Economic Impact,* Brussels, Belgium.

10

GARCH Error Based ARIMA Forecast for GDP in Sri Lanka

CHANDAN KUMAR MUKHOPADHYAY* & AMIT KUNDU**

Abstract

ARIMA (4,1,8) Model has been estimated as the univariate process for GDP series in Sri Lanka for the period 1970-2005. The model has been used for generating one period ahead forecasts for the GDP series. The forecasts are not "efficient" because of heteroscedasticity of residual. GARCH (1,1) Model has then been estimated and used for generating one period ahead forecasts for the GDP series. The forecasts adequately capture volatility of GDP series and are found to be "efficient".

Key Words: ACF, ARIMA, ARMA, PACF, ARCH, GARCH.

* Professor, Department of Economics, North Bengal.

** Registered Ph.D. Scholar, Department of Economics, North Bengal University.

Introduction

Autoregressive Integrated Moving Average (ARIMA) model was introduced by Box and Jenkins in 1960s for forecasting a variable. ARIMA method is an extrapolation method for forecasting and, like any other such method, it requires only the historical time series data on the variable under forecasting. This is one of the sophisticated extrapolation methods, since it incorporates the features of all other methods. However, it does not require the investigator to choose the initial values of any variable and values of various parameters a priori. Further it is robust to handle any data pattern. As one would expect, this is quite a difficult model to develop and apply as it involves transformation of the variable, identification of the model, estimation through non linear method, verification of the model and derivation of forecasts.

The paper presents an attempt for estimating an ARIMA model for GDP in the economy of Sri Lanka and using it for one period ahead forecasting.

Theoretical Basis of ARIMA Model:

The publication by Box and Jenkins of Time Series Analysis: Forecasting and Control ushered in new generation of forecasting tools. Popularly known as the Box-Jenkins methodology, but technically known as the ARIMA methodology, the emphasis of these methods is not on constructing single-equation or simultaneous–equation models but on analyzing the probabilistic, or stochastic, properties of economic time series on their own under the philosophy of letting the data speak for themselves.

Unlike the regression models, in which Y_t is explained by k regressors, X_1 , X_2, X_3, ...,X_k, the BJ-type time series models allow Y_t to be explained by past, or lagged, values of Y_t itself and stochastic error terms, For this reason, ARIMA models are sometimes called atheoretic models because these are not derived from any economic theory-while economic theories are often the basis of simultaneous-equation models.

Let $\{Y_t\}$ be a time series sequence for t = 1,....T. If we model Yt as

$$Y_t - \delta = \alpha_1 (Y_{t-1} - \delta) + u_t$$

where δ is the mean of Y and where ut ~ i i d N (0, $\sigma^2\varepsilon$), then we say that Yt follows a first order autoregressive, or AR(1). Here the value of Y at time t depends on its value in the previous time period and a random term. In other words, this model says that the forecast value of Y at time t is simply some proportion (α1) of its value at time (t-1) plus a random shock or disturbance at time t. Again the values are expressed around their mean values.

But if we consider this model,

$$Y_t - \delta = \alpha_1 (Y_{t-1} - \delta) + \alpha_2 (Y_{t-2} - \delta) + u_t$$

then we say that Y_t follows a second order autoregressive, or AR(2) process.

In general we can have

$$Y_t - \delta = \alpha_1 (Y_{t-1} - \delta) + a_2 (Y_{t-2} - \delta) + ...+ ap (Y_{t-p} - d) + u_t$$

in which case Yt is a *p*th- order autoregressive, or AR(p), process.

The AR process just discussed is not the only mechanism that may have generated Y. Suppose we model Y_t as follows:

$$Y_t = \mu + \beta_1 u_{t-1} + v_t$$

where μ is a constant and u_t, as before, is the white noise stochastic error term. Here Y at time t is equal to a constant plus a moving average of the current and past error terms. Thus, in the present case, we say that Y_t follows a first-order moving average, or an MA (1), process. But if Y_t follows the expression

$$Y_t = \mu + \beta_1 u_{t-1} + \beta_2 u_{t-2} + v_{1t}$$

then it is an MA(2) process. More generally,

$$Y_t = \mu + \beta_1 u_{t-1} + \beta_2 u_{t-2} +.......+ \beta_q u_{t-q} + v_{2t}$$

is an MA(q) process. In short, a moving average process is simply a linear combination of white noise error terms.

Of course, it is quite likely that Y possesses characteristics of both AR and MA and is, therefore, ARMA. Thus, Y_t follows an ARMA (1,1) process if it can be written as

$$Y_t = \theta + \alpha_1 Y_{t-1} + \beta_1 u_{t-1} + w_t$$

where θ presents the constant term.

In general, in an ARMA(p,q) process, there will be p autoregressive and q moving average terms.

Economic time series are usually nonstationary, since these are integrated. These need first order differencing for attaining stationarity. If a time series is integrated of order 1, its first differences are I(0), and it is stationary. Similarly, if a time series is I(2), its second difference is I(0). In general, if a time series is I(d), after differencing it d times we obtain an I(0) series.

Therefore, if we have to difference a time series d times to make it stationary and then apply the ARMA(p,q) model to it, we say that the original time series is ARIMA(p,d,q). It is then an autoregressive integrated moving average time series, where p denotes the number of autoregressive terms, d represents the number of times the series has to be differenced before it becomes stationary, and q is the number of moving average terms.

ARIMA Structure

The Box-Jenkins (BJ) Methodology

The ARIMA structure of a stationary variable may be obtained through the following procedure consisting of four separate steps.

Step 1. Identification. This relates to finding out the appropriate values of p,d and q. The correlogram and partial correlogram may be an aid in this task.

Step 2. Estimation. Having identified the appropriate p and q values, the next stage is to estimate the parameters of the autoregressive and moving average terms included in the model.

Step 3. Diagnostic checking. Having chosen a particular ARIMA model, and having estimated its parameters, one needs to examine whether the chosen model fits the data reasonably well, for it is possible that another ARIMA model might do the job as well. This is why Box-Jenkins ARIMA modeling is more an art than a science.

Step 4. Forecasting. One of the reasons for the popularity of the ARIMA modeling is its success in forecasting. In many cases, the forecasts obtained by this method are more reliable than those obtained from the traditional econometric modeling, particularly for short term forecast.

ARCH Model

In the estimation of any ARIMA model the variance of the disturbance term is assumed to be homoscedastic. But in some cases variance of the error term is not a function of an independent variable but instead varies over time in a way that depends on how large the errors were in the past. As a matter of fact, many econometric time series exhibit periods of unusually large volatility followed by periods of relative tranquity. In such circumstances, the assumption of homoscedasticity is inappropriate. It is particular kind of heteroscedasticity in which the variance of the regression error depends on the volatility of the errors in the recent past. Engle suggested the use of Autoregressive Conditional Heteroscedasticity (ARCH) model to take care of such heteroscedasticity in order to raise the efficiency of forecasts.

Let us consider the estimation of an ARMA (1,1) model

$$Y_t = \beta_0 + \beta_1 Y_{t-1} + \beta_2 u_{t-1} + v_t \qquad (1)$$

A second equation then relates the variance of the error term to the amount of volatility observed in the recent periods such that

$$\gamma^2_t = \alpha_0 + \alpha_1 \varepsilon_{2t-1} \quad (2)$$

Eqn (2) means that variance of et (?2t) has two components – a constant and last period's volatility which is modeled as last period's squared residual (ARCH term). By taking this information about the conditional heteroscedasticity of et in account, one can obtain more efficient estimates of β_0, β_1 and β_2 in eqn(1).

Since the variance of et in eqn(2) depends only on last period's volatility, this model is referred to as ARCH(1). More generally, the variance could depend on any number of lagged volatilities. Consequently, ARCH(p) model is

$$\gamma^2_t = \alpha_0 + \alpha_1\varepsilon^2_{t-1} + \alpha_2\varepsilon^2_{t-2} + \text{------} + \alpha_p\varepsilon^2_{t-p} \quad (3)$$

GARCH Model

Equation (3) can be recognized as a distributed lag model for γ^2_t. Many of the lagged values of ε^2_t can be replaced with one or two lagged values of γ^2_t. This leads to the Generalized Autoregressive Conditional Heteroscedasticity (GARCH) model.

The simplest GARCH model is the GARCH (1,1) model.

$$\gamma^2_t = \alpha_0 + \alpha_1\varepsilon^2_{t-1} + \Phi_1\gamma^2_{t-1} \quad (4)$$

As long as Φ1 <1, eqn(4) can be written as

$$\gamma^2_t = \alpha_0/1 - \Phi_1 + \alpha_1 \sum_{j=1}^{\infty} \Phi_1^{j-1} \gamma^2_{t-j} \quad (5)$$

Eqn(5) indicates that the variance to-day depends on all past volatilities, but with geometrically declining weights.

In general, there may be any number of ARCH terms and any number of GARCH terms. Consequently, the GARCH (p,q) model becomes

$$\gamma^2_t = \alpha_0 + \alpha_1\varepsilon^2_{t-1} + \alpha_2\varepsilon^2_{t-2} + \text{------} + \alpha_p\varepsilon^2_{t-p} + \Phi_1\gamma^2_{t-1} + \text{--------} + \Phi_q\gamma^2_{t-q} \quad (6)$$

$$= \alpha_0 + \alpha_1 \sum_{i=1}^{b} \alpha_1 \varepsilon^2_{t-i} + \sum_{i=1}^{q} \Phi_i \gamma^2_{t-i}$$

Data

The study involves the use of annual data set for GDP in Sri Lanka. The data cover the period running from 1970 to 2005. The data have been collected from various issues of IFS (International Financial Statistics) where the base period is 2000.

Building ARIMA Model for GDP Data and Forecasting

To fit an ARIMA model requires a sufficiently large data set. In this study, we used the data for GDP for the period 1970 to 2005. The model identification needs examination of stationarity of the series concerned.

STATIONARITY:

The ACF and PACF of the GDP data set are being presented through the Figure-1. It is observed from the Figure-1 that

(i) the ACF exhibits a dying-out pattern for the spikes,

(ii) there exists only one single spike at lag one.

These observations indicate that the GDP series is non-stationary and needs differencing. The ACF and PACF of the first differenced series of GDP are being given by the Figure-2.

The Figure-2 shows that

(i) the ACF is free from the dying-out pattern of spikes, and

(ii) the PACF does not contain any significant spike at lag one.

These observations testify for the stationarity of the first differenced GDP series. Consequently the GDP series is I (1) and d=1.

Figure - 1
Correlogram of GDP at Level Data

Sample: 1970 2005
Included observations: 36

Autocorrelation / Partial Correlation

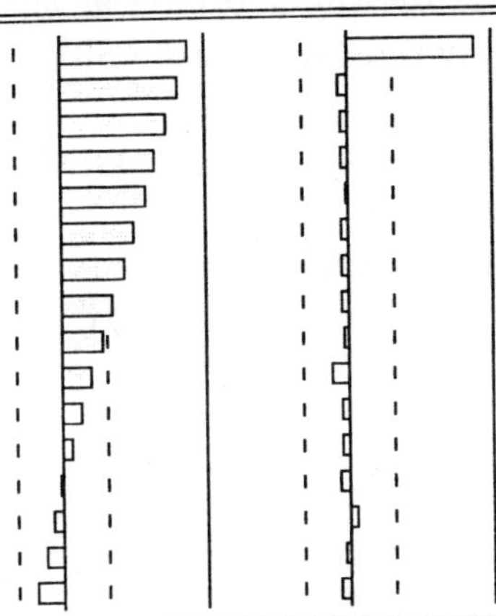

	AC	PAC	Q-Stat	Prob
1	0.924	0.924	33.401	0.000
2	0.845	-0.066	62.124	0.000
3	0.764	-0.055	86.295	0.000
4	0.682	-0.049	106.16	0.000
5	0.605	-0.015	122.30	0.000
6	0.527	-0.055	134.96	0.000
7	0.450	-0.047	144.49	0.000
8	0.374	-0.043	151.33	0.000
9	0.301	-0.038	155.90	0.000
10	0.217	-0.129	158.38	0.000
11	0.136	-0.045	159.40	0.000
12	0.058	-0.052	159.59	0.000
13	-0.019	-0.068	159.61	0.000
14	-0.077	0.056	159.98	0.000
15	-0.129	-0.032	161.06	0.000
16	-0.180	-0.063	163.29	0.000

Figure - 2
Correlogram of GDP at 1st Difference

Sample: 1970 2005
Included observations: 35

Autocorrelation / Partial Correlation

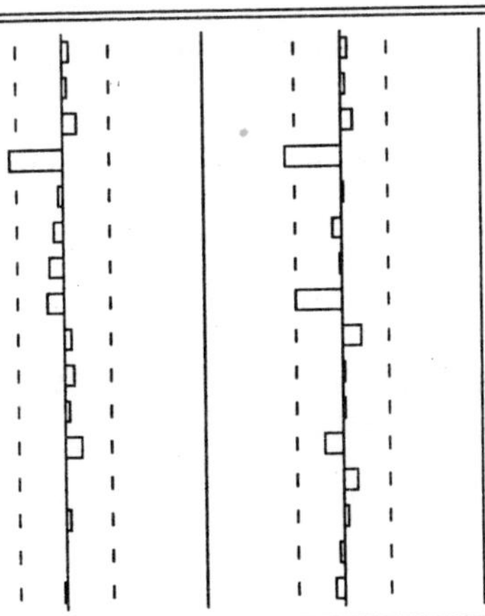

	AC	PAC	Q-Stat	Prob
1	0.048	0.048	0.0866	0.769
2	0.041	0.039	0.1525	0.927
3	0.099	0.096	0.5515	0.907
4	-0.398	-0.413	7.1593	0.128
5	-0.032	0.013	7.2041	0.206
6	-0.077	-0.062	7.4698	0.280
7	-0.107	-0.011	7.9990	0.333
8	-0.128	-0.338	8.7850	0.361
9	0.052	0.136	8.9195	0.445
10	0.067	0.019	9.1504	0.518
11	0.026	0.023	9.1856	0.605
12	0.128	-0.140	10.101	0.607
13	0.005	0.105	10.103	0.686
14	0.026	0.029	10.145	0.751
15	-0.002	-0.025	10.145	0.810
16	-0.019	-0.065	10.171	0.858

Identification of the Model:

AR(p) Structure:

It is further observed from the Figure-2 that

(i) the PACF contains two significant spikes. One occurs at lag 4 while the other occurs at lag 8,

(ii) the ACF contains only one significant spike at lag 4.

These indicate that the first differenced GDP (ΔY_t) series defines an AR(4) structure.

Consequently, the estimable AR (4) model is

$$\Delta Y_t = \alpha + \beta \Delta Y_{t-4} + u_t \qquad (7)$$

Results of Estimation

The estimated equation is as follows:

$$\Delta Y_t = 0.090018 - 0.399407\, \Delta Y_{t-4} \qquad (8)$$

S.E. (0.015167) (0.166463)

t-Stats (5.935112) (-2.399375)

Prob. (0.0000) (0.0231), R_2 = 0.165636, DW= 1.789285, F= 5.757001

Findings:

The equation (8) shows that

(i) $\hat{\beta}$ is found be significant at 5% level,

(ii) $\hat{\alpha}$ is significant at 1% level,

(iii) the equation is free from autocorrelation since DW=1.789285.

Figure – 3
Correlogram of Residual of Eqation-8

Sample: 1970 2005
Included observations: 31

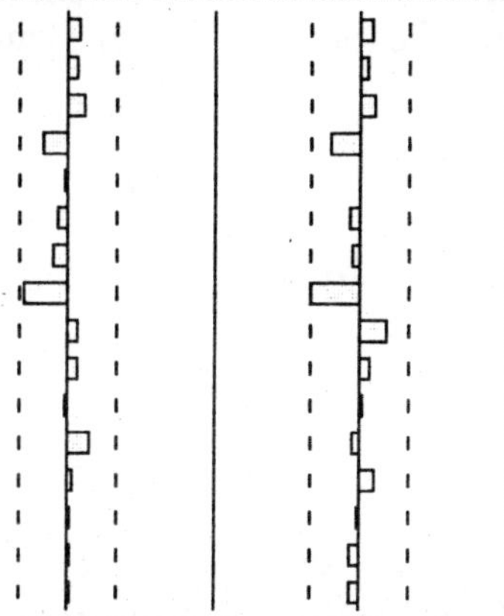

Autocorrelation / Partial Correlation (lag)	AC	PAC	Q-Stat	Prob
1	0.098	0.098	0.3250	0.569
2	0.063	0.054	0.4637	0.793
3	0.115	0.105	0.9449	0.815
4	-0.179	-0.207	2.1598	0.706
5	-0.018	0.008	2.1731	0.825
6	-0.064	-0.058	2.3393	0.886
7	-0.102	-0.046	2.7871	0.904
8	-0.312	-0.350	7.1111	0.525
9	0.074	0.193	7.3636	0.599
10	0.071	0.075	7.6064	0.667
11	-0.011	0.018	7.6130	0.747
12	0.148	-0.046	8.7946	0.720
13	0.040	0.098	8.8842	0.782
14	0.023	-0.013	8.9172	0.836
15	0.010	-0.064	8.9234	0.881
16	0.009	-0.076	8.9292	0.916

MA(q) Structure:

The ACF and PACF of the residuals of the equation (8) are being plotted in Figure-3. The Figure-3 indicates that

(i) the ACF is marked by a singular significant spike at lag 8,

(ii) the PACF contains one significant spike at lag 8

These observations testify for MA (8) structure for ΔY_t. Consequently, the estimable MA (8) model is

$$\Delta u_t = \partial + \gamma \Delta u_{t-8} + v_t \qquad (9)$$

Results of estimation

The estimated equation is as follows:

$$\Delta u_t = -0.000426 - 0.355612\, \Delta u_{t-8} \qquad (10)$$

S.E.	(0.013519)	(0.214305)
t-Stats	(-0.031502)	(-1.659379)
Prob.	(0.9752)	(0.1119)

, $R^2 = 0.115921$, DW= 1.834467, F= 2.753537

Findings:

The estimated equation (10) shows that

(i) $\gamma^\wedge$ is found be significant at 10% level,

(ii) the equation is free from autocorrelation since DW=1.834467

These testify for the justification of MA(8) structure for ΔY_t.

ARIMA (4,1,8) model

ΔY_t, therefore, consists of ARIMA(4,1,8) structure and the relevant estimable model is

$$\Delta Y_t = \alpha + \beta \Delta Y_{t-4} + \Delta u_{t-8} + v_t \quad (11)$$

Results of Estimation

The estimated equation is as follows:

$\Delta Yt =$	0.112024	$- 0.709029 \Delta Y_{t-4}$	$- 0.567504 u_{t-8}$	(12)
S.E.	(0.020599)	(0.218223)	(0.257132)	
t-Stats	(5.438337)	(-3.249102)	(-2.207055)	
Prob.	(0.0000)	(0.0040)	(0.0392)	

R^2 =0.348771, DW=1.645927, F=5.355571

Findings from the Equation (12):

The estimated equation (12) shows that

(i) $\alpha^\wedge$ is significant at 1% level,

(ii) $\beta^\wedge$ is found be significant at 5% level,

(iii) $\gamma^\wedge$ is found be significant at 10% level,

(iv) the equation is free from autocorrelation since DW=1.645927,

(v) the equation is good fit since F-statistic is significant at 1% level.

Consequently, it appears that Yt is generated by an ARIMA (4,1,8) process. This equation can be used for making forecasts for the GDP in Sri Lanka.

ARIMA (4,1,8) Forecasts for Y_t

ARIMA (4, 1, 8) model as given by the equation (12) has been used for generating one period ahead forecast for Y_t. The time plots of GDP (Y_t) and the corresponding forecast (Y_f) are being presented through the Figure-4. Y_f is found to be almost coinciding with Y_t over the period concerned.

Figure - 4

The Time Plots Of The GDP Level Data and the Corresponding ARIMA (4,1,8) Forecasts

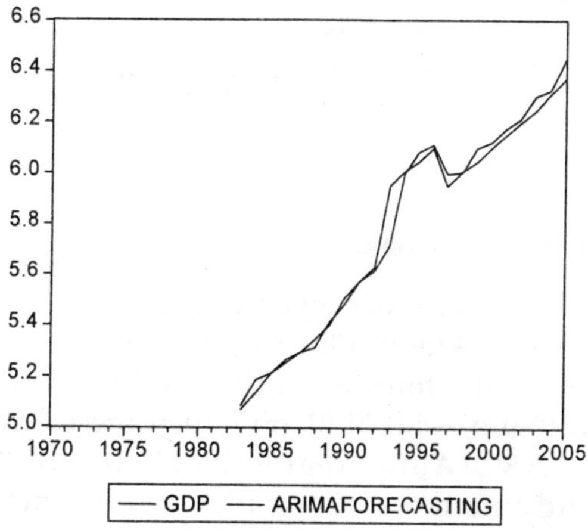

The Figure-4 shows that

(i) the ARIMA (4,1,8) forecasts almost coincide with the GDP level data until 1992,

(ii) there exists an unusual volatility in the GDP level since 1993 to 1997. The forecasts fail to capture such volatility. The presence of such volatility can be identified through the observation of the time plot of forecast errors presented by the Figure-5.

(iii) GDP data set is marked by the absence of unusual volatility over the range 1998-2005. The forecast, over this period, almost coincide with the corresponding GDP level.

Figure-5

The Time Plot of Forecast Errors

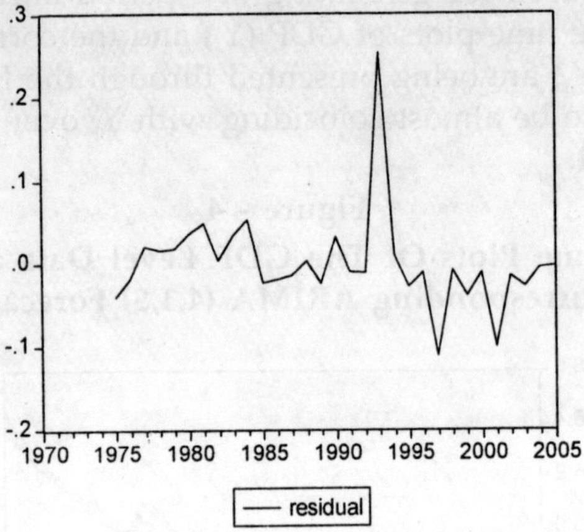

Efficiency of Forecasts:

Forecasts become efficient when there exists no more scope of ploughing back any information from the residuals to improve upon the forecast. If the residuals (e_t) are white noise such that $e_t \sim$ iid N (0, $\sigma^2\varepsilon$), then these errors would have no AR (Auto regressive) structure at all. Consequently, no more information can be obtained from the errors and the errors would not represent any significant loss of information.

The ACF and PACF of the residuals of ARIMA (4,1,8) equation (eqn12) are given by the Figure-6. The Figure-6 shows that both the ACF and PACF are free from any significant spike at any lag. Consequently, the residuals are generated by an ARIMA (0,0,0) process and offer no systematic and deterministic information for improving upon the forecast.

The forecasts become unbiased and and efficient if the forecast residuals are free from auto-correlation and heteroscedasticity. ARIMA (0,0,0) structure for the residuals indicates that residuals are free from autocorrelation. It, therefore, becomes imperative to examine if the residuals are heteroscedastic.

Figure – 6

Correlogram of Forecast Residual

Sample: 1970 2005
Included observations: 23

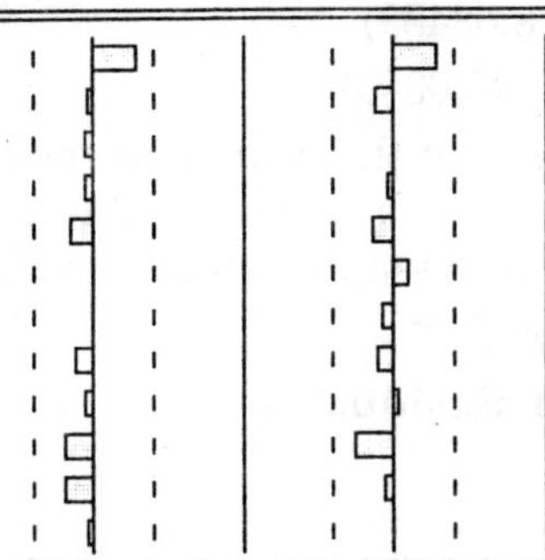

Autocorrelation	Partial Correlation		AC	PAC	Q-Stat	Prob
		1	0.288	0.288	2.1636	0.141
		2	-0.030	-0.122	2.1876	0.335
		3	-0.048	-0.003	2.2531	0.522
		4	-0.044	-0.035	2.3119	0.679
		5	-0.151	-0.146	3.0361	0.694
		6	0.006	0.103	3.0375	0.804
		7	-0.005	-0.069	3.0385	0.881
		8	-0.115	-0.113	3.5483	0.895
		9	-0.046	0.028	3.6351	0.934
		10	-0.190	-0.264	5.2378	0.875
		11	-0.185	-0.052	6.8778	0.809
		12	-0.030	0.008	6.9243	0.863

Heteroscedasticity of the Residuals:

The presence of high volatility followed by low volatility is indicative of heterocsedastic variance of the residuals. Consequently, the forecasts fail to be efficient. This necessitates the estimation of the equation (11) by taking care of heteroscedasticity of the residuals. This can be accomplished through the estimation of ARCH or GARCH Model.

ARCH(p) Structure for Forecast Errors

The ACF and PACF of the variance of the residuals are being presented through the Figure-7. The ACF and PACF are found to be free from any significant spike. However, the spike at lag 1 in the ACF and PACF, though not significant, may be taken as signifying ARCH (1) structure. Consequently, the estimable ARCH (1) equation is

$$h_t \;=\; \alpha \;+\; \rho e^2_{t-1} \;+\; \upsilon_t \qquad (13)$$

Estimation ARCH Model:

The estimated equation is as follows

$$h_t \;=\; 3.17E\text{-}14 + 0.171429e^2_{t-1} \qquad (14)$$

S.E.	(2.95E-14)	(0.009175)
z-stat	(1.072063)	(18.68483)
Prob	(0.2837)	(0.0000)

The equation (14) shows that the estimated coefficient is significant at even 1% level. Consequently the residual variance is ARCH (1) by nature and heteroscedastic.

Figure-7

Correlogram of Residual Square

Sample: 1970 2005
Included observations: 23

Autocorrelation	Partial Correlation		AC	PAC	Q-Stat	Prob
		1	0.329	0.329	2.8332	0.092
		2	-0.136	-0.274	3.3407	0.188
		3	-0.239	-0.111	4.9825	0.173
		4	-0.136	-0.046	5.5418	0.236
		5	-0.126	-0.157	6.0466	0.302
		6	-0.089	-0.067	6.3144	0.389
		7	0.047	0.042	6.3948	0.494
		8	0.288	0.226	9.5823	0.296
		9	0.117	-0.113	10.144	0.339
		10	-0.088	-0.028	10.487	0.399
		11	-0.070	0.079	10.724	0.467
		12	-0.163	-0.223	12.118	0.436

The Correlogram of The Residuals of The Equation(14)

The Correlogram of the residuals of the equation (14) is given by the Figure-8. It is observed from the figure that the residuals are free from significant spike at any lag. Consequently, the degree of moving average of the ARCH model is zero.

Figure-8

Correlogram of residual of the above equation (equation-14)

	AC	PAC	Q-Stat	Prob
1	0.046	0.046	0.2478	0.619
2	0.016	0.014	0.2767	0.871
3	0.008	0.006	0.2838	0.963
4	-0.089	-0.090	1.2407	0.871
5	0.042	0.050	1.4498	0.919
6	0.002	0.000	1.4502	0.963
7	-0.055	-0.055	1.8228	0.969
8	-0.031	-0.035	1.9441	0.983
9	0.048	0.063	2.2369	0.987
10	-0.030	-0.036	2.3507	0.993
11	0.070	0.063	2.9862	0.991
12	-0.040	-0.049	3.1981	0.994
13	-0.043	-0.026	3.4361	0.996
14	-0.073	-0.086	4.1451	0.995
15	-0.025	-0.002	4.2267	0.997
16	0.135	0.133	6.6683	0.979
17	-0.001	-0.016	6.6685	0.987
18	-0.003	-0.018	6.6701	0.993
19	-0.029	-0.023	6.7844	0.995
20	0.008	0.024	6.7941	0.997
21	-0.057	-0.077	7.2534	0.998
22	-0.010	-0.014	7.2675	0.999

GARCH (1,1) Model

In order to test for the presence of a 1st order GARCH term in the conditional variance, the following equation (15) is subject to estimation.

$$h_t = \alpha + \alpha_1 \varepsilon^2_{t-1} + \alpha_2 h_{t-1} + c_t \quad (15)$$

where h_t = residual variance.

Results of Estimation

The estimated equation is as follows:

$$h_t = 0.674720 + 6.05E{+}15\varepsilon^2 t{-}1 - 288.2676h_{t-1} \quad (16)$$

S.E.	(0.292203)	(2.23E+15)	(106.0772)
t-Statistic	(2.309075)	(2.720867)	(-2.717527)
Prob.	(0.0323)	(0.0136)	(0.0137)
R-squared	0.365804		
DW		1.727975	
F-stat		5.479599	

Findings:

It is observed from equation-16 that

(i) $\alpha\hat{}_1$ is significant at 1% level,

(ii) $\alpha\hat{}_2$ is also significant at 1% level,

(iii) DW = 1.727975 indicates that the estimation is free from autocorrelation.

These observations testify for the GARCH (1,1) structure of the residual variance.

Estimation of ARIMA (4,1,8) Equation With GARCH (1,1)

The estimated ARIMA (4,1,8) equation (eqn11) based on the GARCH(1,1) equation (eqn15) is given through the Table 1. The estimated equations are given by eqation-17 and equation-18.

Table-1

GARCH(1,1) ESTIMATION OF THE EQUATION(11)

Dependent Variable: GDPD
Method: ML - ARCH (Marquardt)
Sample(adjusted): 1983 2005
Included observations: 23 after adjusting endpoints
Convergence achieved after 1 iteration
Variance backcast: ON

	Coefficient	Std. Error	z-Statistic	Prob.
GDP4	-0.399406	1.58E-05	-25209.52	0.0000
RESIDUAL8	1.000000	1.59E-06	628872.2	0.0000
C	0.090018	8.55E-06	10525.55	0.0000
	Variance Equation			
C	3.11E-14	7.57E-14	0.410716	0.6813
ARCH(1)	0.150000	0.084746	1.769985	0.0767
GARCH(1)	0.600000	0.179778	3.337444	0.0008

R2	1.000000	Mean dependent var	0.059882
Ad R2	1.000000	S.D. dependent var	0.073985
S.E. of regression	2.54E-07	AIC	-27.17909
Sum squared resid	1.10E-12	SIC	-26.88287
Log likelihood	318.5595	F-statistic	3.72E+11
D-W stat	1.304278	Prob(F-statistic)	0.000000

The Estimated Equations

The estimated equations are

$$\Delta Y_t = 0.090018 - 0.399406\Delta Y_{t-1} + 1.000000\mu_{t-8} \quad (17)$$

S.E. (8.55E-06) (1.58E-05) (1.59E-06)

z-Statistic (10525.55) (-25209.52) (628872.2)

Prob. (0.0000) (0.0000) (0.0000)

$$h_t = 3.11E\text{-}14 + 0.150\Delta^2_{t-1} - 0.600h_{t-1} \quad (18)$$

S.E. (7.57E-14) (0.084746) (0.179778)

z-Statistic (0.410716) (1.769985) (3.337444)

Prob. (0.6813) (0.0767) (0.0008)

R-squared 1.000000, DW 1.304278, F-stat 3.72E+11

Findings From the Estimated equation (17):

It is observed from the estimated equation (17) that

(i) z- statistics of $\alpha\hat{}_1$ and $\alpha\hat{}_2$ are significant at 1% level.

(ii) R^2 =1 and Adjusted R^2 =1

(iii) Sum of square residuals is 1.10E-72

(iv) Log Likelihood Ratio is 318.5595.

All these observations indicate that the estimated equation (17) is good fit.

GRACH (1,1) Forecasts:

Figure-9 presents the time plots of GARCH (1,1) forecasts. The Figure-10 presents the time-plots of the GDP level data and the corresponding GARCH (1,1)error based ARIMA(4,1,8) forecasts. It is found that the forecast plot almost completely coincides with the GDP plot.

Figure-11 presents the time plots of GDP level data and the ARCH (1) error based ARIMA (4,1,8) forecasts. The volatility of the GDP series has not been completely captured by the forecasts based on ARCH (1) error. However this variability has been fully captured by GARCH (1,) forecasts. The time plot of the GARCH (1,1) forecasts errors is presented through the Figure-12. The variance of the forecast errors is the most minimum since the corresponding RMSE=3.18-E11. Forecasts errors almost collapse at zero level. As a result the GARCH (1,1) based ARIMA(4,1,8) forecasts become "efficient".

Figure-9

The Time Plot of GARCH Forecasting

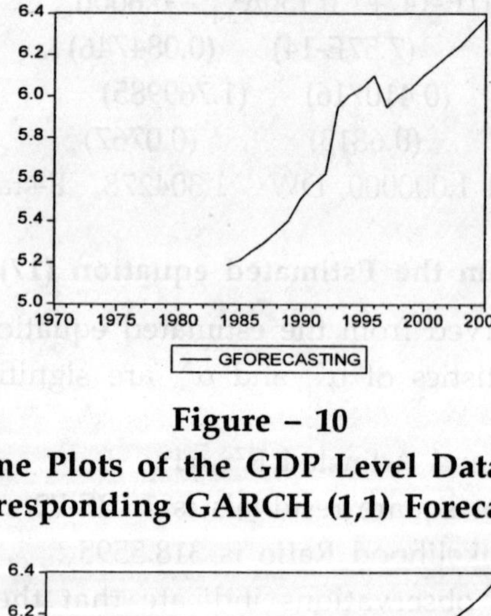

Figure – 10

The Time Plots of the GDP Level Data and the Corresponding GARCH (1,1) Forecasting

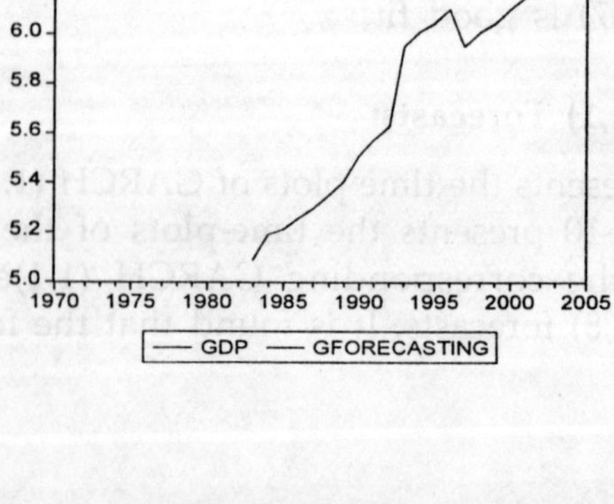

Figure - 11
The Time Plots of the GDP Level Data, ARIMA(4,1,8) and the Corresponding GARCH(1,1) Forecasting

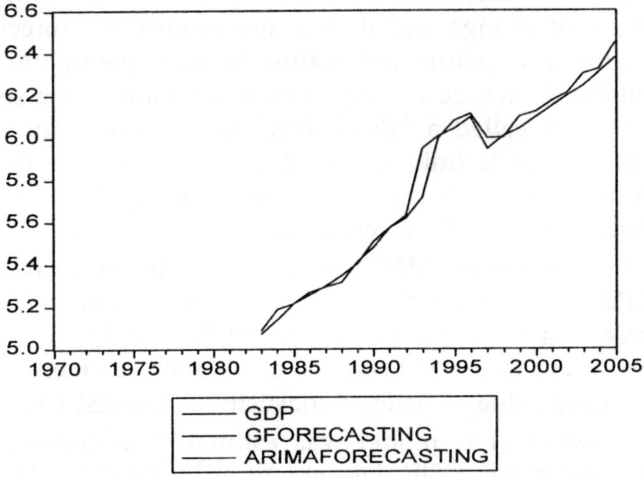

Figure-12
Time Plot of GRACH Forecasting Error

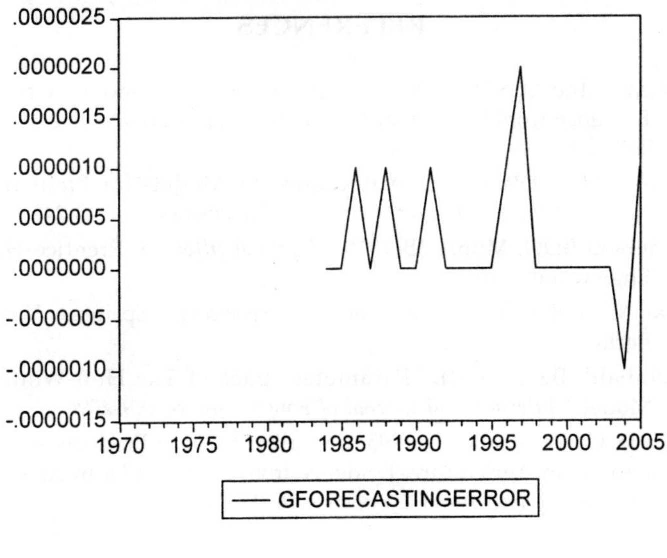

Conclusion

ARIMA model offers a good technique for predicting the magnitude of the variable. Its strength lies in the fact that the method is suitable for any time series with any pattern of change and it does not require the forecaster to choose a priori the value of any parameter. Its limitations include its requirement of a long time series. Often it is called a "Black Box" model. Like any other method, this technique also does not guarantee perfect forecasts. Nevertheless, it can successfully be used for forecasting long time series data.

In this study GDP was found to be generated by ARIMA (4,1,8) model and this model was used for forecasting GDP. However, the ARIMA (4,1,8) forecasts were found to be far from being efficient. The inefficiency was mainly due to heteroscedasticity of forecast residuals.

GARCH (1,1) model was estimated to capture the volatility in the GDP dataset. Accordingly GARCH (1,1) forecasts were have been found to be "efficient". GARCH (1,1) model, therefore, appears to be the appropriate model for forecasting GDP in the economy of Sri Lanka.

REFERENCES

Abhayaratne, A.S.P., 1996. Foreign Trade and Economic Growth Evidence from Sri Lanka, 1960-1992. *Applied Economics Letters* 3, 567-570.

Akaike, H., 1969. Fitting Autoregressive Models for Prediction. *Annals of the Institute of Statistical Mathematics* 21, 243-247.

Anderson BDO, Moore JB(1979). *Optimal filtering*. Prentice-Hall, Englewood Cliffs.

Aoki, M. (1987). *State Space Modeling of Time Series*. Springer- Verlag, Berlin.

Archibald, B.C. (1900). "Parameter Space of The Holt-Winters' Model." *International Journal of Forecasting*, 6, 199-209.

Arnade, C., Vasavada, U., 1995. Causality Between Productivity and Exports in Agriculture: Evidence from Asia and Latin America. *Journal of Agricultural Economics* 46, 174-186.

Assimakopoulos V, Nikolopoulos K (2000). "The Theta Model: a Decomposition Approach to Forecasting." *International Journal of Forecasting*, 16, 199-209.

Bahmani-Oskooee, M., Mohtad, H., Shabsigh, G., 1991. 'Export, Growth and Causality in LDCs: a Re-examination'. *Journal of Development Economics* 36, 405-415.

Blalock, G., Gertler, P.J., 2004. 'Learning from Exporting Revisited in A Less Developed Setting'. *Journal of Development Economics* 75, 397-416.

Boero, G. and Marrocu, E,: '2002, The Performance of Non-linear Exchange Rate Models: A Forecasting Comparison', *Journal of Forecasting* 21, 512-3-542.

Bowerman BL, O'Connel RT, Koehler AB (2005). *Forecasting Time Series and Regression: An Applied Approach.* Thomson Brooks/ Cole, Belmont CA.

Box, George, and Gwilym Jenkins. *Time Series Analysis, Forecasting, and Control*. San Francisco: Holden Day, 1976.

Box, G.E.P. and Jenkins, G.M.: 1970, *Time Series Analysis, Forecasting and Control,* Holden- Day, San Francisco.

Brailsford, T. J. and Faff, R.W. (1996): "An Evaluation of Volatility Forecasting Techniques", *Journal of Banking and Finance,* 20, 419-438

Brannas, K. and De Gooijer, J. G.: 1994, 'Autoregressive- Asymmetric Moving Average Model for Business Cycle Data', *Journal of Forecasting* 13, 529-544.

Brockwell, P.J., Davis, R.A. (1991). *Time series: Theory and Methods.* Springer-Verlag, New York, 2nd edition.

Chatfield C, Yar M (1991). "Prediction Intervals for Multiplicative3 Holt-Winters." *International Journal of Forecasting*, 7, 31-37.

Choi, I., 1993. 'Asymptotic Normality of The Least-Squares Estimates for Higher-Order Autoregressive Integrated Process with Some Applications'. *Econometric Theory* 9, 263-282.

Clements, M.P. and Hendry, D.F.: 1999, *Forecasting Non-stationary Economic Time Series,* MIT Press, Cambridge, MA.

Clements, M. P., Franses, P.H. and Swanson, N.R.: 2004, 'Forecasting Economic and Financial Time-Series with Non-linear Models', *International Journal of Forecasting* 20, 169-183

Deutsch, M., Granger, C.W.J. and Terasvirta, T.: 1994, 'The Combination of Forecasts Using Changing Weights', *International Journal of Forecasting* 10, 47-57.

Diebold, F., and R. Mariano (1995): "Comparing Predictive

Accuracy". *Journal of Business and Economic Statistics,* 13, 253-263.

Enders, Walter. "ARIMA and Cointegration Tests of Purchasing Power Parity." *Review of Economics and Statistics* 70 (Agu. 1988), 504-08.

Gardner Jr, E.S., McKenzie E (1985). "Forecasting Trends in Time Series." Management Science, 31(100, 1237-1246.

Garner Jr, E.S. (1985). "Exponential Smoothing: The State of The Art." *Journal of Forecasting,* 4, 1-28.

Goodrich RL (2000). "The Forecast Methodology." *International Journal of Forecasting,* 16(4), 533-535.

Granger, C.W.J., 1963. "Economic Processes Involving Feedback". *Information and Control* 6, 28-48.

Granger, C.W. J. and Pesaran, M.H.: 2000, "Economic and statistical measures of forecast accuracy", *Journal of Forecasting* 19, 537-560.

Granger, C.W. J. and Terasvirta, T.: 1991, 'Experiments in Modeling Non-linear Relationships Between Time Series', in M. Casdagli and S. Eubank(eds), *Nonlinear Modeling and Forecasting,* Addison-Wesley, Redwood City, pp. 189-197.

Hamilton, J.D.: 1994, *Time Series Analysis,* Princeton University Press, Princeton, NJ.

Hannan EJ, Rissanen J (1982). "Recursive Estimation of Mixed Autoregressive-Moving Average Order." *Biometrika,* 69(1), 81-94.

Harvey, A.C. (1989): *Forecasting, Structural Time Series and Kalman Filter*. Cambridge University Press.

Harvey, D., S. Leybourene, and S. Newbold (1997): "Testing the Equality of Prediction Mean Squared Errors". *International Journal of Forecasting,* 13, 281-291.

Hendry DF (1997). "The Econometrics of Macroeconomic Forecasting." *The Economic Journal,* 107(444), 1330-1357.

Hendry, D.F. and Clements, M.P.: 2003, 'Economic Forecasting: Some Lessons From Recent Research', *Economic Modeling* 20, 301-329.

Hyndman, R.J., Billah, B. (2003). Unmasking the theta method." *International Journal of Forecasting,* 19(2), 287-290.

Hyndman, R.J., Koehler, A.B., Snyder, R.D. (2008). *Forecasting with Exponential Smoothing: The State Space Approach.* Springer.

Hyndman RJ, Koehler AB, Snyder RD, Grose S (2002). "A state Space Framework for Automatic Forecasting Using Exponential Smoothing Methods." *International Journal of Forecasting,* 18(3), 439-454.

Islam, M.N., 1998. 'Export Expansion and Economic Growth: Testing for Cointegration and Causality'. *Applied Economics* 30,415-425.

Lall, S. 1996. *Learning from the Asian Tigers*. Macmillan, London.

Lall, S., 2004. 'Reinventing Industrial Strategy: The Role of Government Policy in Building Industrial Competitiveness'. Working Paper (-2004), Trade and Industrial Policy Strategies, Johannesburg.

Liu, L.M. (1989). "Identification of Seasonal ARIMA Models Using a Filtering Method." *Communications in Statistics,* Part A : Theory & Methods, 18, 2279-2288.

Maddala, D.S.: 1977, *Econometrics,* McGraw-Hill, New York.

Makridakis, S. Wheelwright, S.C., Hyndman, R.J. (1998). *Forecasting: Methods and Applications.* John Wiley & Sons, New York, 3rd edition.

Melard, G., Pasteels, J.M. (2000). 'Automatic ARIMA Modeling Including Intervention, Using Time Series Expert Software." *International Journal of Forecasting,* 16, 497-508.

McLeod, A., and W. Li, "Diagnostic Checking ARMA Time Series Models Using Squared Residual Correlations." *Journal of Time Series Analysis* 4, (1983), 269-73.

Mincer, J. and Zarnowitz, V.: 1969, 'The Evaluation of Economic Forecasts', in J. Mincer (ed.), *Economic Forecasts and Expectations,* National Bureau of Economic Research, New York.

Ord, J.K., Lowe, S. (1996). "Automatic Forecasting." *American Statistician,* 50(1), 88-94.

Petrucelli, J., and S. Woolford. "A Threshold AR(1) Model." *Journal of Applied Probability* 21(1984), 270-86.

Pindyck, R.S, D.L. Rubinfeld (2001) *Econometric Models and Economic Forecasts* (4th Edn), Irwin-McGraw-Hill, N. York.

Sharma, S.C., Dhakal, D., 1994. 'Causal Analysis Between Exports and Economic Growth in Developing Countries'. *Applied Economics* 26, 1145-1157.

Siegel, S. and Castellan, N.J. (1988): *Nonparametric Statistics.* McGraw-Hill: London.

Watson, M. W. and Engle, R.F.: (1985) 'Testing for Regression Coefficient Stability with a Stationary AR(1) Alternative', *Review of Economics and Statistics* 67, 341-346.

West, Mike, and Jeff Harrison. *Bayesian Forecasting and Dynamic Models.* New York: Springer-Verlag, 1989.

West, K.D.: 2006, 'Forecast Evaluation', in G. Elliott, C. W. J. Granger and A. Timmermann (eds.), *Handbook of Economic Forecasting,* Elsevier, Amsterdam.

11

A Mathematical Exposition of the Lechatelier Principle for the Determination of Short- and Long-Run Price Elasticity Relationship in Factor and Commodity Markets

TAMASH RANJAN MAJUMDAR*

Abstract

The present paper provides a mathematical exposition of the LeChatelier Principle for the determination of the relationship between short-and long-run price elasticities for the factor-demand and the commodity-supply functions derived from profit maximization hypothesis. The analysis shows that the long-run price elasticity with fewer restrictions on variables than in the short-run is at least as large as the short-run price elasticity.

Key Words: LeChatelier Principle, Restricted Profit Function, Hotelling's Lemma, First-order Envelope Property.

---

* Lecturer, Department of Economics, North Bengal University.

Introduction

The idea that long-run demand and supply are typically more elastic than short-run demand and supply is common in economics. An intuitive explanation of this widely observed phenomenon is that, in the long-run, the agents can exercise greater freedom of action as they operate under fewer constraints and this will result in the above conjectures about short run and long run. The LeChatelier principle proves this intuitive proposition rigorously. This name is derived after noticing the similar tendency of thermodynamic system to exhibit the same types of responses. This principle has its first application in economics in the neoclassical theory of the firm, where it is used for the study of factor-demand and commodity-supply behaviour in response to instantaneous rates of change in parameter values, such as wage rates and prices. However, this principle has been applied later on to a wide range of optimization problems outside the area of demand and supply theories. In addition, the basic LeChatelier principle has been extended to incorporate discrete changes in parameter values (Milgrom and Roberts,1990,1995).

The LeChatelier principle is originally due to French chemist Henri Louis LeChatelier who analysed the effects of additional constraints of thermodynamic systems. It is interesting to note that the first unconscious use of this principle has been made by Marshall in his analysis of conjectures about short run and long run. Paul Samuelson formally recognized that the mathematical structure of the LeChatelier principle in classical thermodynamics was similar to the maximization models in economics (Suen, Silberberg, Tseng, 1998). His use of this principle in economic optimization problems appeared first in his magnum opus *Foundations of Economic Analysis* (1947), in the context of unconstrained maximization of profits. It is important to note in this connection that this analysis was a part of his pioneering work on the method of comparative statics in economics. This method deals with constraints on maximizing behaviour. It seeks to explain changes in the equilibrium solution of an optimization problem (economic or thermodynamic) when parametric indices of exogeneous conditions change. It is worth noting here that Samuelson's first use of the LeChatelier principle was limited to infinitesimal price changes only as he considered smooth optimization problems. Subsequently, he showed that the principle also applied to problems in linear programming, where parameter changes could be discrete (Samuelson, 1948, 1960). Samuelson's use of the LeChatelier principle has proven to be a very powerful tool and found widespread use in modern economics. Indeed, the attempt for drawing analogy between neoclassical equilibrium economics and the thermodynamics goes back to Samuelson.

The Economics of the LeChatelier Principle : An Informal Analysis

It seems necessary at the initial stage to offer an informal analysis of the economics of the LeChatelier principle before we analyse it formally. Consider a simple two-variable input demand function, where the variables are capital and labour. Suppose now that the price of labour falls. In the short-run, if the capital input is fixed, the direct effect of the price change will be to lead to more labour being employed. In the long-run, changes (increase or decrease) in capital usage may occur which can lead to further increase in the use of labour by the profit maximizing firm. This analysis holds regardless of whether the two factors are substitutes or complementary.

We can offer some intuitive arguments to explain why labour demand should become more elastic when capital is adjusted. First suppose capital and labour are substitutes to each other in the sense that lowering the price of one decreases the demand for the other. Then in the long-run the firm will reduce its use of capital in response to the lower price of labour. Because the inputs are substitutes, reducing the amount of capital raises the use of labour, and this result in a further increase in labour's employment. Thus, the long-run adjustment of demand is greater than the short-run one. Now suppose that capital and labour are complementary to each other in the sense that lowering the price of one increases the demand for another. Then in the long-run, the firm will increase its use of capital in response to a reduction in the price of labour. As the inputs are complementary to each other, an increase in the use of capital would be followed by a commensurate rise in the use of labour, and this would again result in a further increase in the employment of labour. Thus, the long-run employment of labour again goes beyond the short-run equilibrium level.

Milgrom and Roberts (1996) note that these intuitive arguments amount to observing that the extra adjustments involved in long-run demand create a positive feedback that is missing from short-run demand. The feedback argument makes no appeal to small price changes, divisible inputs, convex production technologies, or competitive markets for the fixed input. A similar type of argument can also be made for explaining the relationship between the long-run and short-run supply elasticity- the firm will respond more to a price change in the long run since, by definition, it has more factors to adjust in the long-run than in the short-run (Varian, 1992). This is intuitively the economics involved with the LeChatelier principle.

The Mathematical Version of the LeChatelier Principle

Formally, the standard version of the LeChatelier principle might start with the following unconstrained optimization problem (Janison, 2006) :

$$\max y = f(x_1,..........,x_n) - \sum_{i=1}^{n} \alpha_i x_i \qquad (1)$$

where the Hessian of f is negative definite. Then if we let $x^*_{i,r}$ be the optimal value of the ith variable subject to r independent constraints (r = 1,2,..........,n), we have that

$$\frac{\partial x^*_{i.o}}{\partial \alpha_i} \leq \frac{\partial x^*_{i,1}}{\partial \alpha_i} \leq .... \leq \frac{\partial x^*_{i.n-i}}{\partial \alpha_i} \leq \frac{\partial x^*_{i.n}}{\partial \alpha_i} = 0............(2)$$

for all i = 1,2,.....................,n. In the above expression, $x^*_{i,0}$ represents the optimal value of the ith variable subject to no constraint. The term $x^*_{i,1}$ represents the optimal value of the ith variable subject to one constraint, $x^*_{i,2}$ represents the optimal value of subject to two constraints, and so on. Notice that the constraints are constructed so that the x^*_i are optimal regardless of the number of constraints. Notice that equation (2) represents that

$\frac{\partial x^*_i}{\partial \alpha_i}$ becomes smaller as the number of constraints on the optimal value of the variable increases.

Equation (2) gives the mathematical expression of the LeChatelier Principle. For the two-input case, the equation says that the optimal quantity of an input x_1 to the production function f will vary more with its price α_1 when the quantity of another input x_2 is allowed to vary than when the quantity of x_2 is fixed (at its original maximizing level). Given the fact that

$$\frac{\partial x^*_i}{\partial \alpha_i} < 0$$

that is to say, demand decreases with a rise in price, we also get the result that $\frac{\partial x^*_{i,0}}{\partial \alpha_i}$

is more negative than $\frac{\partial x^*_{i,1}}{\partial \alpha_i}$, an alternative version of the LeChatelier Principle. For the general n-variable case, equation (2) says that the value of demand reduction following a price increase can not be increased as additional constraints (i.e. additional fixed factors in this case) are introduced and may be decreased. Alternatively stated, the slope of the demand curve falls, as the number of constraints rises, or conversely, the slope of the demand curve without constraints rises. It is worth re-emphasising that the LeChatelier Principle as expressed by equation

(2) holds valid provided the Hessian matrix of the production function f is negative definite.

Short -Versus long- run profits

Having defined and interpreted the LeChatelier Principle mathematically, we now outline the formal proof of the LeChatelier results that elasticities of factor- demand and commodity-supply functions derived from profit maximization hypothesis are lower in the short-run than in the long- run. Assuming that the firm produces only one output, the profit function can be written as

$$\Pi(p,w) = \max_{x\geq 0}[py - wx]$$

$$= \max_{x\geq 0}[pf(x) - wx] \qquad \text{......(3)}$$

where $y = f(x)$ is the production function facing the firm, p is the (scalar) price of output (y), w is the vector of factor prices, and the inputs are measured by the (non-negative) vector $x = (x_1, \ldots, x_n)$.

Suppose that the input vector x is partitioned into two components with x^1 containing perfectly variable inputs and x^2 containing those inputs that are fixed or subject to some availability constraints. Thus we have

$$x = (x^1, x^2)$$

also we have $w = (w^1, w^2)$

where w^1 and w^2 are the vectors of prices of the variable and fixed inputs.

Now the short run profit function, also known as the restricted profit function, can be written as

$$\pi^s = \pi^s(p, w, x^2) \qquad \text{......(4)}$$

When all factors are variable, the firm will optimize in the choice of x^2. Hence the long run profit function only depends on the factor prices and the price of the output.

$$\pi^L = \pi^L(p, w)\text{.......................................}(5)$$

We can express this long-run function in terms of the short-run profit function in the following way. Let $x^2(p,w)$ be the optimal choice of the fixed factors, that is to say, $x^2(p,w)$ are solutions to the problem.

$$\pi(p,w) = \max_{x^2} \pi^s(p.w.x^2)\text{..........................}(6)$$

Then the long - run profit function can be written as

$$\pi^L(p,w) = \pi^s(p,w\ ,x^2(p,w))\text{........................}(7)$$

Hotelling's lemma implies

$$x_i^L\ (p,w) = x_i^s(p,w^1,x^2(p,w))\text{..............}(8)$$

This is the fundamental relationship between the short-run and long-run factor demands.

$$y^L(p,w) = y^s(p,w^1,x^2(p,w))\text{.........................}(9)$$

This is the fundamental identity between the short-run and long-run commodity supply functions.

Let us now see how we can use Hotelling's lemma (6) to derive the LeChatelier result relating to factor-demand elasticity. We differentiate equation (8) with respect to $w_1 \in w^1$ to obtain

$$\frac{\partial x_i^L}{\partial w_i} = \frac{\partial x_i^s}{\partial w_i} + \left(\frac{\partial x_i^s}{\partial x_j}\right)\left(\frac{\partial x_j}{\partial w_i}\right)\text{....................................}(10)$$

This equation reveals that the slope of the short-run and long-run factor demand functions differ by a term representing the product of two effects: the change in x_j resulting from a change in w_i , and the change in x_i that would be induced by a (parametric) change in x_j. This product is easily seen to represent the marginal effect on x_i of allowing x_j (the fixed factor) to vary as w_i changes. Now to derive the sign of this product term algebraically, we consider first the following reciprocity condition,

$$\frac{\partial x_i}{\partial w_j} = \frac{\partial x_j}{\partial w_i} \text{...}(11)$$

which could be obtained using Young's theorem. Next we differentiate (8) with respect to w_j to get

$$\frac{\partial x_i}{\partial w_j} = \left(\frac{\partial x_i^s}{\partial x_j}\right)\left(\frac{\partial x_j}{\partial w_j}\right)$$

$$\therefore \frac{\partial x_i^s}{\partial x_j} = \frac{\partial x_i / \partial w_j}{\partial x_j / \partial w_j} \text{...}(12)$$

Substituting (12) into (10), we obtain

$$\frac{\partial x_i}{\partial w_i} = \frac{\partial x_i^s}{\partial w_i} + \frac{(\partial x_i / \partial w_j)(\partial x_j / \partial w_i)}{\partial x_j / \partial w_j} \text{.......................}(13)$$

Using the reciprocity condition (11) into (13), we obtain

$$\frac{\partial x_i^L}{\partial w_i} = \frac{\partial x_i^s}{\partial w_i} + \frac{(\partial x_j / \partial w_i)^2}{\partial x_j / \partial w_j} \text{...................................}(14)$$

Since the last term must be negative, equation (14) says that $\frac{\partial x_i^L}{\partial w_i}$ is more negative than $\frac{\partial x_i^s}{\partial w_i}$, the LeChatelier principle. It is evident that the LeChatelier principle illuminates the fundamental relation ship between the long-run and the short-run factor demand functions. Now given that $x_i^L(.)$ and $x_i^S(.)$ will be tangent at the initial point (by the first-order envelope property), we have

$$\left|\frac{w_i}{x_i^L}\frac{\partial x_i^L}{\partial w_i}\right| \geq \left|\frac{w_i}{x_i^S}\frac{\partial x_i^S}{\partial w_i}\right| \text{...}(15)$$

This expression explicitly says that the long-run price elasticity is at least as large as the short-run price elasticity with respect to factor-demand function.

To deduce the second LeChatelier result relating to supply elasticity, we differentiate equation (9) with respect to p to obtain

$$\frac{\partial y^L}{\partial p} = \frac{\partial y^s}{\partial p} + \left(\frac{\partial y^s}{\partial x_j}\right)\left(\frac{\partial x_j}{\partial p}\right) \text{..}(16)$$

Now differentiating equation (9) again with respect to $w_j \in w^2$, we obtain

$$\frac{\partial y^L}{\partial w_j} = (\frac{\partial y^s}{\partial x_j})(\frac{\partial x_j}{\partial w_j})$$

$$\therefore \frac{\partial y^s}{\partial x_j} = \frac{\partial y^L / \partial w_j}{\partial x_j / \partial w_j} \qquad \text{.......(17)}$$

Substituting (16) into (15), we obtain

$$\frac{\partial y^L}{\partial p} = \frac{\partial y^s}{\partial p} + \frac{(\partial y^L / \partial w_j)(\partial x_j / \partial p)}{\partial x_j / \partial w_j} \qquad \text{.......(18)}$$

Using the following reciprocity condition given by Hotelling's lemma $\frac{\partial y^L}{\partial w_j} = -\frac{\partial x_j}{\partial p}$

into equation (17), we obtain

$$\frac{\partial y^L}{\partial p} = \frac{\partial y^s}{\partial p} - \frac{(\partial x_j / \partial p)^2}{\partial x_j / \partial w_j} \qquad \text{.......(19)}$$

Since the second term on the right-hand side is non-negative, it follows from equation (18) that

$$\frac{\partial y^L}{\partial p} \geq \frac{\partial y^s}{\partial p} \qquad \text{.......(20)}$$

This expression implies that long-run supply response to a change in price is at least as large as the short-run supply response. Now the first-order envelope property says that $y^L(.)$ and $y^s(.)$ are tangent to each other at the initial point. This amounts to observing that

$$\frac{p}{y^L}\frac{\partial y^L}{\partial p} \geq \frac{p}{y^s}\frac{\partial y^s}{\partial p} \qquad \text{.......(21)}$$

This expression explicitly says that the long-run price elasticity is at least as large as the short-run price elasticity with respect to output-supply function.

Concluding Remarks

The LeChatelier principle plays a prominent role in modern economics. Roughly speaking, it involves the idea that any imposed rigidity in one variable of an optimization model causes a reduction in the responsiveness to prices for other variables of the model. This is true irrespective of whether any two variables are substitutes or complements. In this paper, a local version of this principle has been applied for determining two comparative static results: (i) The relationship between the short-and long –run factor-demand elasticities; (ii) the relationship between short-and long –run output- supply elasticities. The derivation of these results is based on a set of assumptions, viz. the continuity of the objective function, the convexity of production technologies, competitive markets for inputs and infinitesimal continuous changes in price. These results show that the long-run price elasticity is at least as large as the short-run price elasticity as there are fewer restrictions on the variables in the long-run than in the short-run.

REFERENCES

Jamison, J. (2006): 'The LeChatelier Principle in Lattices', *Economics Bulletin*, Vol. 3.

Milgrom, Paul and Roberts, John (1990): 'The Economics of Modern Manufacturing: Technology, Strategy and Organization', *American Economic Review*, Vol. 80.

Milgrom, Paul and Roberts, John (1996): 'The LeChatelier Principle', *American Economic Review*, Vol. 86.

Robert G. Chambers (1988): *Applied Production Analysis: A Dual Approach*, Cambridge University Press

Samuelson, Paul A (1947): *The Foundations of Economic Analysis*, Cambridge, M.A, Harvard University Press

Samuelson, Paul A (1960): 'An Extension of the LeChatelier Principle', *Econometrica*, Vol. 28.

Samuelson, Paul A (1966): 'The LeChatelier Principle in Linear Programming', in *The Collected Papers of Paul Samuelson*, MIT Press.

Silberberg, Eugene (1990): *The Structure of Economics*, 2nd Edition, New York: McGraw-Hill.

Suen W, Eugene Silberberg, Paul Tseng (2000): 'The LeChatelier Principle: The Long and the Short of it', *Economic Theory*, Vol.16.

Varian, H.R (1992): *Microeconomic Analysis*, 3rd Edition, W.W. Norton and Co.

12

Relationship Between Budget Deficit and Interest Rate in the Economy of Sri Lanka—An Econometric Study

CHANDAN KUMAR MUKHOPADHYAY* &
KANCHAN DATTA**

Abstract

There has been a plethora of studies concerning the relationship between budget deficit and interest rate. An expansionary fiscal policy followed by the Government to finance the deficit leads to a shift of the IS curve to the right, resulting in an increase in interest rate. On the other hand, Ricardian Equivalence Theorem negates any such relation. This study involves IFS data, where the real interest rate is used. This study is based on a battery of tests like, ADF, PP unit root test, Correlogram followed by the estimation of Co-integration, Vector ECM, Granger Causality. This study rejects the Ricardian Equivalence Theorem and finds that there exists a long run as well as short run dynamics in the relationship where unidirectional Granger Causality runs from Budget Deficit to Interest Rate over the period 1979-2001 in the economy of Sri Lanka.

* Professor, Department of Economics, North Bengal University.
** Lecturer, St. Joseph's College, Darjeeling.

Key Words: Ricardian Equivalence, Unit Root, Co-integration, Vector Error Correction, Granger Causality.

Introduction

At the theoretical level, an extensive debate has developed to explain the relationship between budget deficit and interest rate. Neoclassicals hold that budget deficit leads to an increase in interest rate which in turn results in crowding out of private investment.

Keynesians, on the other hand, stress upon rise in interest rate following a budget deficit. However they believe that such rise in interest rate stimulates savings and helps capital formation. Again the proponents of the 'Ricardian Equivalence Theorem' argue that budget deficit does not have any impact on interest rate at all.

With an increase in Government purchases by an amount ΔG, the immediate impact is to increase the demand for goods and services by ΔG. But since the total output is fixed by inelastic supply of factors of production in the short run, the increase in government expenditure must be met by a decrease in some other category of demand .Since tax is unchanged and so disposable income, hence consumption also remaining unchanged. Therefore the increase in government purchases must be met by an equal amount of decrease in investment. To induce fall in investment, interest rate must rise. Hence, the increase in Government purchases causes the interest rate to rise and investment to decline. Government purchases are said to crowd out investment. For example, let us consider the market for loanable funds. Since the increase in government purchases is not accompanied by an increase in taxes, the Govt. finances the additional spending by borrowing i.e. by reducing private savings. With public saving remaining unchanged, Govt. borrowing reduces national saving. It is reflected by a leftward shift in the supply of loanable funds available for investment. This is shown in the fig below.

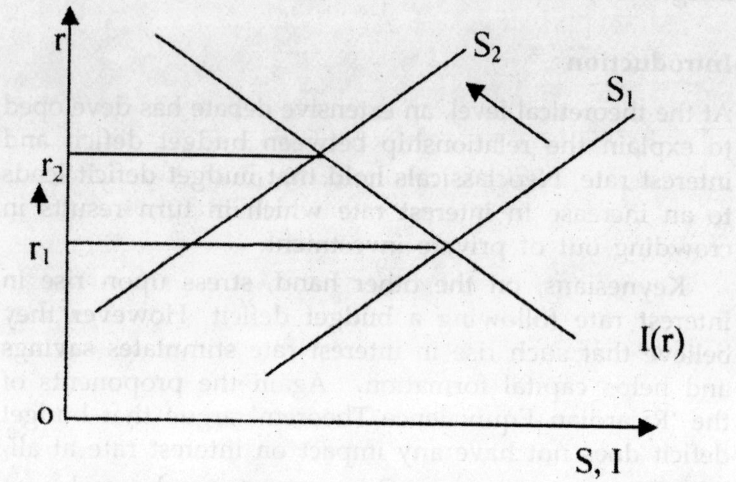

At the initial interest rate, the demand for loanable funds exceeds the supply. The equilibrium interest rate rises to the point where investment schedule crosses the new saving schedule. Thus an increase in government purchases causes the interest rate to rise from r_1 to r_2.

These views can also be explained with the help of the IS-LM frame work.

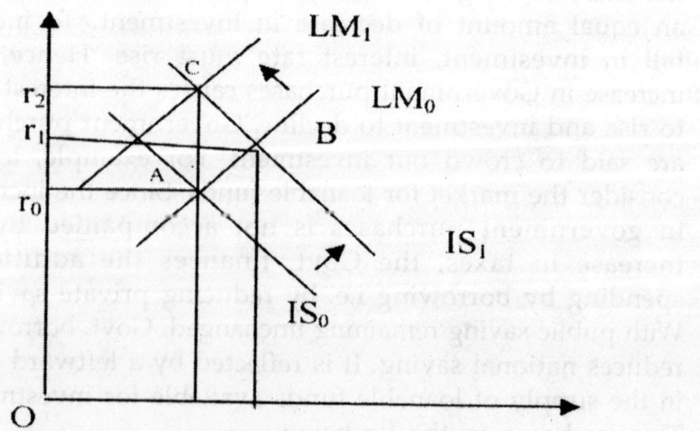

We start at A. An expansionary fiscal policy (i.e. an increase in G or a reduction of T) shifts IS_0 curve to IS_1. Now, according to Keynesian view, new equilibrium will be at B such that both output and interest rate will rise. But according to the classical view, C is the new equilibrium point. Thus the outcome of the policy had been no change in output but full crowding out of investment .However, the rise in interest rate in the classical case is much greater than it is in Keynesian view.

Economists again hold that impact of fiscal deficit on interest rate depends not only on the level of deficit but also on the financing pattern of deficit. Government can finance deficit by: *(i)* printing money and or *(ii)* through the creation of debt, both internal and external. But excessive of any of the financing modes results in the macro-economic imbalances. For example, printing new notes leads to inflationary pressure in the economy while domestic debt financing leads to a decrease in the price of bonds, resulting in a rise in interest rate and crowding out of private investment. Excessive financing of deficit through external debt may lead to current account deficit and depreciation of exchange rate.

However, the outcome may vary depending upon whether the economy is closer to full employment position with supply bottle-necks or passing through a recession. If the economy is near full employment situation, it is quite likely that the rise in aggregate demand caused by government spending would raise interest rates. On the other hand, if the economy is burdened with excess capacity or passing through a severe recession, impact of government spending on interest rate may be quite minimal.

EMPIRICAL STUDIES:

Theoretically four possibilities are in existence.

1) Budget Deficit Granger Causes Interest Rate
2) Interest Rate Granger Causes Budget deficit.

3) There is a bi-directional causality between Budget Deficit and Interest Rate, and
4) There is no relation between these two variables, and so these are independent of each other.

Many scholars have empirically tested this relationship and found contradictory results. Evans (1985), Tanzi (1985), Dalamagas (1987), Ahamad (1994), Kulkarni and Eric Lee (1996) found no positive link between rate of Interest and deficit. While Ostrosky (1979), Cebula (1990), Correia Nunes, Jose and Stemitsiotis (1995) did find evidence for the Link between Budget Deficit and rate of Interest.

Those who got the evidence of this link hold that with economic growth, increasing budget deficit may create over time a shortage of funds available for investment. If this imbalance between supply of funds and intended investment is not met, long term rate of interest rises. Ostrosky, Cebula and others hold that the global integration of financial market makes the supply of funds curve infinitely elastic. That is why, Budget Deficit fails to generate any appreciable change in interest rate.

The empirical investigation of the relationship between budget deficit and the interest rate has generally been confined to developed countries. Earliest work by Tanzi (1985) in the context of the US economy, observed that for the period 1960 to 1984, the sensitivity of the interest rate to fiscal deficit diminished over the years.

Cebula (1990) and Correia, et al (1995) showed that deficit, inflation, short run rate of interest Granger cause long term rate of nominal interest rate. This study was based on Multivariate Loanable Funds Model.

Cebula (1997) further examined the direction of causality between interest rate and budget deficit in the economy of US, over the period 1973 to 1991 and found that there was bi-directional causality between rate of interest and the deficit.

In the context of developing countries studies are few on the link between BD and IR. Mustaq Ahmed (1994) in the economy of Pakistan found that there was no link between rate of interest and deficit.

In Indian context, Ranjan Goyal, (2004) got two way causality between Fiscal Deficit and Interest Rate. Lekha S Chakraborty (2002) made an attempt to address the issue upfront and with 2-variable VAR model, she concluded that budget deficit did not induce rise in rate of interest, and the causality runs from real rate of interest to deficit. In an another study for India and for a number of other countries Surajit Das (2004) found that the interest rates did not necessarily depend on the fiscal deficit .

According to Prabhat Patnaik (2001) the size of fiscal deficit affects the level of the interest rate. This proposition has an appealing simplicity: A fiscal deficit means fresh demand for loans by the government, and hence an increase in the supply of government securities: This increase, must lead to fall in the prices of securities, and a rise in interest rate. Apparently this is an obvious proposition, but theoretically complex and erroneous. So from the empirical studies we got mixed response. In this paper an attempt has been taken to measure the relationship and nature of causality between Budget Deficit and Interest Rate in Srilanka.

Data and Methodology of the Study

The data of BD (Budget Deficit) and Interest Rate range for the period of 1979-2001 and of annual observations. The data have been collected from various issues of International Financial Statistics (IFS), BD is taken as a percentage of real GDP, where as Interest Rate is taken as lending rate. It is converted into real terms while inflation is measured in terms of CPI with base 1995 =100. Symbolically, it is denoted by IR.

Stationarity of the relevant data sets has been tested through study of Correlogram, Augmented Dickey Fuller test and Phillips–Perron tests. These tests have been performed in order to test the presence of 'unit roots' in the datasets concerned.

Co integration between BD and IR has been examined for ascerting the existence of long run relationship between these variables. Short run dynamics have been examined through the estimation of Vector Error Correction Model (VECM). Then Engle-Granger Causality tests have been performed in order to identify the nature and direction of causal relation between the variables concerned.

Graphical Presentation

The time plots of BD and IR are presented through Figure 1.

Figure-1
TIME PLOTS OF BD AND IR

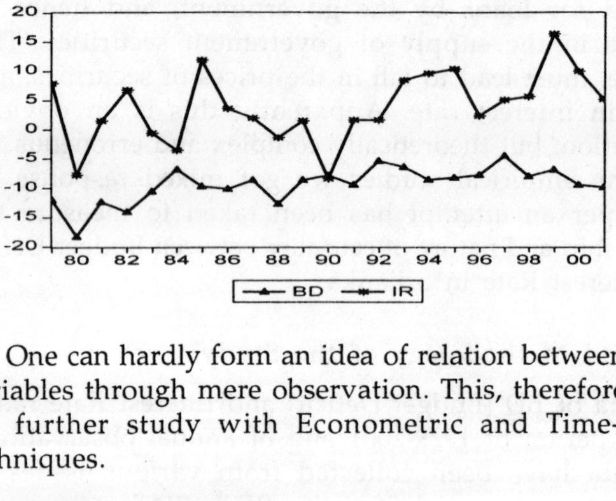

One can hardly form an idea of relation between these variables through mere observation. This, therefore ,calls for further study with Econometric and Time-Series techniques.

Stationarity: Correlogram Study

The ACF and PACF of both the series at level are being presented by Figure 2 and Figure 3 respectively.

Figure-2
CORRELOGRAM OF BD

Sample: 1979 2001
Included observations: 23

Correlogram of BD

Autocorrelation | Partial Correlation

	AC	PAC	Q-Stat	Prob
1	0.478	0.478	5.9825	0.014
2	0.347	0.153	9.2783	0.010
3	0.230	0.022	10.805	0.013
4	-0.066	-0.291	10.936	0.027
5	0.101	0.256	11.264	0.046
6	0.178	0.205	12.332	0.055
7	0.060	-0.146	12.460	0.086
8	0.133	-0.059	13.136	0.107
9	-0.060	-0.131	13.284	0.150
10	-0.181	-0.053	14.738	0.142
11	-0.197	-0.141	16.594	0.120
12	-0.229	-0.014	19.340	0.081

FINDINGS

It is observed from the Figure -2 that:

(i) ACF is free from any dying out pattern of spikes.

(ii) there exists only one single significant spike in the ACF and PACF at lag one.

These observations testify that BD is stationary at level i.e BD is I(0).

Figure-3
CORRELOGRAM OF IR

Sample: 1979 2001
Included observations: 23

Correlogram of IR

Autocorrelation | Partial Correlation

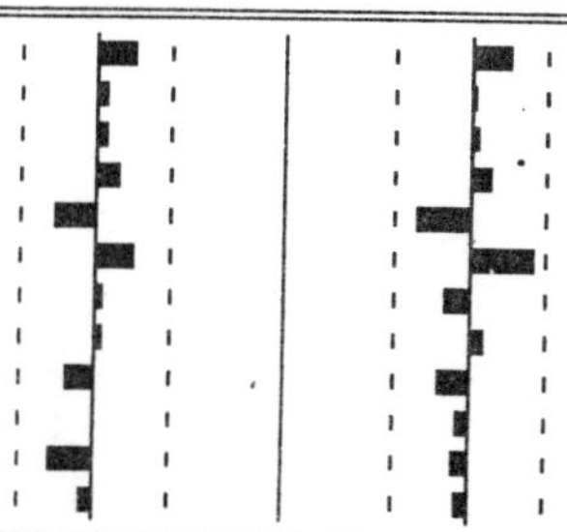

	AC	PAC	Q-Stat	Prob
1	0.212	0.212	1.1715	0.279
2	0.057	0.012	1.2596	0.533
3	0.049	0.036	1.3281	0.722
4	0.116	0.102	1.7335	0.785
5	-0.225	-0.287	3.3436	0.647
6	0.206	0.356	4.7808	0.572
7	0.034	-0.145	4.8224	0.682
8	0.026	0.067	4.8490	0.774
9	-0.158	-0.168	5.8785	0.752
10	0.003	-0.057	5.8789	0.825
11	-0.238	-0.085	8.5931	0.659
12	-0.058	-0.062	8.7692	0.723

FINDINGS

The Figure -3 shows that

(i) ACF is free from any dying out pattern of spikes.

(ii) no significant spike occurs at any lag in the ACF and PACF.

These observations testify for the stationarity of the IR series at level. Consequently, IR is also I(0).

Study of Stationarity: Unit Root Tests

Stationarity of the time series data on BD and Interest rate has further been enquired into through 'Unit root tests' . These tests include ADF (Augmented Dickey – Fuller) and Phillips –Perron tests. The results are presented through Table 1-4.

Table 1

RESULTS OF THE ADF TEST (UNIT ROOT TEST) ON IR

Variable	*Order*	*Exogenous*	*Lag length*	*ADF Test statistic*	*Prob.**
IR	level	Const.	0	-3.642791	0.0132
IR	level	Cont+lr.trd	0	-4.734430	0.0054
IR	level	None	0	-2.951017	0.0051

*MacKinnon (1996) one-sided p-values (Automatic based on SIC, Max lag =8).

FINDINGS FROM THE TABLE -1

It is observed from the Table -1 that

(i) ADF test statistic is -3.642791 with probability 0.0132 with exogenous constant.

(ii) ADF test statistic is -4.734430 with probability 0.0054 with exogenous constant and time trend.

(iii) The same test statistic is-2.951017with probability 0.0051with exogenous none.

According to these findings, the null hypothesis of the unit Root in IR series is rejected at 5% with intercept and at 1% level of significance with intercept and time trend and at 1% with none exogenous respectively.

All these findings further confirms that Real Interest rate series is stationary at level.

Table 2

RESULTS OF THE ADF TEST (UNIT ROOT TEST) ON BD

Variable	*Order*	*Exogenous*	*Lag length*	*ADF Test statistic*	*Prob.**
BD	level	Const.	0	-2.717928	0.0870
BD	level	Cont+lr.td	0	-3.550730	0.0584
BD	level	None	1	-1.591412	0.1031

*MacKinnon (1996) one-sided p-values. (Automatic based on SIC, Max lag=8).

FINDINGS FROM THE TABLE -2

The Table-2 indicates that

(i) ADF test statistic is -2.717928 with probability 0.0870 with exogenous constant.

(ii) the same test statistic is -3.550730 with probability 0.0584 with constant and time trend .

(iii) ADF test statistic is -1.591412 with probability 0.1031 with exogenous none.

All these findings again confirm the stationarity of BD series at level at level.

Table 3

RESULTS OF THE PHILLIPS-PERRON (PP) UNIT ROOT TEST ON IR

Variable	*Order*	*Exogenous*	*PP Statistic*	*Prob*.*	*Band.*
IR	level	Const.	-3.642791	0.0132	0
IR	level	Cont+lr.td	-4.724769	0.0056	1
IR	level	None	-2.951017	0.0051	1

*MacKinnon (1996) one-sided p-values.

FINDINGS FROM THE TABLE -3

The Table-3 shows that

(i) PP test statistic is -3.642791 with probability 0.0132 while exogenous is constant.

(ii) PP test statistic is -4.724769 with probability 0.0056 while exogenous is constant and time trend.

(iii) PP test statistic is -2.951017 with probability 0.0051with exogenous none.

These observations also support the ADF test results confirming the stationarity of IR series at level. There exists no structural shift in the data set causing non-stationarity.

Table 4

RESULTS OF THE PHILLIPS-PERRON (PP) UNIT ROOT TEST on BD

Variable	*Order*	*Exogenous*	*PP Statistic*	*Prob*.*	*Band.*
BD	level	Const.	-2.717928	0.0870	0
BD	level	Const+lr.trd	-3.559878	0.0574	1
BD	level	None	-0.717141	0.3944	6

*MacKinnon (1996) one-sided p-values

Findings from the PP Test Results in Table 4

It is observed from table 4 that

(i) the Budget Deficit data series is stationary at level in the first two exogenous(intercept and constant with time trend). So BD is I(0), at 1% level of significance according to Phillips Peron Unit root test results.

(ii) no structural shift in the BD data set is evident causing non-stationarity.

THE STUDY OF CO-INTEGRATION

The study in this section is devoted to examining the existence of a long run relationship between IR and BD. Before estimating such relation, it becomes pertinent for us to know if such relation really existed. This involves test of co-integration. The co-integrating equation is

$$BD_t = \alpha + \beta\ IR_t + U_t \qquad (1)$$

where U_t is the error term and can be expressed as the linear combination of IRt and BDt since

$$U_t = BD_t - \alpha - \beta\ IR_t \qquad (2)$$

If U_t, the residual, does not contain unit root and is stationary, the series IR_t and BD_t are said to be co-integrated*. In such case a long run stable relationship between these two variables is expected to exist.

ESTIMATION OF THE EQUATION (2)

The equation (2) is estimated and the results of estimation are being presented through Table 5.

Table 5

RESULTS OF ESTIMATED REGRESSION EQUATION – 1

Variable	*Coefficient*	*S.E.*	*t-stat*	*Prob.*
Constant	-9.984893	0.738	-13.529	0.0000
β	0.148830	0.104	1.428	0.1678

The B^ is not significant. The correlogram of the residuals of the estimated equation is given by Fig-4. The Fig -4 shows that the residuals are stationary.

Figure-4

CORRELOGRAM OF U_t

Sample: 1979 2001
ncluded observations: 23

Correlogram of UT

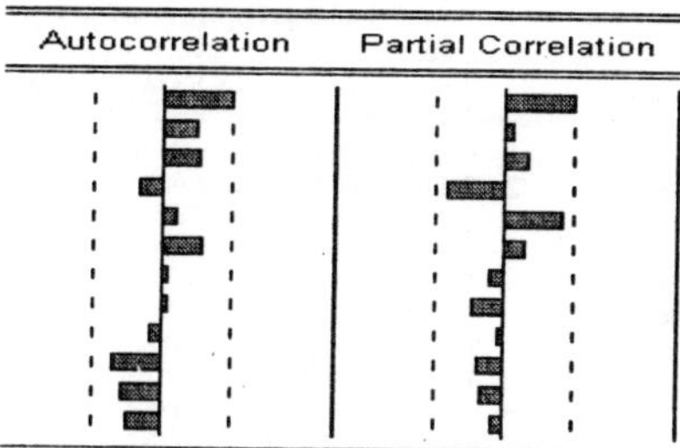

	AC	PAC	Q-Stat	Prob
1	0.416	0.416	4.5202	0.033
2	0.213	0.048	5.7591	0.056
3	0.225	0.146	7.2117	0.065
4	-0.135	-0.348	7.7636	0.101
5	0.092	0.338	8.0366	0.154
6	0.244	0.126	10.055	0.122
7	0.033	-0.089	10.095	0.183
8	0.034	-0.192	10.139	0.255
9	-0.073	-0.038	10.359	0.322
10	-0.296	-0.151	14.222	0.163
11	-0.246	-0.141	17.126	0.104
12	-0.199	-0.079	19.204	0.084

* If two variables are I(0), then these two are automatically co-integrated

CO-INTEGRATION BETWEEN IRt (DEPENDENT VARIABLE) AND BD (INDEPENDENT VARIABLE)

Now let us consider another cointegrating equation

$IR_t = \delta + \gamma\ BD_t + V_t$ (3)

$V_t = IR_t - \delta - \gamma\ BD_t$ (4)

The results of the estimation is presented through the Table -6

Table 6
RESULTS OF ESTIMATED REGRESSION EQUATION – 3

Variable	*Coefficient*	*S.E.*	*t-stat*	*Prob.*
Constant	9.501	4.106	2.31	0.03
γ	0.5951	0.4166	1.438	0.1678

FINDINGS:

It is observed from the table -6

(i) γ^ is not significant.

(ii) the residuals of the co- integrating equation (V_t) are stationary as exhibited by the correlogram of residuals given by the Fig-5.

Consequently, IR is Co-integrated with BD and, therefore, IR is found to maintain a long run relationship with BD.

Figure-5
CORRELOGRAM OF V_t

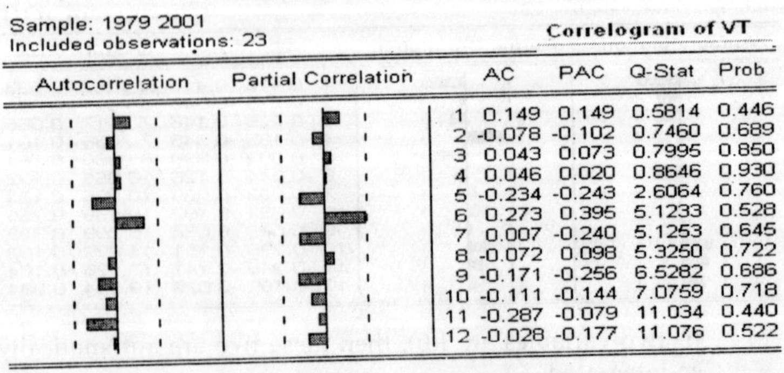

Sample: 1979 2001
Included observations: 23

Correlogram of VT

	AC	PAC	Q-Stat	Prob
1	0.149	0.149	0.5814	0.446
2	-0.078	-0.102	0.7460	0.689
3	0.043	0.073	0.7995	0.850
4	0.046	0.020	0.8646	0.930
5	-0.234	-0.243	2.6064	0.760
6	0.273	0.395	5.1233	0.528
7	0.007	-0.240	5.1253	0.645
8	-0.072	0.098	5.3250	0.722
9	-0.171	-0.256	6.5282	0.686
10	-0.111	-0.144	7.0759	0.718
11	-0.287	-0.079	11.034	0.440
12	-0.028	-0.177	11.076	0.522

SHORT RUN DYNAMICS: VECTOR ERROR CORRECTION MODEL ESTIMATION

In the short run, there may be disequilibrium even when long run equilibrium relationship exists. This motivates the study of the short run relationship between the variables concerned. Consequently, a model that combines both long run and short run behavior of the variables are examined through the estimation of the Error Correction Model (ECM). In this study we have estimated Vector Error correction models which consists of the following equations.

$$\Delta BD_t = \gamma_2 + \rho_2 z^{\wedge}_{t-1} + \beta_1 \Delta BD_{t-1} + \beta_2 \Delta BD_{t-2} + \beta_3 \Delta IR_{t-1} + \beta_4 \Delta IR_{t-2} + \varepsilon^2_t \quad (5)$$

$$\Delta IR_t = \gamma_1 + \rho_1 z^{\wedge}_{t-1} + \alpha_1 \Delta IR_{t-1} + \alpha_2 \Delta IR_{t-2} + \alpha_3 \Delta BD_{t-1} + \alpha_4 \Delta BD_{t-2} + \varepsilon_{1t} \quad (6)$$

The results of estimation of the equations are being presented through the Table 7.

Table 7

RESULTS OF ESTIMATION OF THE VECTOR ERROR CORRECTION MODEL

Dependent variable	*Explanatory variables*	*Coefficients*	*S.E*	*t-statistics*
ΔBD_t	Constant (γ_1)	0.292815	0.5071	0.58017
	$z^{\wedge}_{t-1}$*	-0.235903	0.08345	-2.82676
	ΔBD_{t-1}*	-0.578521	0.22513	-2.56970
	ΔBD_{t-2}	-0.320465	0.18950	-1.69114
	ΔIR_{t-1}	0.127592	0.10318	1.23657
	ΔIR_{t-2}	0.139452	0.08619	1.61794
R^2 = 0.520061, F statistic = 3.034079				
ΔIR_t	Constant (γ_2)	0.159686	1.55406	0.10275
	$z^{\wedge}_{t-1}$	-0.146957	0.25696	-0.57190
	ΔIR_{t-1}	-0.337032	0.31771	-1.06081
	ΔIR_{t-2}	-0.236241	0.26539	-0.89015
	ΔBD_{t-1}	0.494729	0.69321	0.71368
	ΔBD_{t-2}	0.807861	0.58348	1.38454
R^2 =0.361517, F statistic = 1.585397				

FINDINGS FROM TABLE 7

It is observed from Table-7 that,

(i) $Z^{\wedge}_{t-1}$ is significant in the 1st cointegrating equation, which implies that there exists short run dynamics between BD and IR.

(ii) Z_{t-1} is not significant in the 2nd equation, which implies that the short run shocks in BD cannot produce significant deviation in IR from its long run relationship with BD.

(iii) The coefficient of Z_{t-1} in the 1st cointegrating equation is negative and its absolute value is less than one. This indicates that short run positive shocks in IR_t leads to a fall in the value of BD below the long run equilibrium level in the following period.

(iv) $| Z_{t-1} | <1$ indicates that these shocks exhibit a converging short run dynamics which implies a stable long run relationship between BD and IR.

(v) In the 1st cointegrating equation, the coefficient of ΔBD_{t-1} is significant at 1% level while all other coefficients fail to be significant even at 10% level.

(vi) In the 2nd cointegrating equation all the coefficients fail to be significant even at 10% level.

(vii) observations in(v) and (vi) indicate the absence of any short-run causality between IR and BD.

GRANGER CAUSALITY TEST: THE MODEL

This test has been performed with the estimation of the equations

$$BD_t = \theta_2 + \alpha_{1i} BD_{t-i} + \alpha_{2i} \Sigma IR_{t-i} + \varepsilon_{2t} \qquad (7)$$

$$IR_t = \theta_1 + \beta_{1i} IR_{t-i} + \beta_{2i} \Sigma BD_{t-i} + \varepsilon_{1t} \qquad (8)$$

where $i=0,1,2,3,4$

Estimation of the Equation (7)

The causality equation (7) can be written as

$$BD_t = \theta_1 + \alpha_0 BD_{t-1} + \alpha_1 IR_{t-1} + \alpha_2 IR_{t-2} + \alpha_3 IR_{t-3} + \alpha_4 IR_{t-4} \varepsilon_{1t} \quad \ldots\ldots(9)$$

The results of the estimation of the equation (7) are being presented through Table 8.

Table 8

D.V.	*Expla.vari*	*Coeffi.*	*S.E*	*t-stat*	*Prob*
BD_t	Constant	-5.934	2.182	-2.72	0.018
	BD_{t-1}	0.265	0.236	1.122	0.282
	IR_{t-1}	-0.056	0.088	-0.638	0.535
	IR_{t-2}	0.026	0.092	0.285	0.780
	IR_{t-3}	-0.062	0.098	-0.633	0.538
	IR_{t-4}	0.046	0.089	0.520	0.612

R^2 = 0.115924, AIC= 4.596097, SIC=4.845031, F=0.341, Prob.= 0.879
Adjusted R^2 -0.224106,RSS = 58.28,DW = 2.234

Findings from the Table 8

The Table 8 shows that

(i) the coefficient of BD_{t-1} is not significant even at 10% level.

(ii) coefficients of IR_{t-1}, IR_{t-2}, IR_{t-3} and IR_{t-4} also fail to be significant even at 10% level.

All these observations testify that IR fails to Granger cause BD_t.

Estimation of the Equation 8

The equation (8) can be presented as

$$IR_t = \theta_2 + \beta_0 IR_{t-1} + \beta_1 BD_{t-1} + \beta_2 BD_{t-2} + \beta_3 \cdot BD_{t-3} + \beta_4 BD_{t-4} + \varepsilon_{2t} \quad (10)$$

The results of the estimation of this equation (10) are being presented through the Table 9.

Table 9

D.V	*Expla.vari*	*Coeffi.*	*S.E*	*t-stat*	*Prob*
IR t	Constant	21.013	5.244	4.006	0.0015
	IR_{t-1}	0.1288	0.203	0.6331	0.5376
	BD_{t-1}*	0.9817	0.522	1.8775	0.0831
	BD_{t-2}**	1.7425	0.528	3.297	0.0058
	BD_{t-3}	-0.4507	0.431	-1.045	0.3150
	BD_{t-4}	-0.2334	0.376	-0.6205	0.5456

R^2 = 0.6329, AIC= 5.974, SIC=6.27, =4.483, rob.= 0.221865
Adjusted R^2 = 0.4917, RSS = 232.48, DW = 2.578
D.V= Dependent Variable

Findings from the Table 9

It is observed from the Table 9 that

(i) β_0^ the coefficient of IR_{t-1} is not significant even at 10% level.

(ii) β_1^, the coefficient of BD_{t-1} is significant even at 10% level.

(iii) β_2^ , the coefficient of BD_{t-2} is significant at 1% level of significance.

(iv) β_3^ and β_4^ are not significant even at 10% level.

All these findings indicate that BD Granger Causes IR.

Confirmation of the Nature of Granger Causality

The findings on the nature of Granger Causality between BD and IR has been confirmed through F-Test. The results of the test are being presented through Table 10.

Table 10: Results of the Granger Causality Test Between IR and BD (Using F Statistics)

Null hypothesis	*Obser.*	*Lag length*	*F statistic*	*Probability*
(1) IR does not Granger cause BD	19	4	(1) 0.57824	(1) 0.68520
(2) BD does not Granger cause IR	19	4	(2) 5.2488	(2) 0.015
(1) IR does not Granger cause BD	18	5	(1) 0.53092	(1) 0.74815
(2) BD does not Granger cause IR	18	5	(2) 4.4119	(2) 0.0390

It is observed from the Table 10 that

(i) the Null Hypothesis (IR does not Granger cause BD) with lag length 4 and 5 cannot be rejected even at 10% level.

(ii) the Null Hypothesis (BD does not Granger cause IR) with lag length 4 and 5 is rejected at 1% level.

These findings further confirm that there exists a uni-directional causal relationship between real interest rate and budget deficit and the causality runs from Budget Deficit to Real Interest rate.

Summary and Conclusion

This study shows that

(i) The BD and IR series at level are stationary and therefore, both the variables are I(0).

(ii) BD and IR series are co-integrated implying that there exists a long-run relationship between BD and IR.

(iii) short run shocks transmitted through the BD channel significantly affect IR. However, these shocks are convergent and, therefore, the IR maintains a stable relationship with BD.

(iv) short–run shocks transmitted through the IR channel fails to affect BD.

(v) BD_t Granger Causes IRt while IRt is not found to Granger Cause BDt. Consequently, there exists a unidirectional causality between budget deficit and real interest rate in the economy of Sri Lanka where variation in Budget deficit Granger causes variation in real interest rate.

This study shows that budget deficit in the economy of Sri Lanka causes variation in real interest rate. However the transmission mechanism of the shocks in the budget deficit to real interest rate has not been investigated in this study. The study is done following Friedman's idea that the economy is a 'Black Box' and it is hardly known how a budget deficit shock is transmitted through the economy. This requires a further study with the construction of a 'Structural Model'.

REFERENCES

Ahamad, Mustaq (1994): 'The Effects of Government Budget Deficits on Interest Rates: A Case Study Of a Small Open Economy'. *Economia International,* Vol XL VII.

Ahking, Francis W. and Stepen M. Miller (1985):' The Relationship between Government Deficits, Money Growth, and Inflation.' *Journal of Macroeconomics,* 7(4), Fall, pp. 447-67.

A. Koutsoyannis, *Theory of Econometrics: An Introductory Exposition of Econometric Methods,* 2nd edition, ELBS with McMillan, 1993.

Barrow, R. (1989) "The Ricardian Approach to Budget Deficit", *Journal of Economic Perspectives,* Vol. 3, pp. 37-54.

Cebula, J. Richard (2000): 'Structural Budget Deficits and the Ex Ante Real Long-Term Interest Rate:An Analysis of the Direction of 'Causality.' *Public Finance,* Vol. 52 (1), pp. 36-49.

Corria, Nunes, Jose and Loukas Stemitsiotis (1995): 'Budget Deficit and Interest Rates: Is there a Link? International Evidence', *Oxford Bulletin of Economics and Statistics,* 57(4), November.

D.N. Gujarati, *Basic Econometrics,* TATA McGraw-HILL, Edition 2004.

Dickey, David, and W.A. Fuller (1981): "The Likelihood Ratios Statistics for Auto Regressive Time Series with a Unit Root." *Econometrica* Vol. 49.

Engle, Robert F. and C.W.J Granger (1987): "Cointegration and Error Correction Representation, Estimation and Testing, " *Econometrica* 55(2) March

Evans, Paul (1985): `Do Large Deficits Produce High Interest Rate?' *American Economic Review,* Vol 75, No1.

Fuller, W.A. (1976): *Introduction to Statistical Time Series.* Wiley, NewYork.

Granger, C.W.J. (1969) "Investigating Causal Relationship by Econometric Models and Cross Spectral Methods", *Econometrica,* Vol. 37.

Kerry Patterson (2000): *An Introduction to Applied Econometrics—A Time Series Approach,* Macmillan.

Kulkarni, G. Kishore and Lee Erickson (1996): 'Is Crowding out Hypothesis Evident in LDCs? A Case of India', *Indian Economic Journal,* Vol 43, No1.

L.S. Chakraborty, "Fiscal Deficit and Rate of Interest - An Econometric Analysis of the Deregulated Financial Regime.", *EPW* 2002, May 11.

Mac Kinnon, J.G. (1991): 'Critical Values Of Cointegration Tests' in RF Engle and CWJ Granger (eds), *Long Run Economic Relationship: Readings in Cointegration,* Chapter 13, Oxford University Press, New York.

N.G. Mankiw, *Macro Economics,* Worth Publishers, 6th edition, 2007.

Prabhat Patnaik, "On Fiscal Deficits and Real Interest Rates", *EPW,* 2001.

Phillips, PCB and Pierre Perron (1987), "Testing for A Unit Root in Time Series Regression", *Biometrika,* vol. 75.

Ranjan Goyal, "Does Higher Fiscal Deficit Lead to Rise in Interest Rates?- An Empirical Investigation." *EPW* 2004

Tanzi, V. (1985) "Fiscal Deficit and Interest Rates in the United States: An Empirical Analysis." IMF staff papers. Vol 32, no 4.

Walter, E. (1995) *Applied Econometric Time Series.* John Wiley and Sons. NewYork, USA.

Wood, John (1981): 'Interest rates and Inflation,' *Economic Perspective,* Vol. 5.

13

Fiscal Synchronization in Maldives— A Study with Vector Autoregression, Impulse Response Function and Variance Decomposition

CHANDAN KUMAR MUKHOPADHYAY* & BISWAJIT MAITRA•

ABSTRACT

The paper examines if there existed any long-run causal relationship between expenditure and revenue in the economy of Maldives over the period 1980-2006. Expenditure and revenue series are found to be CI(0). The VAR model has found the evidence that Fiscal Synchronization Hypothesis is followed in Maldives. The Impulse Response Functions indicate that revenue shocks are more important in constituting the long-run base of both revenue and expenditure profiles. Variance Decomposition study confirms that shocks transmitted through revenue channel account for the major part of

---

* Professor, Department of Economics, North Bengal
• University Registered Ph. D Scholar, Department of Economics, North Bengal University

variations in both revenue and expenditure above their corresponding long-run levels.

Key Words: Cointegration, Fiscal synchronization, Impulse Response Function, VAR, Variance Decomposition, Granger Causality.

Introduction

Fiscal policy has a prominent and far-reaching role in economic development. Two main fiscal instruments are government expenditure and government revenue. Efficacy of fiscal policy depends on how government regulates these instruments through budgetary management. Persistent budget deficits must eventually be met by higher taxes or lower spending. The question of which of these two methods the government should choose to satisfy the intertemporal budget constraint has recently received considerable attention. For effective policy formulation, the relationship between these two parameters needs to be examined.

Variants of Hypotheses

A study of literature reveals four schools of thought regarding the relationship between government revenue and government expenditure.

(1) Tax-and-Spend Hypothesis

This hypothesis suggests that the amount of tax revenue determines the size of government expenditure. More specifically, the view is that, rise in taxes propels the growth of government spending. So, there is a unidirectional causal relationship running from government tax revenue to government expenditure. Friedman (1978), Buchanan and Wagner (1977, 1978) hold this view.

According to Friedman (1982), a cut in tax leads to higher deficits which would influence government to reduce its level of spending. Buchanan and Wagner (1978) share the same view that taxes Granger cause government expenditure but the causal relationship is negative. Their point of view is that, following a cut in taxes, the public will perceive that cost of government programs has fallen. As a result, they will demand more programs from the government which, if undertaken, will result in an increase in government spending. Consequently, budget deficit cannot be reduced by simply raising taxes as this only results in more spending, leaving the deficit at the highest level acceptable by the public.

(2) Spend-and-Tax Hypothesis

This view postulates that government expenditure actually Granger causes tax revenue. Government takes the expenditure decision first, and then imposes tax on the people. So, there exists a unidirectional causality running from government expenditure to government revenue. This view is based on the observations that any large-scale exogenous disturbances (like wars, political disturbances or natural disasters, etc.) induce an increase in government spending and, therefore, an increase in tax revenues. The solution suggested here for problems of budget deficits is that government spending should be reduced. This hypothesis is motivated by Peacock and Wise man (1961 and 1979), Barro (1974, 1978). Barro argues that, if agents do not suffer from fiscal illusion, they will recognize that the current level of debt-financed expenditure ultimately implies an increase in current and future taxation. Therefore, it is implicitly assumed that expenditure changes cause corresponding changes in revenue.

(3) Fiscal Synchronization Hypothesis

This hypothesis holds that government expenditure and government revenue are interdependent and these are determined simultaneously. So, there exists a bi-directional causal link between the variables concerned. Specifically, government expenditure can Granger cause government revenue and/or government revenue can Granger cause government expenditure. In this hypothesis, the public determines the levels of government spending and taxation by weighing the benefits of the government services against their costs. Musgrave (1969), Meltezer and Richard (1981) have supported this view.

(4) *Fiscal Neutrality*

The 'Fiscal Neutrality School' holds that government expenditure and government revenue are independent. There is no relationship between them at all (Baghestani and Mc.Nown).

Objectives of the Study

The main objectives of the present study are:

(i) to examine if there existed any long run relationship between expenditure and revenue in the economy of Maldives over the period 1980 - 2006. With this end in view, we have studied Co-integration between expenditure and revenue in Maldives.

(ii) to enquire into the dynamic short-run relationship between expenditure and revenue in Maldives through the Vector Auto-Regression Model, Impulse Response Function and Variance Decomposition. More specifically, in this section we seek to identify which one of the hypotheses mentioned above holds for Maldives over the period of our study.

Data and Variables

This study is based on the annual time series data involving government expenditure (Et) and government revenue (Rt) in Maldives. Data-sets have been collected from different issues of International Financial Statistics (IFS) published by the IMF. GDP Deflator (2000 = 100) has been used. For estimating models, we have converted the data-sets into (natural) Logarithmic forms.

Organization of the Paper

Section II is devoted to the study of Co-integration. Section III deals with short-run dynamics through the estimation of Vector Auto-regression Model (VAR). Section IV presents the analysis with Impulse Response Functions. Section V constitutes the study with Variance Decomposition. Section VI presents the Summary and Conclusion.

II

STUDY OF COINTEGRATION

In our study, both the time series data-sets for expenditure and revenue of Maldives are found non-stationary at level and these attains stationarity upon first differencing. Consequently, both these series are I(1). Engle and Granger (1987) hold that one can run a regression between two variables even though both are non-stationary if the series are integrated of the same order. If the linear combination of the non-stationary variables were stationary, the variables are said to be 'Co-integrated'. Engle-Granger techniques are being applied for the study of co-integration.

Engle-Granger Model of Cointegration

Engle-Granger approach involves two step method of co-integration between expenditure and revenue. In the first step, following two equations are estimated

$$E_t = \alpha + \beta R_t + u_t \tag{1}$$

$$R_t = \gamma + \delta E_t + v_t \tag{2}$$

In the second step, the residuals series and from the estimated equations are subject to 'Unit Root Tests'. If the residuals do not contain any unit root, the series are said to be co-integrated.

Estimation of Equations (1) and (2)

Equations (1) and (2) have been estimated through the OLS method. The corresponding estimated equations (3) and (4) are

$$E_t = 0.436 + 0.903\, R_t \tag{3}$$

SE (0.087) (0.029)

t [4.986] [31.09]

R^2 = 0.97, DW= 1.501, F-statistic = 966.7

$$R_t = -0.395 + 1.079\, E_t \tag{4}$$

SE (0.109) (0.034)

t [-3.614] [31.09]

R^2 = 0.97, DW= 1.480, F-statistic = 966.7

Time plots of residuals of the estimated equations (3) and (4) have been presented through Figures (1) and (2) respectively. These figures show that the residuals do not have any trend. The stationarity of these residuals has been examined through the ADF test and the PP unit root test. Tables (1) and (2) present the results of ADF and PP tests on residuals.

Figure 1: Time Plot of Residuals $\hat{u}_t$

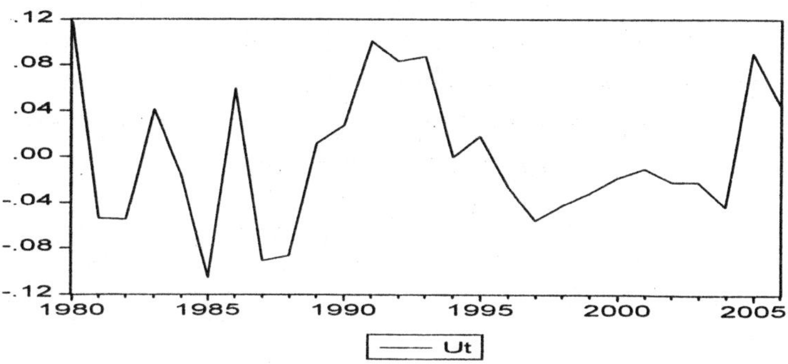

Figure 2: Time Plot of Residuals $\hat{v}_t$

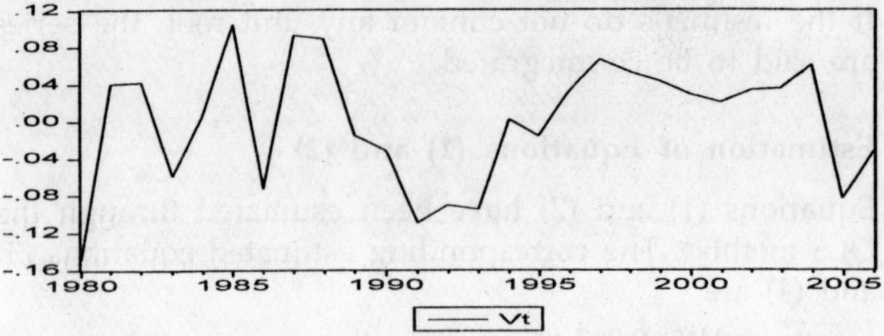

Table 1: Adf Unit Root Test on Residuals Lag Length Automatic† Based on Modified AIC, Max Lag = 8

Variables	*Null Hypothesis*	*ADF Test statistic*	*Lag Length*	*Critical Values*		
				1%	*5%*	*10%*
$\hat{u}_t$	has a unit root (Intercept)	-4.42	0	-3.71	-2.98	-2.62
$\hat{v}_t$	has a unit root (Intercept)	-4.62	0	-3.71	-2.98	-2.62

*MacKinon (1996) one sided p-values.

Table 2: Philips-Perron Unit Root Test on Residuals

Variables	*Null Hypothesis*	*Bandwith*	*PP Test statistic*	*Critical Values*		
				1%	*5%*	*10%*
$\hat{u}_t$	has a unit root (Intercept)	1	-4.4	-3.71	-2.98	-2.62
$\hat{v}_t$	has a unit root (Intercept)	1	-4.62	-3.71	-2.98	-2.62

*MacKinon (1996) one sided p-values.

Findings

It is observed from the Table - 1 and Table - 2 that

(i) the null hypothesis of 'unit root (with intercept)' for the residual $\hat{u}_t$ is rejected at 1% level by the ADF test. So $\hat{u}_t$ is stationary.

(ii) the null hypothesis of 'unit root (with intercept)' is rejected for the residual $\hat{v}_t$ at 1 % level of significance. It testifies for stationarity of $\hat{v}_t$.

(iii) Philips-Perron test rejects the null hypothesis of 'unit root (intercept)' for both the residuals $\hat{u}_t$ & $\hat{v}_t$ at 1% level. Thus the Philips-Perron test also confirms the stationarity of the residuals, $\hat{u}_t$ and $\hat{v}_t$

Stationarity of Residuals - Correlogram Analysis

The stationarity of the residuals have been examined through the plots of their corresponding Autocorrelation Functions (ACF) and the Partial Autocorrelation Functions (PACF) at different lags. Figure-3 and Figure - 4 embody the Correlograms of the residuals and respectively

Figure 3: Correlogram of $\hat{u}_t$

Autocorrelation | Partial Correlation

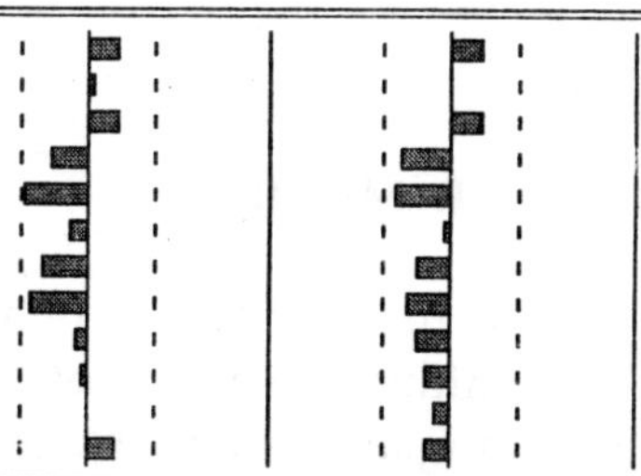

	AC	PAC	Q-Stat	Prob
1	0.169	0.169	0.8567	0.355
2	0.025	-0.004	0.8757	0.645
3	0.169	0.170	1.8033	0.614
4	-0.214	-0.286	3.3582	0.500
5	-0.362	-0.307	8.0282	0.155
6	-0.099	-0.030	8.3902	0.211
7	-0.256	-0.182	10.961	0.140
8	-0.324	-0.253	15.275	0.054
9	-0.070	-0.190	15.489	0.078
10	-0.031	-0.143	15.533	0.114
11	0.007	-0.083	15.536	0.159
12	0.157	-0.140	16.826	0.156

Figure 4: Correlogram of $\hat{v}_t$

Autocorrelation | Partial Correlation

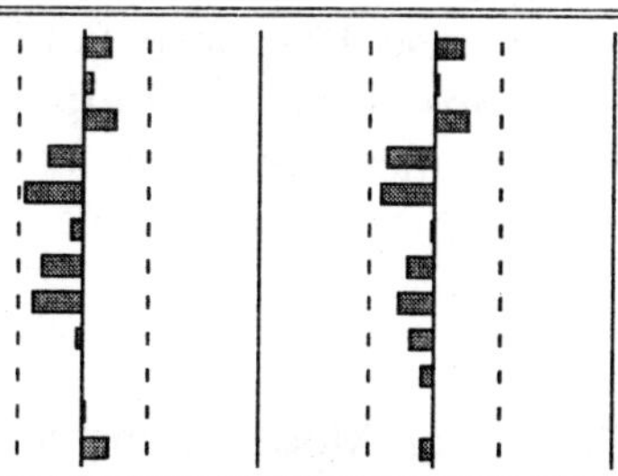

	AC	PAC	Q-Stat	Prob
1	0.162	0.162	0.7937	0.373
2	0.044	0.018	0.8543	0.652
3	0.186	0.181	1.9841	0.576
4	-0.206	-0.280	3.4241	0.490
5	-0.357	-0.318	7.9567	0.159
6	-0.081	-0.009	8.2005	0.224
7	-0.249	-0.153	10.631	0.156
8	-0.302	-0.210	14.381	0.072
9	-0.039	-0.134	14.448	0.107
10	-0.008	-0.062	14.451	0.153
11	0.018	-0.004	14.467	0.208
12	0.149	-0.082	15.620	0.209

It is observed from the Figure-3 and 4 that

(i) the relevant ACFs are free from the dying out pattern of spikes

(ii) the PACFs do not contain any singular significant spike at lag 1

These observations testify for the stationarity of $\hat{u}_t$ and $\hat{v}_t$.

The findings of stationarity of residuals through ADF, PP tests and ACF, PACF plots, therefore, confirm CI(0) relationship between expenditure and revenue in Maldives at levels. So, expenditure maintains a long run relationship with government revenue. Similarly, government revenue is also in long-run relationship with government expenditure. In the following section we have enquired into the nature and stability of such relationship.

III

STUDY WITH VAR MODEL

In order to find the long run dynamic relationship between expenditure and revenue in Maldives we cannot make any a-priori assumption of endogenous and exogenous variables. For this purpose, we have applied the Vector Auto-Regression Model (VAR) which treats all variables symmetrically without making reference to the issue of dependence versus independence. Different tools employed in VAR analysis, such as Impulse Response Functions and Variance Decompositions can be helpful in understanding interrelationships among economic variables and in the formulation of more structured economic model.

The Model

The relevant Vector Auto-Regression Model on expenditure (Et) and revenue (Rt) consists of the following equations

$$E_t = \alpha_1 + \sum_{i=1}^{k} \beta_{1i} E_{t-1} + \sum_{i=1}^{k} \gamma_{1i} R_{t-i} + u_{1t} \quad (3)$$

$$R_t = \alpha_2 + \sum_{i=1}^{k} \beta_{2i} R_{t-i} + \sum_{i=1}^{k} \gamma_{2i} E_{t-i} + u_{2t} \quad (4)$$

Here E_t, and R_t represent government expenditure and government revenue at time t respectively. E_{t-i}, R_{t-i}, represent government expenditure and government revenue at time t-i, i = 1,2,3, ..., respectively. u_{1t}, u_{2t} are the stochastic error terms, called impulse or innovations or shocks in the VAR model. These equations do not represent any joint relationship between E_t and R_t. These equations, therefore, represent "Seemingly Unrelated Regression" (SUR) model. The estimation of the model considers and uses the contemporaneous Var-Covariance matrix (Ω) of the error terms involved such that (Ω) = Var-Cov (u_{1t}, u_{2t}), where is a positive definite matrix.

Selection of Lag Length

In the estimation of VAR model, the selection of maximum lag length (k) is important. In our study we have followed Enders (1995) method of lag selection and started with eight lags. We have reduced the lags one by one given that estimated t-statistic for the coefficient involved is insignificant. In lag 3 many parameters have been found statistically significant. Therefore, we have taken the 3rd lag in the VAR estimation.

Estimation and Results of the VAR Model

Results of the estimation of the VAR model are being presented through the Table 3.

Table 3: Results of the VAR Estimation (Equation 3)

Dependent variable	*Explanatory Variables*	*Coefficients*	*'t' statistics*	*Standard errors*
	Constant	0.439	1.501	0.292
	E_{t-1}	0.365	1.376	0.265
	E_{t-2}	-0.102	-0.439	0.232
E_t	E_{t-3}	0.047	0.208	0.227
	R_{t-1}	-0.126	-0.281	0.448
	R_{t-2}	1.149	2.230	0.515
	R_{t-3}	-0.423	-0.822	0.515

DW = 1.91, R^2 = 0.978, Adjusted R^2 = 0.970, F-statistic = 127.25

Findings From the VAR Estimation

It is observed from the Table - 3 that

(i) $\left|\sum_{1}^{3} \hat{\beta}_{1i}\right| < 1, \left|\sum_{1}^{3} \hat{\gamma}_{1i}\right| < 1$. So the lag structures are consistent.

(ii) F - statistic = 127.25 $> F_{0.05}^{7,27}$, which indicates that the estimated equation is good fit.

(iii) DW = 1.91 which indicates that the system is free from autocorrelation

(iv) $\hat{\gamma}_{12}$, the coefficient of R_{t-2}, is significant at 5% level.

Economic Interpretations

The coefficient of R_{t-2} is positive and significant at 5% level. It implies that a rise in government revenue in the previous year leads to a rise in current government expenditure even in the presence of lagged terms of the government expenditure in the equation concerned. Therefore, Revenue Granger causes Expenditure in the period of our study.

Study on 'Reverse Causation'

We have observed how variation in government expenditure is triggered by variation in government revenue. It does neither confirm nor ignore the possibility that the variation in revenue is caused by variation in expenditure. So there exists a possibility of reverse causation. We seek to address this issue henceforth. With this end in view, we estimate Equation (4) of the VAR model where revenue appears as the dependent variable. The Table - 4 presents the results of such estimation.

Table 4: Results of the VAR Estimation (Equation- 4)

Dependent variable	*Explanatory Variables*	*Coefficients*	*'t' statistics*	*Standard errors*
	Constant	0.206	1.156	0.178
	Rt-1	0.843	3.083	0.273
Rt	Rt-2	0.156	0.497	0.314
	Rt-3	0.040	0.129	0.314

Et-1	0.144	0.889	0.161
Et-2	-0.330	-2.326	0.142
Et-3	0.101	0.730	0.138

DW = 2.03, R^2 = 0.992, Adjusted R^2 = 0.991, F-statistic = 403.07

Findings from the Table 4

It is observed from the Table (4) that

(i) $\left|\sum_{1}^{3}\hat{\beta}_{2i}\right| < 1$ $\left|\sum_{1}^{3}\hat{\gamma}_{2i}\right| < 1$ So the lag structures are consistent.

(ii) F - statistic = 403.07 > $F_{0.05}^{7,22}$, which indicates that the estimated equation is good fit.

(iii) DW = 1.89, which indicates that the system is free from autocorrelation

(iv) $\hat{\beta}_{21}$, the coefficient of Rt-1 , is significant at 1% level

(v) $\hat{\gamma}_{22}$, the coefficient of Et-2 , is significant at 5 % level

Economic Interpretation

It is, therefore, observed from the estimated equation (4) that

(i) R_t is a function of R_{t-1} since $\hat{\beta}_{21}$ is significant. So, R_t, in its univariate structure, represents AR (1) process.

(ii) positive and significant coefficient of R_{t-1} indicates that current revenue is positively related to previous period revenue.

(iii) The coefficients obtained from the estimated model actually imply elasticity coefficients. $\hat{\beta}_{21}$= 0.843 implies that elasticity of government revenue with respect to one year lagged expenditure is 0.843. The expression $\hat{\gamma}_{21}$ = -0.330 states that the change in government revenue, following a change in government expenditure, is less than unity. In other words, long run equilibrium level of revenue

cannot be permanently altered by the change in expenditure. This further means that variation in government revenue, following variation in expenditure, is converging to long run equilibrium level.

(iv) the significant value of $\hat{\gamma}_{21}$ essentially indicates that immediate past period lagged expenditure affects current revenue significantly even in the presence of lagged terms of revenue in the vector of regressors. It implies that 'Expenditure Granger Causes Revenue' in Maldives over the period of our study.

It, therefore, appears that

(i) in the economy of Maldives, the variation in government expenditure is found to cause and is caused by variation in government revenue over the period concerned.

(ii) both expenditure and revenue are truly 'endogenous' in the system. Consequently, the shocks in any endogenous variable cause variation in other endogenous variable.

Better insights about the relationship between expenditure and revenue can be obtained through the study of the corresponding Impulse Response Functions and Variance Decomposition. The following sections present the study on these accounts.

IV

STUDY WITH IMPULSE RESPONSE FUNCTIONS (IRF)

Meaning and Relevance of IRF

A shock to the 'i'-th variable not only directly affects the i-th variable itself but the shock is also transmitted to all of the other endogenous variables through the dynamic (lag) structure of the VAR. An Impulse Response Function traces the effect of a one time shock to one of the innovations on current and future values of the endogenous variables. In other words, Impulse Response Function traces the response of a variable through time to an unanticipated change in itself or other interrelated variables. Therefore, the Impulse Response Function can be used in VAR system to describe the dynamic behaviors of the whole system with respect to shocks in the residuals of the time series.

Graphical Presentation of Impulse Response Functions

The relevant Impulse Response Functions of the estimated VAR model consisting of Equations (3) and (4) are shown in Figure - (5) through Figure - (8)

Figure 5

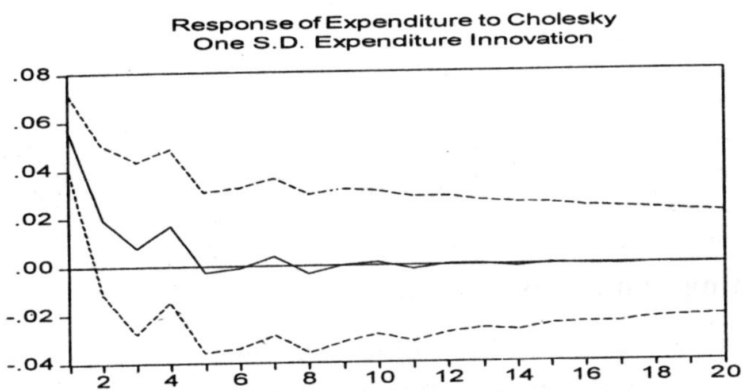

Figure 6

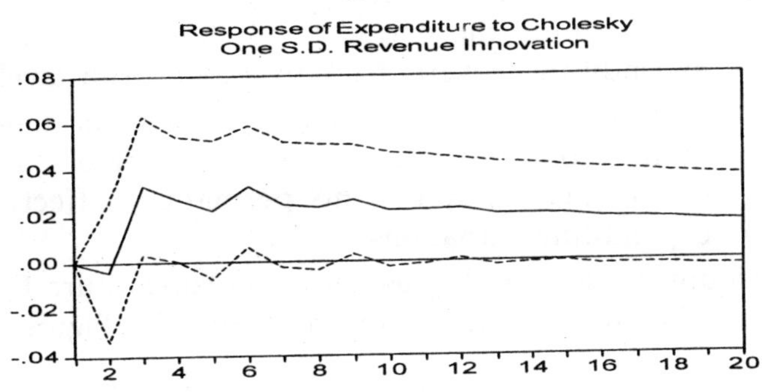

Figure 7

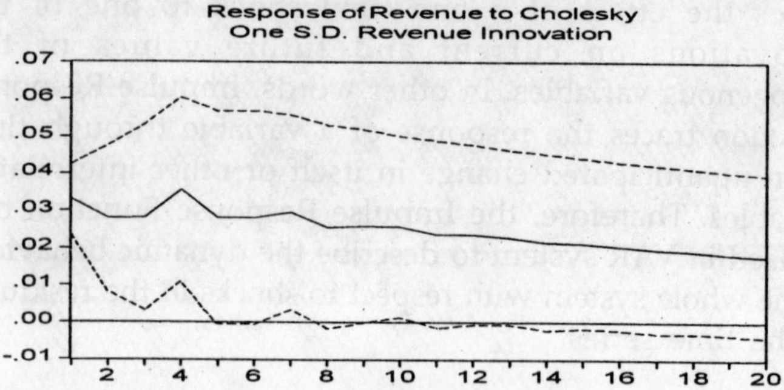

Figure 8

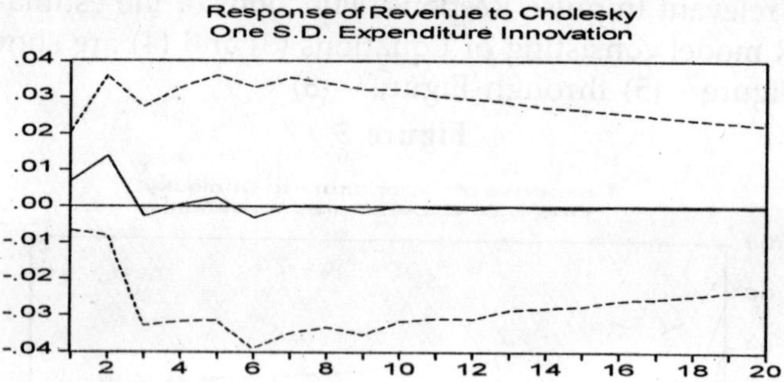

Findings and Explanations

It is observed from the Figure (5) that

(i) expenditure (E_t) declines immediately following a positive impulse in E_{t-1}. Such declining trend persists upto the period t = 3. After this period, expenditure reverts back to its long run level.

(ii) such variation in E_t is short lived since Et almost attains long run trend after the period t = 5. Consequently, it has no permanent effect on expenditure variations.

Figure (6) depicts the responses of expenditure E_t to impulses in revenue R_t. It appears from the Figure (6) that

(i) following a positive impulse in revenue, Et remains unchanged at t = 1. But it slightly declines below the initial base line at t = 2.

(ii) since at t = 2, Et registers a rise and after some rises and falls, the expenditure level rises above the long-run base by about 3.5% for. This indicates that revenue shock appears to cause permanent changes in the expenditure profile.

Figure (7) shows that

(i) revenue rises immediately at t = 1 by 3 % following a short run shock in its own innovation.

(ii) with a decline at t = 2 and a rise in t = 3, revenue almost reverts back to the base it attained at t = 1. Consequently, the variation in Rt, following any shock transmitted through the revenue channel, is permanent.

It is observed from the Figure (8) that

(i) for a positive expenditure shock, revenue increases immediately at t = 1. At t = 2, it declines slowly and reverts back to its long-run base.

(ii) the shock transmitted through expenditure channel fails to produce any long-lasting effect on revenue profile.

Economic Interpretation

It, therefore, appears that

(i) Et , in response to any impulse transmitted through expenditure channel, quickly attains the long-run equilibrium level after a very short-lived variation.

(ii) expenditure exhibits delayed response to shocks transmitted through revenue channel since at t = 1 period, expenditure remains unchanged. However, such revenue shocks cause permanent change in expenditure profile since expenditure rises permanently by about 3.5% above its initial long-run base

(iii) positive shock, transmitted through the revenue channel, causes immediate variation in revenue profile . Responses of revenue are long-lasting in view of the fact that such revenue shocks cause a permanent rise in the revenue profile by about 3 % above the initial long-run base.

(iv) shocks, transmitted through the expenditure channel, cause short-lived variation in revenue profile. The revenue profile returns back to its initial long-run base at t=3.

All These Observations Testify That

(i) the shocks, transmitted through revenue channel, cause permanent variations in both revenue and expenditure profiles. Following positive revenue shocks, both the revenue and expenditure profiles attain permanently higher levels above their corresponding initial long-run bases.

(ii) the shocks, transmitted though expenditure channel, are short-lived since these cause temporary variations in both revenue and expenditure profiles. Following any positive expenditure shocks, both revenue and expenditures profiles, after some short lived variations, revert back to the initial long run base within a very short-period.

V

STUDY WITH VARIANCE DECOMPOSITION

Meaning and Relevance of Variance Decomposition

Impulse Response Functions show how shocks to one endogenous variable can affect other endogenous variables in the VAR system. Variance Decomposition, on the other hand, separates the variations in an endogenous variable into various components representing effects of different shocks.

The Forecast Error Variance Decomposition reflects the proportion of forecast error variance of a variable which is explained by an unanticipated change in itself as opposed to that proportion attributable to change in other, perhaps interrelated variables. In other words, the Forecast Error Variance Decomposition tells us the proportion of the movement in a sequence in response to its own shocks versus shocks of other variables.

Variance Decomposition of Expenditure

The percentile decomposition of variance of expenditure across different lags is given by the Table 5. Figure 9 presents graphical presentation of such decomposition.

Table 5: Variance Decomposition of Expenditure

Period	*S.E.*	*Expenditure*	*Revenue*
1	0.0553	100.000	0.000
2	0.0587	99.494	0.505
3	0.0678	76.003	23.996
4	0.0748	67.350	32.649
5	0.0781	61.924	38.075
6	0.0845	52.878	47.121
7	0.0881	48.873	51.126
8	0.0912	45.753	54.246
9	0.0949	42.220	57.779
10	0.0975	40.072	59.927
11	0.1000	38.128	61.871
12	0.1025	36.274	63.725
13	0.1045	34.910	65.089
14	0.1064	33.643	66.356
15	0.1083	32.509	67.490
16	0.1099	31.580	68.419
17	0.1114	30.721	69.278
18	0.1128	29.961	70.038
19	0.1141	29.302	70.697
20	0.1153	28.696	71.303

Figure 9

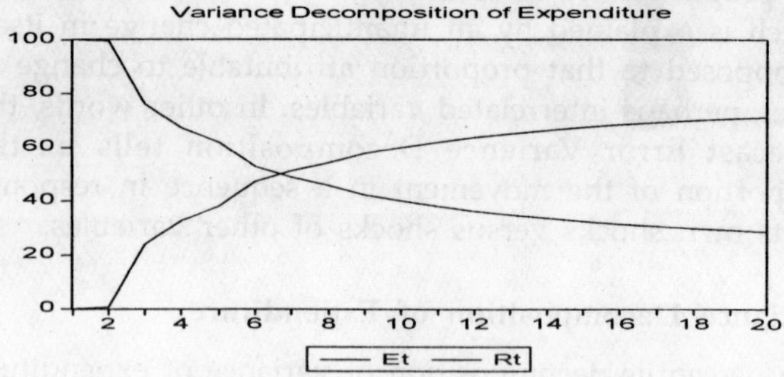

Findings From the Table 5 and Figure 9.

It is observed from the Table 5 and Figure 9 that

(i) variation in expenditure in the short-run (upto t = 6) is mainly due to shocks transmitted through the expenditure channel.

(ii) variation in expenditure in the long-run (for and) is mainly due to the shocks transmitted through the revenue channel.

(iii) shocks, transmitted through revenue channel, account for more than 70% of total variations in expenditure (about its long-run base level)

(iv) shocks, transmitted through expenditure channel, account for less than 30% of total variations in expenditure in the long-run.

(v) expenditure exhibits its delayed response to revenue shocks while its response to expenditure shocks is immediate.

Economic Interpretations

It, therefore, follows that

(i) the long run base of the expenditure profile is mainly constituted by revenue considerations. It confirms the Granger Causality running from revenue to expenditure.

(ii) short run variations in expenditure are caused by

economic compulsions for increasing expenditure. These compulsions are transitory by nature and may not be contributing to the long-run expenditure profile.

Variance Decomposition of Revenue

The decomposition of Revenue Variance across different lags is given by the Table 6. The corresponding graphical presentation is available in the Figure 10.

Table 6: Variance Decomposition of Revenue

Period	*S.E.*	*Expenditure*	*Revenue*
1	0.0553	4.2553	95.744
2	0.0587	11.389	88.610
3	0.0678	8.5197	91.480
4	0.0748	5.9439	94.056
5	0.0781	5.1064	94.893
6	0.0845	4.5747	95.425
7	0.0881	3.9731	96.026
8	0.0912	3.6178	96.382
9	0.0949	3.3449	96.655
10	0.0975	3.0901	96.909
11	0.1001	2.9041	97.095
12	0.1025	2.7463	97.253
13	0.1045	2.6075	97.392
14	0.1064	2.4961	97.503
15	0.1083	2.3977	97.602
16	0.1099	2.3118	97.688
17	0.1114	2.2389	97.761
18	0.1128	2.1737	97.826
19	0.1141	2.1161	97.883
20	0.1153	2.0657	97.934

Figure 10

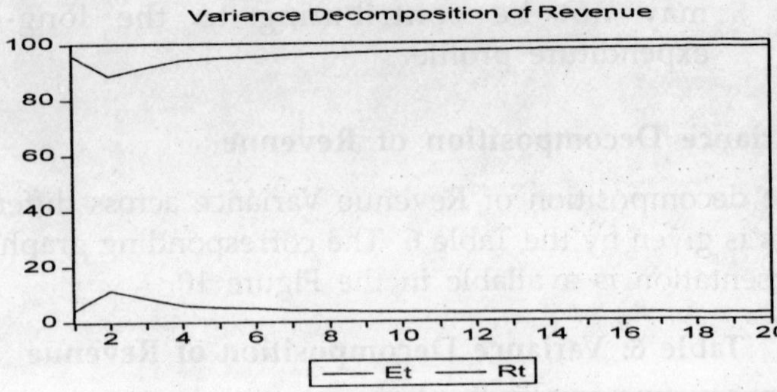

Findings From the Table 6 and Figure 10.

It is observed from the Table 6 and Figure 10 that

(i) the response of revenue to shocks, transmitted through the revenue and expenditure channels, is immediate.

(ii) the short-run and long-run variations in revenue are dominated by its responses to shocks transmitted through revenue channel.

(iii) revenue shocks account for at least 96% of total variations in revenue profile both in the long-run and in the short-run.

(iv) expenditure shocks account for about only 2% of the total variation in revenue in the long run.

Economic Interpretations

It, therefore, appears that

(i) Granger causality running from expenditure to revenue is very weak.

(ii) 'Revenue Profile' is mainly constituted by revenue considerations and not by expenditure considerations.

VI

SUMMARY AND CONCLUSIONS

The study with the VAR Model shows that Revenue Granger Causes Expenditure and Expenditure also Granger Causes Revenue. Therefore, there exists a bi-directional causality between revenue and expenditure.

However, 'Impulse Response Function Analysis' shows that, following impulses in expenditure, both revenue and expenditure profiles revert back to their initial long-run bases in a very short-period.

Again, 'Impulse Response Function Analysis' confirms that both revenue and expenditure are raised to a new level which is higher than the original base, following positive shocks transmitted through revenue channel. This indicates that revenue shocks are more important in constituting the long-run bases of both revenue and expenditure profiles.

Finally, 'Variance Decomposition' study confirms that shocks transmitted through revenue account for major part of variations in both revenue and expenditure above their corresponding long-run levels. In case of short-run variations in expenditure, revenue shocks were found to be dominant.

All these findings testify for the fact that there is a strong Granger Causality running from Revenue to Expenditure. However, the Granger Causality from Expenditure to Revenue is very weak. Consequently, all the findings testify that the 'Tax-and-Spend hypothesis' is the prevalent feature of the fiscal system in the economy of Maldives over the period of our study (1980 – 2006).

REFERENCES

Anderson, William, Mayler S. Wallace, and J.T. Warner (1986), "Government Spending and Taxation: What Causes What?" *Southern Economic Journal,* Vol. 52, pp. 630-639.

Baghestani, H. and R. Mc Nown (1984), "Do Revenue Expenditure Respond to Budgetary Disequilibria?", *Southern Economic Journal* 60, pp. 311-322.

Barro, R.J., (1979), "On the Determination of Public Debt", *Journal of Political Economy,* 81, pp 940-971.

Barro, Robert J.,(1989), "The Ricardian Approach to Budget Deficits", *Journal of Economic Perspective,* Vol. 3 (Spring), pp. 37 – 54.

Blackley, P.R. (1986), "Causality Between Revenue and Expenditures and Size of the Federal Budget", *Public Finance Quarterly* 14, pp. 139-156.

Buchanan, J. and R. Wagner (1977), *Democracy in Deficit: The Political Legacy of Lord Keynes,* (New York: Academic Press).

Buchanan, James M., and Richard E. Wagner, ed., 1978, *Fiscal Responsibility in Constitutional Democracy* (Leiden, Netherlands: Martinus Nijhoff Social Sciences Division).

Chaudhury, A.R., (1988) "Expenditure and Receipts in State and Local Government Finances: Comment", *Public Choice* 59, pp. 277-285.

Darrat, A.F. (1998), "Tax and Spend, and Spend and Tax? An Enquiry into the Turkish Budgetary Process", *Southern Economic Journal* 64, pp. 940 - 956.

Das A and Sangeeta (1998-1999), "Temporal Causality Between Government Taxes and Spending: An Application of Error Correction Models", *Prajnan,* Vol. XXVII, No. 1.

Dhanasekaran, K., (2001) "Government Tax Revenue, Expenditure and Causality: The Experience of India", *Indian Economic Review,* Vol. XXXVI. No. 2, pp. 359-379.

Dickey, D. A., D.A. Fuller (1981) "The Likelihood Ratio Statistics for Autoregressive Time Series with a Unit Root", *Econometrica,* Vol. 49 No.4, pp 1057-72.

Dore Ousmane and Jean-Claude Nachega (2000) "Budgetary Convergance in the WAEMU: Adjustment Through Revenue or Expenditure?" IMF Working Paper, International Monetary Fund.

Engle, R.F. and C.W.J. Granger, (1986) "Co-integration and Error Correction: Representation, Estimation and Testing", *Econometrica,* Vol. 55, No. 2, March, pp. 81-111.

Friedman, Milton, 1978, "The Limitations of Tax Limitation," *Policy Review,* Summer, 7-14.

Granger, C.W.J., (1986), "Developments in The Study of Co-integrated Variables", *Oxford Bulletin of Economic and Statistics*, Vol. 48, pp. 213 - 228.

Joulfinian, D and R. Mookerjee, (1990), "The Government Revenue Expenditure Nexus: Evidence From a State", *Public Finance Quarterly*, Vol. XVIII, No. 1, January, pp. 92-103.

Kirchgassner, G. and S. Prohl "Causality Between Expenditure and Revenues: Empirical Evidence From Switzerland" University of St. Gallen, Swiss Institute of International Economics and Applied Economic Research, SIAW – HSG.

Manage, Neela, and Michael L. Marlow (1986), "The Causal Relationship Between Federal Expenditures and Receipts", *Southern Economic Journal*, Vol. 52 (January), pp. 617-29.

Martin, Marc-Jean, J. Krishnakumar and N. Soguel (2004) "Application of Granger Causality Test to Revenue and Expenditure of Swiss Cantons" Departement d'econometrie, University de Geneve, 40 Boulevard du Pont-d'Arve, CH – 1211 Geneve 4.

Meltzer, Allan, and Richard, Scott (1991), "A Rational Theory of the Size of Government", *Political Economy* (New York: Oxford University Press)

Moalusi, D.K. (2004), *Causal Link Between Government Spending and Revenue: A Case Study of Botswana*, Department of Economics, Fordham University.

Mukhopadhyay, C. K. and B. Maitra, "Causal Relationship Between Government Revenue and Government Expenditure in India – An Econometric Study for the Periods 1950 – 2005" Working Paper Series, Vol. 2, October, 2006, Department of Economics, University of North Bengal.

Mukhopadhyay, C.K. and B. Maitra "Fiscal Synchronization Hypothesis in the Economy of Sri-Lanka (1957-2004) – An Econometric and Time Series Analysis", *Journal of South Asian Economy*, Vol. 1, March, 2007

Musgrave, Richard A. (1969), "Principals of Budget Determination, in The Public Economy", *An Introduction to Government Finances*, ed. By William Henderson and Helen Cameron (New York: Random House)

Narayan, P. K. and Seema Narayan "Government Revenue and Government Expenditure Nexus: Evidence from Developing Countries", *Applied Economics*, Vol. 38, Issue 3, Feb. 2006, pp. 285-291.

Naidu, C. R., Md. Mohsin and V. J. Naidu (1994-95), "Government Expenditure in Andhra Pradesh: An Analysis of Growth and Determinants", *Prajnan,* Vol. XXIII, No. 3, 332-352.

Peacock, Alan T., and Jack Wiseman, (1961), *The Growth of Public Expenditure in the United Kingdom,* Princeton University Press, Princeton, New Jersey.

Phillips, P.C.B. (1986), "Understanding Spurious Regression in Econometrics", *Journal of Econometrics,* December, pp. 311-340.

R. Rati (1988), "Additional Evidence on Causality Between Government Revenue and Government Expenditure", *Southern Economic Journal,* Vol. 54, No.3 (Jan., 1988), 763-769.

14

Vector Autoregression Model for Exchange Rate—A Study with Impulse Response Functions and Variance Decomposition

CHANDAN KUMAR MUKHOPADHYAY* & BISWAJIT MAITRA•

ABSTRACT

The study attempts to find the dynamic adjustment of Rupee/Dollar exchange rate variation following internal and external monetary shocks. Applying Vector Autoregressive Model and Impulse Response Functions with co-integrated filtered time series (quarterly), study aims at identifying the nature of these shocks and their impulses. It is found that short run variations in exchange rate are mainly a monetary phenomenon. In the short run variation of exchange rate, domestic monetary shocks dominate the foreign monetary shock. Exchange rate maintains stable long run equilibrium relations with lagged exchange rate, domestic and foreign money supply.

Key Words: Cholesky Decomposition, Impulse Response Function, Innovation, VAR.

* Professor, Department of Economics, North Bengal University

• Registered Ph.D. Scholar, Department of Economics, North Bengal University.

1.1 Introduction

Christopher Sims has developed the Vector Autoregressive Model (VAR), where true simultaneity among a set of variables necessitates that these are to be treated on equal footing. There should not be any a prior distinction between endogenous and exogenous variables. Economic theories contain behavioral, structural, and/or reduced form relationships that can be incorporated into a VAR analysis. The VAR model is designed for forecasting of the interrelated variables by analyzing the dynamic impact of the random disturbances of the system.

In our analysis we have taken three macro economic variables, namely, Rupee/Dollar exchange rate, money supply in India (Home country) and the money supply in USA (Foreign country). Monetary Approach to Exchange Rate Determination (MAER) holds that domestic as well as foreign money supply can influence exchange rate. Again in the presence of 'Activist' nature of the monetary policy in the home county, the variation of exchange rate can also affect the variation of money supply in that country. Therefore, in order to find the exchange rate dynamics in India, we cannot make any a-priori assumption of endogenous and exogenous variables.

1.2 The Model

The model of Vector Auto Regression (VAR) for Rupee/Dollar Exchange Rate (E_t) is as follows. Here Et, Mt and Ft represent Rupee/Dollar exchange rate, domestic (India) money supply (M2) and foreign (US) money supply (M2) at time t respectively. Again E_{t-i}, M_{t-i}, F_{t-i} represent Rupee/Dollar exchange rate, domestic money supply and foreign money supply at time t-i, i = 1,2,3, ------, respectively. These variables are taken in logarithmic form with stationarity attained through appropriate filtering like differencing.

$$E_t = \alpha_1 + \sum_{i=1}^{k} \beta_{1i} E_{t-1} + \sum_{i=1}^{k} \gamma_{1i} F_{t-i} + \sum_{i=1}^{k} \delta_{1i} M_{t-i} + u_{1t} \quad \text{---------------} (1)$$

$$M_t = \alpha_2 + \sum_{i=1}^{k} \beta_{2i} M_{t-i} + \sum_{i=1}^{k} \gamma_{2i} E_{t-i} + u_{2t} \quad \text{---------------} (2)$$

Here, are the stochastic error terms, called impulse or innovations or shocks in the VAR model. These equations do not represent any joint relationship between E_t and M_t. These equations, therefore, represent "Seemingly Unrelated Regression" (SUR) model. The estimation of the model considers and uses the contemporaneous Var-Covariance matrices (Ω) of the error terms involved such that Ω = Var-Cov (u_{1t}, u_{2t}), where Ω is a positive definite matrix.

1.3 Selection of Lag Length

Before estimating VAR, the decision regarding the selection of maximum lag length (k) is important. This is because, inclusions of too many lagged terms consume degrees of freedom and consequently, problem of multicollinearity can arise. On the other hand, inclusion of few lags can lead to selection errors.

Akaike Information Criterion, Schwartz Information Criterion, Hannan-Quinn Information Criterion, Sequential Modified LR test statistic, etc are generally used for the determination of optimum lag length. However, in our study we have followed Enders (1995) and started with eight lags. We have reduced the lags by one and carried out the test, given that estimated t-static for the coefficient involved is insignificant. In 3rd lag few parameters have been found statistically significant. But .in lag 2 many parameters have been found statistically significant. We have compared the optimality of 2nd and 3rd lag by applying lag selection criterion and finally have taken lag 2 in our model. The relevant results are being presented in the Table 1.

Table 1: VAR Lag Order Selection Criterion Endogenous Variables: E_t, F_t, M_t Sample: 1975 (I) – 2005 (IV)

Lag	*AIC*	*SIC*	*HQ*	*LR*
0	-15.22	-15.15	-15.19	N.A
1	-15.55	-15.27	-15.44	55.56
2	-16.31*	-15.82*	-16.11*	102.05*
3	-16.22	-15.53	-15.94	7.33

Note: * indicates lag order selected by the criterion

AIC: Akaike information criterion

SIC: Schwarz information criterion

HQ: Hannan-Quinn information criterion

LR: Sequential modified LR test statistic.

For the 2nd lag all the AIC, SIC, HQ, LR criteria give optimum values and we have used 2nd lags of all the variables (E_t, M_t, F_t) in the estimated VAR model.

1.4 Estimation and Results of VAR Model:

The results of the estimation of the VAR model are being presented through the Tables 2 – 3:

Table: 2
Results of VAR Estimation (Equation 1)
Sample Adjusted: 1976(ii) – 2005(iv)
Included Observations: 119

Dependent variable	*Explanatory Variables*	*Coefficient*	*'t' statistic*	*Standard errors*
E_t	Constant	-0.019	-1.955	0.010
	E_{t-1}	0.163	1.857	0.088
	E_{t-2}	0.117	1.338	0.087
	M_{t-1}	0.066	0.669	0.099
	M_{t-2}	0.314	3.20	0.098
	F_{t-1}	0.075	1.523	0.049
	F_{t-2}	0.076	1.532	0.050

R^2 = 0.32, Adjusted R^2 = 0.29, F-statistic = 9.09, DW = 2.06

Table 3
Results of VAR Estimation (Equation 2)
Sample Adjusted: 1976(11) – 2005(IV)
Included Observations: 119

Dependent variable	*Explanatory Variables*	*Coefficient*	*'t' statistic*	*Standard errors*
M_t	Constant	0.016	2.676	0.006
	M_{t-1}	0.078	1.219	0.064
	M_{t-2}	0.666	10.406	0.064
	E_{t-1}	0.067	1.175	0.057
	E_{t-2}	0.138	2.404	0.057

$R^2 = 0.659$, Adjusted $R^2 = 0.647$, F-statistic = 56.16, DW = 2.06

1.5 Findings

It is observed from the estimated equation (1) that

(i) $\left|\sum_{i=1}^{2}\hat{\alpha}_{1i}\right|+\left|\sum_{i=1}^{2}\hat{\beta}_{1i}\right|+\left|\sum_{i=1}^{2}\hat{\gamma}_{1i}\right|<1$ So the lag structure is consistent.

(ii) F - statistic $= 9.09 > F_{0.05}^{7,121}$, which indicates that the estimated equation is good fit.

(iii) D.W. = 2.01 indicates that the system is free from autocorrelation

(iv) $\hat{\beta}_2$, the coefficient of E_{t-1} is significant at 1% level

(v) the coefficient of M_{t-2} is significant at 1% level.

1.6 Economic Interpretation

The economic significance of these findings is as follows:

(i) Positive and significant coefficient of M_{t-2} indicates domestic monetary shock (at 2 period back) leads to depreciation of exchange rate (i.e., rise in Rupee/ Dollar Exchange rate). This findings supports the main proposition of the MAER model of exchange rate determination.

(ii) Again the positive and the significant coefficient of E_{t-1} implies that a rise in Rupee/Dollar exchange rate leads to a rise in Rupee/Dollar exchange rate in the next period (quarter). This feature of exchange rate represents almost continuous depreciation of Indian Rupee against US Dollar over the period of study.

(iii) The coefficients obtained from the estimated model actually imply elasticity coefficients. $\hat{\delta}_{12} = 0.314$ and $\hat{\beta}_{11} = 0.163$, imply that exchange rate elasticity with respect to one quarter lagged exchange rate is 0.163 and that with respect to two quarter lagged money supply is 0.314. The expression $\hat{\delta}_{12} = 0.314$ states that the change in Rupee/Dollar exchange rate following change in money supply is less than unity. In other words, long run equilibrium level of Rupee/Dollar exchange cannot be permanently altered by the change in money supply. This further means that variation in Rupee/Dollar exchange rate following variation in money supply is converging to long run equilibrium level.

We have observed how exchange rate variation is triggered by variation in money supply. It does neither confirm nor ignore the possibility that the variation in money supply is caused by variation in exchange rate. This is possible if money supply is 'activist' with respect to exchange rate variation. So there exists a possibility of reverse causation. We seek to address this issue henceforth. With this end in view, we estimate equation (2) of the VAR model where money supply appears as the dependent variable.

1.7 Findings from the Table 2

It is observed from the estimated equation (2) that

(i) $\left|\sum_{i=1}^{2}\hat{\alpha}_{2i}\right| + \left|\sum_{i=1}^{2}\hat{\beta}_{2i}\right| + \left|\sum_{i=1}^{2}\hat{\gamma}_{2i}\right| < 1$ So the lag structure is consistent.

(ii) F - statistic = 56.16 > $F_{0.05}^{5,121}$, which indicates that the estimated equation is good fit.

(iii) D.W. = 2.06 indicates that the system is free from autocorrelation

(iv) $\hat{\beta}_{22}$, the coefficient of M_{t-2} is significant at 1% level

(v) the coefficient of E_{t-2} is significant at 1% level

1.8 Analysis and Economic Interpretation

It is, therefore, observed from the estimated equation (2) that

(i) M_t is a function of M_{t-2} since $\hat{\beta}_{22}$ is significant and Mt, in its univariate structure, represents AR (2) process.

(ii) $\hat{\beta}_{22} > 0$ indicates that current money supply is positively related to two period back money supply. A rise in two quarter back money supply is followed by an increase in the current money supply. This finding explains an important feature of Indian monetary policy. In Indian economy expansionary monetary policy had been operative over the period of the study. Money supply increases continuously especially after the nationalization of banks. Thus overall increase in money supply seems to display a nature which fails to conform to Friedman's K% point rule. The univariate probability structure underlying the distribution process for money supply, therefore, indicates an underlying inclination for maintaining a changing (increasing) mean value over the period concerned.

(iii) the significant values of $\hat{\gamma}_{22}$ essentially indicates that two period (quarter) lagged exchange rate affects current money supply significantly even in the presence of lagged money supply in the vector of regressors. It implies that exchange rate Granger causes Indian money supply.

It, therefore, appears that in Indian economy variation in money supply is found to be caused by variation in exchange rate over the period of the study. However, better insights about the relationship between money supply and exchange rate can be obtained through the study of VAR model from Impulse Response Function and Variance Decomposition. In the following section we have discussed these issues in detail.

II
IMPULSE RESPONSE FUNCTION

2.1 Introduction

A shock to the 'i'-th variable not only directly affects the i-th variable itself but the shock is also transmitted to all of the other endogenous variables through the dynamic (lag) structure of the VAR. An Impulse Response Function traces the effect of a one time shock to one of the innovations on current and future values of the endogenous variables. In other words, Impulse Response Function traces the response of a variable through time to an unanticipated change in itself or other interrelated variables. Therefore, the Impulse Response Function can be used in VAR system to describe the dynamic behaviors of the whole system with respect to shocks in the residual of the time series.

In a linear model, the Impulse Responses are not history dependent and the magnitude of the shock does not alter the time profile of the responses. However, the interpretation of the Impulse Response Functions for a nonlinear model is not straightforward. In the non linear model Impulse Responses are history dependent. The effect of a particular shock on the time path of the system depends on the magnitudes of the current and the subsequent shocks. In this case sign of the shocks is important.

2.2 Graphical Presentations of Impulse Response Functions:

The relevant impulse response functions are being

presented through the Figures 1 – 3.

Figure: 1

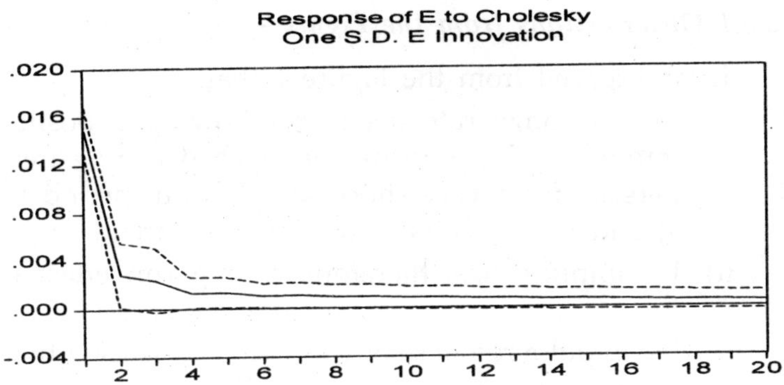

Figure: 2

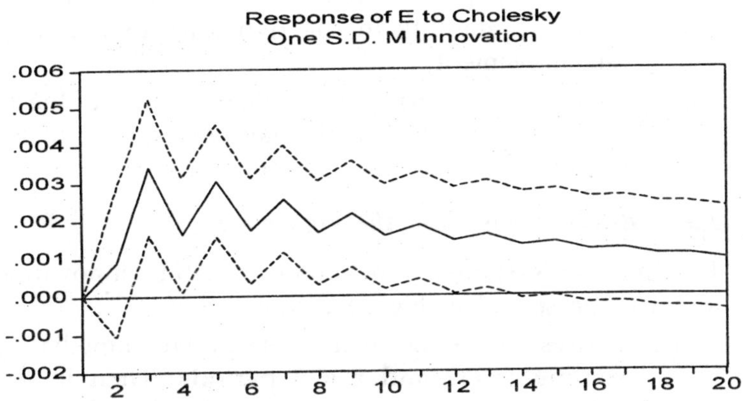

Figure: 3

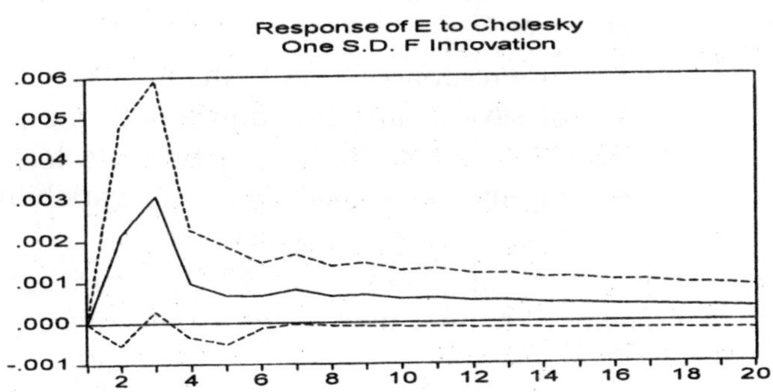

2.3 Explanation of Exchange Rate Dynamics: Impulse Response Functions

2.3.1 *Observations from the Figure - 1*

It is observed from the Figure 1 that

(i) the exchange rate declines following a positive impulse in E_{t-1} immediately. Such declining trend persists for a very short period (until period t = 4) and then reverts to the long run trend.

(ii) E_{t-1} impulse has, therefore, a long run effect on E_t.

(iii) the impulse response of E_t depicts a balancing trend in view of the fact the rise in E_{t-1} is converted by a subsequent decline in E_t. Such counteracting response depicts a trend for the maintenance of long run stability in the dynamics of exchange rate movement.

(iv) the short run variability in Et may not be due to the impulse in E_{t-1} but it may be response of E_{t-1} to impulse from other factors.

2.3.2 *Observations from the Figure - 2*

The Impulse Response Functions to one S.D. innovation in Mt as presented in Figure 2 shows that:

(i) E_t rises following an impulse in Mt immediately at time t = 2 and t = 3 periods. Then in the following period (t = 4) it declines. It indicates a case of overshooting of E_t following a monetary shock.

(ii) the impulse responses of Et to the monetary factors consist of several ups and down over the period (t = 2 to t = 16) until E_t reverts to its long run level. This indicates that short run variability in Et is mainly due to monetary shock.

(iii) the effects of shocks transmitted through the monetary channel have a permanent effect.

2.3.3 *Observations from the Figure - 3*

Figure 3 depicts the responses of Et to impulses in foreign money supply. It appears from the Figure 3 that

(i) Et displays immediate rise (depreciation) following a positive impulse in foreign money supply and it persists in successive periods (periods t = 2 and t = 3).

(ii) such variation in E_t in short-lived since Et almost attains long run trend at period t = 5.

2.3.4 *Economic Interpretations*

It, therefore, appears that

(i) Et, in response to any impulse transmitted through previous period exchange rate quickly attains long run equilibrium level after a very short lived variation.

(ii) Et, in response to any impulse transmitted through foreign money channel, attains long run equilibrium level after significant short run variations in several successive periods.

(iii) E_t, in response to shocks transmitted through domestic money channel, attains long run equilibrium level after significant short run variations in several successive periods.

(iv) Et exhibits overshooting phenomenon in response to impulse transmitted through domestic and foreign money channels.

(v) Short run variation in E_t due to foreign money impulses dominate over three successive (t = 2, 3) periods while effects of domestic money impulses dominate above (t = 3) period variations.

III
VARIANCE DECOMPOSITION

3.1 Introduction

Impulse Response Functions trace the effects of a shock to one endogenous variable on to the other variables in the VAR, while Variance Decomposition separates the variation in an endogenous variable into the component shock to the VAR. Thus Variance Decomposition provides information about the relative importance of each random innovation in the matter of affecting the variables in the VAR.

Unrestricted VARs are not particularly useful for short-term forecasts since they are over parameterized. The Forecast Error Variance Decomposition reflects the proportion of forecast error variance of a variable which is explained by an unanticipated change in itself as opposed to that proportion attributable to change in other, perhaps interrelated variables. In other words, the Forecast Error Variance Decomposition tells us the proportion of the movement in a sequence due to its own shocks versus shocks of other variables.

3.2 Variance Decomposition Table

The variance decomposition of exchange rate variance over 20 quarters is being presented through the Table 4 below. This is also shown with the help of the Figure -5.

Table: 4

Variance Decomposition of E_t

Period	*Standard Error*	E_t	F_t	M_t
1	0.014725	100.0000	0.000000	0.000000
2	0.015117	97.82197	1.997536	0.180496
3	0.015951	90.28806	5.557424	4.154515
4	0.016103	89.26468	5.803723	4.931597
5	0.016440	86.04311	5.728533	8.228357

6	0.016557	85.11755	5.800943	9.081505
7	0.016792	83.09904	5.867822	11.03314
8	0.016897	82.31515	5.935032	11.74981
9	0.017061	80.99158	5.972402	13.03601
10	0.017149	80.34698	6.018041	13.63498
11	0.017267	79.43905	6.048826	14.51213
12	0.017340	78.91937	6.082502	14.99813
13	0.017427	78.27692	6.106359	15.61672
14	0.017486	77.86323	6.131153	16.00562
15	0.017550	77.39760	6.149734	16.45267
16	0.017598	77.07094	6.168241	16.76082
17	0.017646	76.72734	6.182685	17.08998
18	0.017684	76.47076	6.196620	17.33262
19	0.017721	76.21374	6.207844	17.57842
20	0.017751	76.01289	6.218418	17.76869

Figure 4
Graphical Presentation of Variance Decomposition of E_t

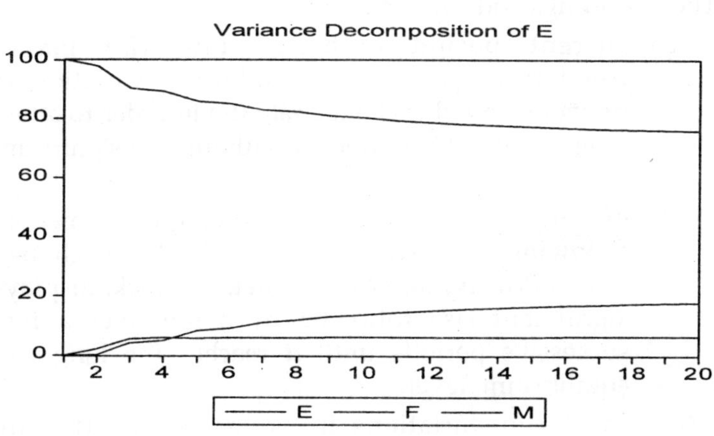

3.3 Explanation of Exchange rate Dynamics: The Variance Decomposition

It is observed from the Table 4 and the Figure 4 that

(i) previous period exchange rate (E_{t-1}) accounts for at least 76 % of the variation in Et.

(ii) foreign money channel accounts for at most 6 % of E_t variations.

(iii) domestic money channel explains not exceeding 17 % of variations in E_t.

(iv) foreign money channel dominates in accounting for short run variations in E_t over the period t = 2,3,4. This implies that short run variation in E_t due to foreign money channel impulses are short lined.

(v) domestic money channel dominates in explaining short run variations in E_t over the period t = 5,6, ... This testifies for long lived short run variations in Et due to domestic money channel impulses.

3.4 Economic Interpretations

These findings indicate that,

(i) current period exchange rate (E_t) makes countervailing movement following variation in previous period exchange rate (E_t) in order to attain long run equilibrium level without any significant lapse of time.

(ii) exchange rate exhibits 'Overshooting Phenomenon' following domestic monetary shocks. Exchange rate, following domestic monetary shock, displays significant rise followed by a fall over a few successive periods until it reaches the long run equilibrium level.

(iii) short run variations in exchange rate (E_t) are 'MONETARY PHENOMENA' since such variations are mainly due to domestic and foreign monetary shocks.

(iv) domestic monetary shocks dominate over foreign monetary shocks in generating short run variations in exchange rate. Domestic monetary shocks explain 17.76% of variations in exchange rate in 20th period, while foreign monetary shock explains at most 6.21% of such variations.

(v) 76% of variations in exchange rate are of long run ones. Again impulses transmitted through (previous) exchange rate channel account for these long run dynamics of exchange rate is marked by an AR(1) process.

(vi) Rupee/Dollar exchange rate declines following a positive impulse from foreign money supply. This appears to be asymmetric in view of the prediction of a rise given by the MAER Theories.

3.5 Conclusions

The main findings from the study of Impulse Response Functions and Variance Decomposition are as follows:

(i) The long run dynamic path of exchange rate is predominantly defined by an AR(1) process.

(ii) The short run variations in exchange rate is mainly a 'monetary phenomenon'.

(iii) Exchange rate displays an 'Overshooting' response following an impulse transmitted through domestic money channel.

(iv) Domestic monetary shocks dominate over foreign monetary shocks in explaining short run variations in exchange rate.

(v) Exchange rate maintains 'stable' long run equilibrium relations with lagged exchange rate, domestic and foreign money supplies since its responses revert to long run path before long following impulses transmitted through all the channels considered.

It, therefore, appears that the univariate ARIMA structure for forecasting exchange rate is appropriate. However, Transfer Function Forecasting for exchange rate, through the inclusion of the effects of the domestic and foreign monetary shocks, is expected to be an efficient one.

REFERENCES

Bilson, J. F. O. (1978), "The Monetary Approach to the Exchange Rate: Some Empirical Evidences", International Monetary Fund Stuff Papers, 25, pp. 48 – 75.

Branson, W. H., H. Halttunen and P. Masson (1977), "Exchange Rate in the Short Run: The Dollar – Deutschemark Rate", *European Economic Review*, 10, pp. 303 - 324.

Calvo, G. A. and C. A. Rodriguez (1977), "A Model of Exchange Rate Determination under Currency Substitution and Rational Expectations", *Journal of Political Economy*, 85, pp. 617 – 25.

Dickey, D.A., and W.A. Fuller (1979), "Distribution of the Estimates for Autoregressive Time Series with a Unit Root", *Journal of the American Statistical Association*, 74, June, pp. 427-31.

Dornbusch, R. (1976), "Expectations and Exchange Rate Dynamics", *Journal of Political Economy*, Vol. 84, pp. 1161 – 76.

Dornbusch, R. (1980), "Exchange Rate Economics: Where Do We Stand?", *Brookings Papers on Economic Activity*, Vol. 1, pp. 143–85.

Dornbusch, R. (1984), "Monetary Policy under Exchange Rate Flexibility", in D. Bigman and T. Taya (eds.), *Floating Exchange Rates and the State of World trade Payments, Cambridge*, Mass.: Harper & Row, Ballinger, pp. 3 – 31.

Dornbusch, R. and S. Fischer (1980), "Exchange Rates and the Current Account", *American Economic Review*, Vol. 70, pp. 960–71.

Edison, H. J. and B. D. Pauls (1993), "A Re-assessment of the Relationship between Real Exchange Rates and Real Interest Rates: 1974–1990", Journal of Monetary Economics, Vol. 31, pp. 165-87.

Engle, R. F. and C. W. J. Granger (1987), "Co-integration and Error Correction: Representation, Estimation, and Testing", *Econometrica*, Vol. 55, No. 2, March, pp. 251-76.

Flood, R. P. and A. K. Rose (1995), "Fixing Exchange Rates: A Virtual Quest for Fundamentals", *Journal of Monetary Economics,* 36, pp. 3 -37.

Frankel, J.A. (1976), "A Monetary Approach to the Exchange Rate: Doctrinal Aspects and Empirical Evidence", *Scandinavian Journal of Economics,* 78, pp. 200-24.

Frankel, J.A. (1979), "On the Mark: A Theory of Floating Exchange Rates Based on Real Interest Differentials", *American Economic Review,* 69, pp. 610–22.

Frankel, J.A. (1982a), "The Mystery of the Multiplying Marks: A Modification of the Monetary Model", *Review of Economics and Statistics,* 64, pp. 515–19.

Frankel, J.A. (1982b), "A test of Perfect Substitutability in the Foreign Exchange Market", *Southern Economic Journal,* Vol. 49, pp. 406–16.

Frankel, J.A. and A. K. Rose (1995), "Empirical Research on Nominal Exchange Rates", in G. Grossman and K. Rogoff (eds.), *Handbook of International Economics,* vol. III, Amsterdam: Elsevier Science, pp. 1689–729.

Friedman, M. (1953), "The Case of Flexible Exchange Rates", in M. Friedman, *Essays in Positive Economics,* Chicago: University of Chicago Press, pp. 157–203.

Hodrick, R. J. (1978), "An Empirical Analysis of the Monetary Approach to the Determination of the Exchange Rate", in J. A. Frankel, and H. A. Johnson (eds.), *The Economics of Exchange Rate: Selected Studies,* Mass.: Addison-Wesley, pp. 97–116.

Kilian, L. and M. P. Taylor (2001), "Why Is It so Difficult to Beat Random Walks Forecast of Exchange Rates?", *Journal of International Economics,* forthcoming.

Koedijk, K. G. and P. Schotman (1990), "How to Beat the Random Walk: An Empirical Model o0f Real Exchange Rates", *Journal of International Economics,* 29, 311–32.

Mark, N. C. (1995), "Exchange Rate Fundamentals: Evidence on Long - Horizon Predictability", *American Economic Review,* Vol. 85, pp. 201 – 18.

McNown, R. and M. Wallace (1989), "Co-integration Tests for Long Run Equilibrium in the Monetary Exchange Rate Model", *Economic Letters,* Vol. 31, pp. 263–7.

Meesa, R. A. (1986), "Testing for Bubbles in Exchange Markets: A Case of Sparkling Rates", *Journal of Political Economy,* 94, pp. 345–73.

Meesa, R. A. and K. Rogoff (1983), "Empirical Exchange Rate Models of The Seventies: Do They Fit Out of Samples?", *Journal of International Economics,* 14, pp. 3–24.

Meesa, R. A. and A.K. Rose (1991), "An Empirical Assessment of Non - linearties in Models of Exchange Rate Determination", *Review of Economic Studies,* 58, pp. 603–19.

Obstfeld, M. and A.C. Stockman (1985), "Exchange Rate Dynamics", in R. Jones and P. B. Kenen (eds.), *Hand Book of International Economics,* Vol. 2, Amsterdam: North Holland, pp. 917–77.

Phillips, P., and P. Perron (1988), "Testing for a Unit Root in Time Series Regression", *Biometrica,* Vol. 75, June, pp. 335–346.

Stockmen, A.C. (1980), "A Theory of Exchange Rate Determination", *Journal of Political Economy,* Vol. 88, pp. 673–98.

Taylor, M.P. (1990), *The Balance of Payments,* Cheltenham: Edward Elgar Publishing Ltd.

Taylor, M. P. (1995), "The Economics of Exchange Rates", *Journal of Economic Literature,* Vol. 33, pp. 13–47.

Van den Berg, H. and S.C. Jayanetti (1993), "A Novel Test of The Monetary Approach Using Black Market Exchange Rates and the Johensen-Juselius Co-integration Method", *Economic Letters,* 41, pp. 413-18.

Woo, W.T. (1985), "The Monetary Approach to Exchange Rate Determination under Rational Expectations: The Dollar-Deutschmark Rate", *Journal of International Economics,* 18, pp. 1-16.